STATEMENT CONCERNING PUBLICATIONS OF
RUSSELL SAGE FOUNDATION

The Russell Sage Foundation was established in 1907 by Mrs. Russell Sage "for the improvement of social and living conditions in the United States of America." In carrying out its purpose the Foundation maintains a staff which, among other duties, conducts studies of social conditions, authorized by the General Director, where new information, its analysis and interpretation seem necessary in order to formulate and advance practicable measures aimed at improvement. From time to time the Foundation publishes the results of these studies in book or pamphlet form.

In formulating the problem for study, in mapping out a plan of work on it, in collecting facts, in drawing conclusions, and in the presentation of findings, authors of Foundation studies, who are always either members of the staff or specially commissioned research workers, have the benefit of the criticism and advice of their colleagues in the organization. Full freedom is given research workers for the final decision on all of these steps, and in presenting and interpreting both factual material and conclusions in their own way. While the general responsibility for management of the Foundation is vested in the board of trustees, the responsibility for facts, conclusions, and interpretations rests with the research workers alone and not upon the Foundation, its trustees, or other members of the staff. Publication under the imprint of the Foundation does not imply agreement by the organization or its members with opinions or interpretations of authors. It does imply that care has been taken that the research on which a book is based has been thoroughly done.

LAWYERS AND THE PROMOTION OF JUSTICE

BY

ESTHER LUCILE BROWN

DEPARTMENT OF STATISTICS
RUSSELL SAGE FOUNDATION

NEW YORK
RUSSELL SAGE FOUNDATION
1938

130 E 22nd St. N.Y City

E. L. HILDRETH AND COMPANY
printers at Brattleboro, Vermont

TABLE OF CONTENTS

LIST OF TABLES

PREFACE

THIS monograph is the fifth in a series dealing with the present status of certain established or emerging professions in the United States. Social Work as a Profession, the first to be published, appeared in 1935, and revised editions were issued in 1936 and 1938. The Professional Engineer and Nursing as a Profession were published in 1936, and Physicians and Medical Care in 1937.

A similar philosophy and method of procedure characterize all the studies. The professions have been viewed primarily in relation to their effectiveness in meeting public needs. At the same time an attempt has been made to determine to what degree members of the various groups work under conditions sufficiently favorable for them to utilize their training and experience for their own continued growth and for the benefit of those whom they serve. The interests of the public and the interests of the professional groups need not be antithetical. In fact, only to the extent that these interests are brought into harmony can either those who receive or those who render the service profit satisfactorily. The significance of this fact is all too often overlooked by a public that is inclined to think only of its desires and needs, and by the professions that sometimes forget that the reason for their existence and for the privileges accorded them is their service to society.

No one would dispute the assumption that adequate preparation constitutes the most important single element of successful practice. Consequently, a large portion of each study has been devoted to the evolution of professional education and problems

5

incident to it. Similarly, since professional associations are capable of doing much to raise standards of practice and of determining what the relation of a group to society shall be, the most important of the national associations have been described at some length.

As professions grow in age, size, and importance, the several states gradually assume varying degrees of responsibility for defining who shall be entitled to practice within the respective jurisdictions and under what conditions. Official control of the medical profession is now relatively extensive and strictly enforced by the appropriate administrative agencies. For the bar, however, the states have not yet evolved so comprehensive or efficient control, and as one result many poor law schools are still permitted to prepare students for the practice of law. So acute is this difficulty that a discussion of rules and procedures governing admission to the bar appears in this volume.

One of the most serious problems at present is the lack of means for accurate determination of how many persons are needed in each professional group, and the lack of a method of regulating, in the interests of the public and of the group, the number and distribution of those admitted. In view of this situation, such data as could be obtained relating to the question of the possible overcrowding of the bar, and to the distribution and earnings of lawyers have been reviewed.

To a degree not true of any other profession, lawyers serve society in diversified ways. Not only are they counselors and advocates for their clients, but members of the bench are chosen from among them. As judges they decide what the law is, and the judicial decisions rendered by them in the higher tribunals become a part of our common law. In addition to these strictly professional functions, large numbers of lawyers enter public life as state legislators and members of Congress. Much of our statutory law is proposed and nearly all of it is drafted by them. The administration of government is also extensively carried on by members of the bar. Thus, on the legal profession devolves large responsibility for the legislative and executive branches, as well as for the judicial branch, of government.

So widespread is their influence and power that the future of the United States lies, in no inconsiderable degree, in the hands of lawyers. It has, therefore, seemed essential in final portions of this book to point, on the one hand, to the failure of bar and bench to accept certain social responsibilities, and to note, on the other, the emergence of several trends that appear to indicate a growing desire within the profession to promote justice more effectively than in the past.

Material presented in this, as in the earlier studies, has been obtained from numerous interviews with members of the profession and attendance at professional meetings, as well as from books, periodicals, proceedings, and unpublished documents. Unfortunately, for the legal profession, particularly, there is very little literature relating to several of the subjects discussed. Members of the bar have largely confined their writing in the past to the law itself. Only recently have they begun to survey professional problems and their own relation to the public. Much effort, therefore, has been expended in assembling and interpreting data so scattered that they have not been readily available to lawyers and have been even less known to the laity. It is hoped that this information will be of assistance to those who are striving to make the legal profession, as well as professions generally, contribute more widely to the welfare both of their members and of society. Vocational counselors, too, may find this volume useful.

7

Anyone who has ever attempted to write about a group of which he was not a member is aware of the multiplicity of problems encountered. He may, however, have one significant asset —an ability to view the group and its achievements and problems more dispassionately than do most of its members. In order to become acquainted with the historical facts and the philosophy essential for obtaining such perspective, assistance from representatives of the group is of the greatest value. To the preparation of this study, a long list of lawyers and a few exceptionally qualified persons who are not members of the bar have rendered such aid. Professor Elliott E. Cheatham of the Columbia University Law School, Mr. Will Shafroth of the staff of the American Bar Association, Mr. Alfred Z. Reed of the Carnegie Foundation, and Dean Albert J. Harno of the University of Illinois Law School spent many hours in discussing professional questions with me, and have read the manuscript in whole or in large part. Dean Charles E. Clark and Professor James Grafton Rogers of Yale University Law School, Dean Leon E. Green of Northwestern University, Professor Edmund M. Morgan of Harvard University, and Dean H. Claude Horack of Duke University helped generously in envisaging new trends in legal education. For much that I have learned of legal service for the poor, I am indebted to Mr. Reginald Heber Smith of Boston, Professor John S. Bradway of Duke University, the directors of several of the legal aid societies, and several members of the National Lawyers Guild, including Professor Karl N. Llewellyn of Columbia University, who are attempting to formulate plans for providing organized legal service for persons of small means. Through many other lawyers and law-school teachers, whom lack of space does not permit me to name, have come information, points of view, and perhaps most important of all—the "feel" of the profession. I also wish to acknowledge the assistance I have received from Dr. Ralph G. Hurlin under whose general direction this series of studies has been made.

ESTHER LUCILE BROWN

LAWYERS AND THE PROMOTION OF JUSTICE

EVOLUTION OF THE LEGAL PROFESSION IN UNITED STATES

LAWYERS were not numerous or important in the American colonies until after the beginning of the eighteenth century, and not until shortly before the Revolutionary War did they begin to play an important role in governmental affairs. In early colonial days the general assembly or legislature constituted the sole court of law; later the royal governor and his deputies acted in that capacity. Even after the establishment of independent courts, officers of the law, with the possible exception of the chief justice, were laymen. Prior to the Revolution it was not deemed advisable that judges be learned in the law.

In England lawyers had long been unpopular as a class, because they were looked upon as instruments for enforcing the subtleties and "iniquities" of that body of law, known as common law, that had evolved from judicial decisions. This attitude the colonists brought with them and perpetuated in the New World. At a time when pioneers were engaged in the arduous task of clearing the wilderness, moreover, there was little place for attorneys. Charles and Mary Beard relate how the Massachusetts Body of Liberties, adopted in 1641, permitted every litigant to plead his own cause. If the litigant was unable to help himself and obtained someone to assist him, he was to give his counsel "noe fee or reward for his paines."[1] In the early years of Maryland a local chronicler rendered thanks that there were no lawyers in that colony and no business to occupy

[1] The Rise of American Civilization. Macmillan Co., New York, 1930, vol. 1, p. 100.

such factious members of a community. When William Penn founded his democratic commonwealth on the banks of the Delaware, an enthusiastic promoter rejoiced that it contained neither doctors nor lawyers, as there was no need either "of the pestiferous drugs of the one or the tiresome loquacity of the other."[1]

Certain groups were particularly hostile toward lawyers. In New England the clergy maintained complete supremacy for a long time over the magistracy and the courts. In New York, Maryland, and Virginia merchants and wealthy landowners and planters were extremely jealous of the exercise of power by others than themselves. So bitter was the feeling toward attorneys that much legislation was enacted against them. Charles Warren, a distinguished member of the Boston bar, who has made an extensive study of the legal profession in the United States prior to 1860, insists, however, that "attorneys" of this period were generally traders, land speculators, and men of a facile pen and tongue, who were employed to talk in court for those desiring assistance.[2] The few that acted in a professional capacity in the early years were minor court officers, such as deputy sheriffs, clerks, and justices. They so often stirred up litigation for the sake of petty court fees, that in most of the colonies statutes were passed prohibiting such persons from serving as lawyers.

Aside from the type of men who became attorneys, Mr. Warren maintains that there were several reasons why law developed but slowly as a profession in this country and lawyers long failed to become an influential group in the community. In the

[1] Beck, James M., May It Please the Court. Macmillan Co., New York, 1930, p. 97.
[2] A History of the American Bar. Little, Brown and Co., Boston, 1913, p. 5.

first instance, law as a science was so rigid that it failed to touch the life of the people. Common law was still feudal and tyrannical, heavily encumbered with the formalism of the Middle Ages, and so obscured from laymen by its use of Latin that the Puritans conceived of it as some "dark and knavish business." Although the statement has frequently been made in judicial decisions that our ancestors claimed the English common law as their birthright and brought it with them to this country, the colonists of Massachusetts, Connecticut, and Rhode Island never recognized it as binding *ipso facto*. From 1620 to 1700 English common law was in force in most of New England only in so far as it was specifically adopted by statute or was accepted by custom. Connecticut never adopted it even by statute. Not until the bar and bench of that state came to be representative of men familiar with English law were its rules made law through judicial decision.

A second difficulty in the path of professional development was the scarcity of law books and reports, and the lack of law schools. Even in England, at the end of the seventeenth century, hardly more than 70 law books and fewer than 100 volumes of law reports had been published. Not many of these were in use in the colonies. The participation and interference, furthermore, of the royal governors in the judicial systems of the colonies did much to prevent the evolution of a trained bar. Finally, the ignorance and lack of legal education of the judges themselves was such that their courts offered little opportunity for the training of competent counsel.

It is little wonder that, under such circumstances, neither lawyers nor the law occupied a position of much significance. With the beginning of the eighteenth century, however, new influences appeared, which rapidly altered the situation. Commerce, export trade, ship building, fishing, and slave trading came to be highly important, and rich merchants began to control community matters. Questions concerning business contracts, business paper, land rights, wills, and political liberties grew to be so vital that they required the attention of skilled lawyers. The need was supplied at first by barristers brought from England. Soon, however, men of distinguished families and college education entered the practice of law, and, although law schools were lacking and law books scarce, they brought about a marked change in the character of the profession. A considerable number of young men, moreover, went to London to study law in the Inns of Court. From the four colonies, Maryland, Pennsylvania, Virginia, and South Carolina, where the tendency to go abroad to study was particularly marked, it is reported that between 1750 and 1775, nearly 150 men attended the Inner and Middle Temple Inns.

So customary did it become for prospective lawyers either to attend American colleges such as Harvard, Yale, Princeton, Brown, and William and Mary, or to study at the English Inns of Court that Mr. Warren declares that in the late eighteenth century most lawyers had had one of these two types of preparation. By virtue of education and training they not only identified themselves with legal work but with politics and public life. They were the spokesmen, writers, and orators of the people when the latter were forced to look for champions in the struggle against the Mother Country. Although there is some slight difference of opinion among historians about the number of lawyers present at the various conventions that played so important a part in the winning of independence from Great Britain and the creation of new forms of government, the following figures, quoted from Charles and Mary Beard, testify to the role of the legal profession in these groups. Of the 24 men who attended the Albany Congress of 1754, 13 were lawyers. In the first Continental Congress, that launched the Revolution, 24 of the 45 delegates were lawyers. In the second Congress, which declared independence from Great Britain, 26 of the 56 delegates were men of legal training, and in the Constitutional Convention of 1787, 33 of the 55 members were lawyers.[1] The profession had raised itself from its lowly status of the seventeenth century to one of prestige and great influence. For a time it enjoyed a social position scarcely second to that of the ministry.

The years between 1789 and 1812 witnessed the growth of the early federal bars, composed chiefly of lawyers from Pennsylvania, Maryland, and Virginia; the initiation of law schools; and the masterful work of great jurists in New York and New England, who laid the foundations of American common law. Three factors, however, obstructed the progress of bench and bar to some degree: recurrence of dislike of lawyers as a class, bitter feeling against England and English common law, and lack of a distinct body of American law.

Mr. Warren remarks that nothing in legal history is more curious than the sudden revival after the Revolutionary War of the old unpopularity and distrust of lawyers. It seemed for a time as if their great services had been forgotten. A large number of the most eminent and older members of the bar were Royalists, and they had either left the country or had retired from practice. Many other distinguished lawyers were actively engaged in politics, or in the army, or had accepted positions on the bench. This left the practice of the law in the hands of men of less distinction and ability.

[1] The Rise of American Civilization, vol. 1, p. 101.

Social and financial conditions after the Revolution, more-over, tended to produce great unrest. Interruption of business caused by the war, high prices, and enormous public debts seri-ously embarrassed all classes of people. Royalists whose estates had been confiscated were making strenuous efforts to have their property restored, while English creditors were trying to recover their claims. The chief law work, therefore, was the collection of debts and the enforcement of contracts. Jails were over-crowded with debtors imprisoned under the rigorous laws of the period. Irritated by excessive litigation, by the increase of suits for debts and mortgage foreclosures, and by heavy fees and court costs, many persons were inclined to attribute all their misfortunes to the existence of lawyers. So bitter was the feel-ing against the legal profession that at the town meeting of 1786 in Braintree, Massachusetts, the following resolution was passed:

We humbly request that there may be such Laws compiled as may crush or at least put a proper check or restraint on that order of Gentlemen denominated Lawyers the completion of whose modern conduct appears to us to tend rather to the destruction than the pres-ervation of this Commonwealth.[1]

In 1787 John Quincy Adams, then a college senior, made the following statement which revealed how strong was public opinion:

At a time when the profession of the Law labours under the heavy weight of popular indignation; when it is upbraided as the original cause of all the evils with which the Commonwealth is distressed; when the legislature have been publicly exhorted by a popular writer to abolish it entirely, and when the mere title of lawyer is sufficient to deprive a man of the public confidence, it should seem this pro-

[1] Adams, Charles F., Three Episodes of Massachusetts History. Houghton Mifflin Co., Boston, 1896, vol. 2, p. 897.

fession would afford but a poor subject for panegyric; but its real utility is not to be determined by the short-lived frenzy of an inconsiderate multitude, nor by the artful misrepresentations of an insidious writer.[1]

Shays' Rebellion, which had broken out in Massachusetts in the preceding year, was directed largely against the courts and lawyers, and military force was required to subdue it. Similar conditions prevailed in other states, and riots were numerous. The debtors of Vermont set fire to their court-houses; those of New Jersey nailed up the doors. Lawyers were mobbed in the streets and judges were threatened.

Parallel with this hatred of lawyers as a class, prejudice once more appeared against the system of English common law on which the courts based their decisions. It was shared, not only by many educated as well as uneducated laymen, but by many American lawyers. After the Revolution, there had been much discussion in the courts concerning the extent to which the common law of England was binding. Some states had adopted in their constitutions such parts of the common law as had formed the law of the colonies prior to 1775. In other states there had been no authoritative declaration, and much uneasiness had resulted. Many persons agreed that English law had no binding force after the Revolution, while some of the anti-Federalists claimed that it had had no power prior to the Revolution unless it had been accorded power by constitution or statute.

In addition to antagonism of everything that savored of England or monarchy, the jealousy of the individual states over any infringement of their jurisdiction by the federal government further accentuated the difficulties of the legal profession.

[1] "Diary of John Quincy Adams." In Proceedings of the Massachusetts Historical Society, Boston, Second Series, vol. 16, November, 1902, p. 343.

The War of 1812 exercised a great influence upon economic and legal history. It gave rise to a vast number of decisions on prize and admiralty law. It turned attention, which had been centered almost exclusively upon shipping and agriculture, to manufacture and invention. As a result, corporation and patent law made their appearance. Because coast-wise trade was ruined by the British blockade, the war promoted the construction of canals, turnpikes, and better means of internal communication. Increased transportation resulted in opening new areas for legal service. Finally, the war cut the legal profession off from the supply of English law reports and books, and thus cast lawyers upon their own resources in the solution of legal problems.[1]

Before the nineteenth century was far advanced, the rapidly growing complexity of American civilization further altered the nature of legal practice. Increasing industrialization, the advent of the railroad, the settlement of the West, new political trends, the rising tide of immigration, the Civil War and reconstruction, the opening of foreign markets and expansion in world trade—all these and many other factors worked marked changes in the type of legal service that was needed. Older forms of practice were largely superseded by new forms, which had been undreamed of a century earlier. The reputation of a lawyer had long depended upon his appearance in court, particularly in trials that had a human and dramatic appeal. He now began to serve as advocate less frequently, because he was greatly needed as an adviser in legal matters. This trend continued, so that today there are attorneys of long experience who have never argued a case before a jury.

One of the most noticeable changes in the bar during the last

[1] Warren, Charles, A History of the American Bar, pp. 212–217, 223, 228, 275–276.

century was the relative increase in the number of lawyers employed by industrial or commercial concerns on a salary or retainership basis. From the days when Abraham Lincoln served as an efficient representative of the directors of the Illinois Central Railroad until the end of the century, lawyers connected with railroads found in that type of practice a peculiarly lucrative source of income. Development of big business in the second half of the century, with its details of corporate organization, financing, failures, and receiverships, opened the door for further legal activities, which have increased in scope and volume and which will be discussed in a later portion of the book.[1]

At present international law, with its claims commissions, arbitration tribunals, World Court, and many branches of commercial transactions, affords another field of legal service which is by no means restricted exclusively to the law firms of large cities.

The greatest expansion of the twentieth century, however, lies in the development of administrative law. As federal and state governments have assumed more power and responsibility, various types of boards, commissions, and bureaus have been created, whose work is done in great part by persons trained in the law. Thus, the largest number of lawyers in the United States, in proportion to population, is in the District of Columbia, and many of them are in the employ of the government. The same situation exists to a lesser degree in the state capitals. Although the legal profession has shown steady resistance to the growth of quasi-judicial governmental agencies, they will undoubtedly continue to increase. Already these agencies "lie all along the route which modern government is traveling," and

[1] See pp. 219–222.

they have opened to the practicing lawyer a large new field for employment.[1]

While the scope of legal practice has been expanding within the areas of business and government, it has become restricted in some other areas.[2] Title examination and conveyancing, which once occupied a large proportion of an attorney's time, are gradually being taken from him by the spread of title insurance and by decrease in the number of persons holding real estate. Banks and trust companies are persistently invading the field of administration and management of estates that lawyers once found profitable. Industrial compensation and liability insurance have largely eliminated certain former sources of income. The probation system and penal boards of various kinds are reducing the need for legal service. Preparation of income tax returns and other documents, and practice before such government agencies as the Interstate Commerce Commission have been taken over in part by specialists without law-school training.

Other changes have also appeared, which center around the relative position of the lawyer in public life and in society. For many years prior to the presidency of Andrew Jackson, the law was conceived of as a stepping stone to public service. Although he was a lawyer and had been judge of the highest court of his state, Jackson supported the theory that government could and should be operated by the common people; trained lawyers were not essential. Rewards in the field of politics and government began to be diverted from the bar by the appearance of a distinct class of politicians and by the development of more carefully organized parties. In later administrations at-

---

[1] Rogers, James Grafton, "Forces Remolding the Lawyer's Life." In American Bar Association Journal, October, 1931, p. 641.
[2] *Ibid.*, p. 640.

torneys were again welcome, but they never entirely regained their former prestige as public servants. They have continued, nevertheless, to enter government positions in sufficient numbers so that many of the most important offices have been filled by members of the bar. Some two-thirds of the presidents of the United States have been lawyers. So have nearly all the federal secretaries of state, as well as all the federal and most of the state judiciary. The legal profession has provided most of the state governors, while its representation in state legislatures has been far greater than that of any other group. The same has been true of Congress. At a recent session 70 per cent of the Senate and 60 per cent of the House of Representatives were lawyers. In spite of such impressive figures, however, few of the ablest and most successful members of the bar have devoted themselves to public affairs.[1]

The lawyer has not only lost some of his prestige as a public servant but the bar has been forced to meet competition from other rapidly advancing professions. There was a long period when the influence of the clergy had waned considerably, and when engineers and physicians were not sufficiently numerous or strongly enough organized to challenge supremacy of the lawyer. During that time he stood at the pinnacle of professional power and authority. Recently he has had to share leadership with other groups, some of which are today pressing strong claims for ascendancy.[2]

LEGAL EDUCATION

The preceding section has briefly described the growth of the

[1] *Ibid.*, p. 641.
[2] Harno, Albert J., Letter to the Law Alumni of the University of Illinois, Urbana, April, 1936, p. 2.

legal profession from colonial days until the present time. We turn now to legal education, changes in which have played an important role in developing professional characteristics.

EARLY DEVELOPMENTS

As there were no colleges that gave lectures in law and no schools devoted to legal training in this country until near the close of the eighteenth century, the prospective colonial lawyer, unless he were able to go to England to study, entered upon one of two forms of apprenticeship as a means of preparing himself for practice.[1] He frequently became a copyist or assistant in the office of a clerk of a court. Thus, he was able to pick up scraps of knowledge about legal practice and read such books as he could borrow. This was the exiguous training that many eminent lawyers received who could not afford the time or money for more comprehensive preparation. Such men generally became well versed in ordinary forms of law and in the leading decisions of the courts. They succeeded as long as cases followed traditional patterns, and the simplicity of the law of the period was a great help to them. They knew little of law as a science, and unusual cases presented grave difficulties.

The second form of apprenticeship was to enter the office of a leading member of the bar, preferably one of the few who had a good law library. There, through study, observation, and occasionally by direct teaching, law students absorbed the principles of law. They were expected to copy pleadings and other documents and to draft briefs. In return, the master gave advice, information, or instruction according to his leisure and inclination. Since he was generally too busy to pay much attention to his students, the chief advantage gained was often from in-

[1] Warren, Charles, A History of the American Bar, pp. 164–167.

formal contacts with him and from association with able lawyers against whom he tried cases.

For the privilege of engaging in this kind of apprenticeship, the student usually paid a fee of perhaps $100 or $200. If the lawyer were a man of great distinction, the amount was sometimes as much as $500. There is still extant a promissory note which reads: "Phil. March 22, 1782. I promise to pay James Wilson Esq. or order on demand one hundred guineas, his fee for receiving my nephew Bushrod Washington as a student of law in his office. G. Washington."[1]

By 1770 the bar in a few states had become more compact in organization and more assured of its power than in earlier years. As a result the legal profession gradually began to formulate rigid rules concerning requirements for office study, which paved the way for the establishment of regular law schools. In Massachusetts the Suffolk bar instituted the movement toward more strict regulations. In 1771 it decreed that "consent of the bar . . . shall not be given to any young gentleman who has not had an education at college, or a liberal education equivalent in the judgment of the bar."[2]

The reputation of the Suffolk bar became so high during the next few years that its members received applications for instruction from many southern students who would have gone to England to study in pre-Revolutionary days. In 1780 it voted that "no gentleman take a student into his office for a less consideration than one hundred pounds sterling," and in 1783 it declared that "no gentleman in future shall have in his office more than three students at the same time."[3] In New Hamp-

---

[1] *Ibid.,* p. 166.
[2] "Record-Book of the Suffolk Bar." In Proceedings of the Massachusetts Historical Society, Boston, First Series, vol. 19, December, 1881, p. 150.
[3] *Ibid.,* pp. 154, 157.

shire, Vermont, Rhode Island, Connecticut, and New Jersey, similar restrictive provisions were put into effect a little later. In some instances these provisions were formulated by bar associations, in others by rule of court or by statute.

Subsequent to the Revolutionary War, American colleges began to offer lectures in law. In 1777 the Assembly of Connecticut proposed to endow three professorships at Yale College in law, medicine, and oratory, if it might have some voice in the appointment of professors and in the government of the College. The plan was never consummated, for the Corporation of Yale declined to yield any of its powers to the Assembly. President Ezra Stiles, who came into office in 1777, however, lectured on law and jurisprudence to the undergraduates.

The College of William and Mary in Virginia is generally credited with founding the first American professorship in law. This occurred in 1779. There was, at the time, only one other such professorship in the entire English-speaking world, the Vinerian chair at Oxford, which had been established in 1758 and whose first incumbent was Sir William Blackstone.

Eleven years after the founding of the professorship at William and Mary, the College of Philadelphia formally appointed James Wilson, an associate justice of the United States Supreme Court, to the position of professor of law. His first lecture, delivered before President Washington and the Cabinet, the governor of Pennsylvania, members of Congress and of the legislature, did not meet with general approbation. His violent criticisms of Blackstone and his extreme Federalist views concerning the power of the national government were apparently not well received by lawyers or by the public. He later discontinued his lectures, probably because of lack of interest on the part of students. It was a quarter of a century later before the

University of Pennsylvania, with which the College of Philadelphia had been consolidated, appointed another professor of law.

In 1793 King's College in New York, today Columbia University, made the well-known James Kent professor of law. His early lectures formed the nucleus of his famous four-volume Commentaries on American Law, the first edition of which was published between 1826 and 1830. Because only two students and his own clerks attended his lectures in 1795 and no one enrolled in 1796, he tendered his resignation, but it was not accepted. During the winter of 1797–1798, six or eight students presented themselves. At the conclusion of this series of lectures he resigned to enter upon a long judicial career. When he retired from the bench in 1823, he was again made professor.

Transylvania University in Lexington, Kentucky, appointed a graduate of William and Mary in 1799 to be "professor of law and politics." For a generation Transylvania was the only organized center of legal education west of the Alleghenies. The professorship seems to have remained in more or less continuous existence until 1879. A few other colleges gave lectures in law but in them, as in the institutions already mentioned, an attempt was rarely made to afford complete and practical education for law students. Before the end of the eighteenth century, however, several private law schools had been opened by individual lawyers where such an education could be obtained. These private schools were essentially a more specialized and elaborate form of law office. They originated in New England, where the system of apprenticeship training was most firmly established, and spread from that area to other states.

No one can say how many of these institutions there were, since it was not always possible to distinguish between a law office and a private school. At least 20 such schools existed at some time during the first half of the nineteenth century, and probably many more. In 1850 there is record of only three that had not either formed a connection with a college or perished. Thereafter they became almost extinct, although another type of proprietary institution appeared at a later period. Even at the time when these schools were most numerous and prosperous, their mortality was high. In the absence of endowment, and before the discovery that an independent law school might attract students by conferring degrees, a private institution was entirely dependent for its success upon its owner or administrator. When he died, grew aged, or turned to some other interest, no definite assets remained upon which a successor might build. The significance of these schools lies in the fact that they served temporarily to provide some systematic instruction in law during a period when colleges were not yet prepared to give it.[1]

The most influential of the private institutions was that founded in 1784 in Litchfield, Connecticut, by Judge Tapping Reeve.[2] Although the school was conducted in a small and most unpretentious building, situated behind Judge Reeve's magnificent home, it always bore the dignified title, the Litchfield Law School. To it, before its abandonment in 1833, came over 1,000 students, many from distant states. In 1813 the enrolment was 55—a figure exceeded by no other American law school for twenty years. Large numbers of its alumni later occupied judicial or governmental positions of great prestige.

---

[1] Reed, Alfred Z., Training for the Public Profession of the Law. Carnegie Foundation for the Advancement of Teaching, New York, 1921, pp. 128, 132–133, 189.
[2] Warren, Charles, A History of the American Bar, p. 360; "Law School at Litchfield," in United States Law Journal and Civilian's Magazine, June, 1823, pp. 401–405.

Professor Joel Parker of the Harvard Law School remarked as late as 1871:

> Perhaps no Law School has had—perhaps I may add ever will have—so great a proportion of distinguished men on its catalogue, if for no other reason, because attendance upon a Law School was then the rare exception, an advantage attained in general only by very ambitious young men, and because there was then much less competition for the offices and honors to which they aspired.[1]

This private institution and some of its scarcely less noteworthy contemporaries exerted a profound influence upon the nature of legal training for half a century. It remained for Harvard College, however, to found the first school of law of the type which, despite many subsequent variations, still dominates American legal education. In 1815 Harvard created a professorship in law for the benefit of college seniors and resident graduates. Isaac Parker, chief justice of the Massachusetts Supreme Court, who occupied the chair, became convinced that attendance at lectures did not furnish adequate theoretical preparation for entering upon legal practice, even if accompanied by practical training in an office. Consequently, he suggested the founding of a separate professional school devoted to the training of lawyers. This was accomplished in 1817.

Harvard thus took a decisive step that was to serve as a precedent for other universities. The number of students, however, was small. For many years it never exceeded 20, and at one time there was only a single student. The legal profession had not yet accepted the idea that law could be learned in a school as well as in a law office. Cambridge, moreover, was inaccessible in the days before railroads. It was more convenient for many

[1] The Law School, Harvard College. Hurd and Houghton, Cambridge, 1871, p. 8.

men to attend courses in the University of Virginia and the College of William and Mary, or in private schools conducted by distinguished lawyers or judges in such towns as Philadelphia, Litchfield, Northampton, Dedham, and Amherst. In 1830, however, as the result of a munificent gift, a new professorship was created at Harvard and Joseph Story, associate justice of the United States Supreme Court, was appointed to it. Under his guidance, the law school shortly became the leading institution in this country. In 1844, just before his death, enrolment reached 163, an unparalleled figure for those days.

By 1840 instruction in professional law was being given in the colleges or universities of William and Mary, Virginia, Transylvania, Harvard, Yale, Cincinnati, and Dickinson.[1] About 350 students were in attendance at these schools. During the next twenty years the founding of university law departments proceeded at an average of nearly one a year. It was evident that the trend had turned from the private school to one connected with an institution of higher learning. Between 1860 and 1870 some institutions were forced to close because of the Civil War. Subsequent to 1870 new schools were established with more rapidity than wisdom. In that year there were 31 schools, in 1880 there were 51, and in 1890, 61. By 1900 the number had jumped to 102. A few of these institutions, particularly those founded after 1890, were independent of university affiliation of any kind.

On the whole, the schools connected with institutions of higher learning were very similar to one another prior to the Civil War. They were conducted by and for practitioners, had

---

[1] Since the material presented by Mr. Reed of the Carnegie Foundation, in Training for the Public Profession of the Law, is the most authoritative source of information about the history of legal education, the remainder of this section has been taken from pp. 151–193 of that volume.

practically no entrance requirements, and were so loosely co-ordinated with the college or university that they were not an integral part of the educational scheme. So difficult was it even to exist that they were glad to receive students on almost any terms. They could not greatly raise their standards, since enrolments would suffer were they to require students to do much more than the minimum of work demanded by the state. Such extra work as was offered was made attractive by the promise of a degree upon its completion.

The length of the school course was most often one year. Although, by rule of court, the required period of legal preparation in Massachusetts from 1810 to 1836 was three years for college graduates and five for all others, Harvard demanded that only a year and a half of this time be spent in the law school. The rest could be passed in a law office before entering, during, or after attending the school. This plan proved to be so impractical that it was discarded in 1839, and the length of the course was thereafter stated as being one and one-half years. The course at Yale extended over two years. These are the only exceptions known to the one-year standard as late as 1840. In 1860, 12 of the 21 university schools were still requiring only one year of work.

By 1870, after a century of experimentation, law schools came to be accepted by the legal profession as a logical method of preparation for the practice of law. This attitude was reflected in bar admission requirements, which state legislatures began to make more strict. The growing complexity of law, moreover, demanded a lengthening of the course of study and a rearrangement of the curriculum.

Just at this time President Charles W. Eliot made Christopher C. Langdell dean of the Harvard Law School. Perhaps no single event in legal education during the second half of the nineteenth century has had greater significance. Upon appointment in 1870, he immediately began extensive reforms. His first act was to establish a progressive course of study. Under the old system subjects had been taught in alternate years to classes composed both of first- and second-year students. He so arranged the curriculum that students were not allowed credit for second-year work until they had passed examinations covering the courses of the first year. The system of engaging lecturers who were practicing lawyers or judges was abandoned, and full-time professors were obtained. It was ruled that no student under nineteen years of age should be admitted to the school, and all who did not have a baccalaureate degree should be required to pass an entrance examination. In 1876 the faculty voted to lengthen the course of study to three years, and in 1893 they decreed that admission should be open only to graduates of approved colleges or to those qualified to enter the senior year of Harvard College. Sooner or later many of the other schools followed these reforms. The present basic pattern of legal education still reflects innovations made in this one school over sixty years ago.

The rise of university law schools in the nineteenth century, as has already been noted, was an almost fatal blow to schools of the Litchfield type. The fact that proprietary institutions did not confer degrees put them at a great disadvantage. That a degree might be awarded by an independent law school does not seem to have been regarded as a possibility prior to the Civil War. For a long time it had been evident, however, that degrees conferred in the name of a university upon graduates of schools only loosely affiliated with a larger organization was often a hollow mockery from the academic point of view. Consequently, the degree came gradually to be looked upon merely as the symbol of a successfully completed professional law course. When this attitude had once become established, the theory that no institution except a university might properly confer the LL.B. was too transparent a pretense to be continued.

In 1866 an independent evening law school, which had been established the year previously, was incorporated as the Iowa Law School with the privilege of awarding a degree in law. When 12 graduates actually received the LL.B. in 1866, a precedent was set which was to attract the attention of practicing lawyers who wished to engage in legal education. This new type of degree-conferring proprietary institution, however, did not assume importance until the eighteen-nineties, when evening law schools began to be more numerous. Since then the appearance of many independent institutions has created a serious problem in legal education, as later pages will indicate.

NUMBER OF SCHOOLS AND OF STUDENTS

When the twentieth century opened 102 degree-conferring law schools, as has already been noted, were in existence in the United States. No fewer than 33 new schools appeared during the next ten years. Several closed their doors, however, during the same period, so that the decade closed with a total of 124 institutions. In 1920 the number had increased to 146. The academic year of 1930–1931 saw 180 law schools in operation; 1936–1937 saw 185 schools. Thus, during the short period of thirty-six years, the number of institutions for the training of lawyers increased by 83.[1]

---

[1] These and subsequent figures appearing in this section have been taken, unless otherwise indicated, from the Annual Review of Legal Education for 1936, published in 1937 by the Section of Legal Education and Admissions to the Bar of the American Bar Association.

Large as this growth has been, it must be borne in mind that these figures represent only degree-conferring law schools. Other institutions prepare students for the law, but their number has never been determined. The problem has always existed of what schools to include in any list, since the very meaning of the term, law school, depends upon the interpretation of the person who uses it. Mr. Reed, who for many years presented statistics of law schools, limited his attention to residential institutions which confer degrees. When the Section of Legal Education and Admissions to the Bar of the American Bar Association undertook in 1936 to continue the annual publication of these data, it decided to use a somewhat different basis of enumeration and defined a law school as an institution having more than 10 students, which provides a definite curriculum and conducts regular classes. It disregarded correspondence schools, small law classes conducted primarily by one man for profit, and review courses offered in many cities for periods of five or six weeks to law-school and office students who wish coaching in preparation for bar examinations. In spite of the fact that several such institutions and a good many review courses are known to exist, the number of their students is probably not sufficiently large to affect greatly the figure for total enrolment in all schools.

Upon counting those institutions that conformed to its definition, the Section of Legal Education found that there were 195 in 1935. Eight of these did not grant degrees. For 1936 it listed 190, of which five were non-degree conferring schools.[1]

It is instructive to note what has been happening to medical schools since 1900 while law schools have increased by 86 per

[1] Data relating to the number of law schools and student enrolment for 1937 appeared too late to be utilized in subsequent analyses in this study. It may be noted, however, that the number of schools decreased from 190 to 185 between 1936 and 1937.

cent.[1] At the beginning of the century there were 160 medical schools or 58 more than the number of law schools.[2] Before 1910, however, the great reform in medical education began to make itself felt and weak schools with totally inadequate financial resources, equipment, and faculty began to close their doors.[3] By the end of the decade, the number of schools had dropped to 131. During the next ten years the reorganization of medical education went on apace, as the result of pressure exerted by the American Medical Association, the Association of American Medical Colleges, state boards of examiners, the Carnegie Foundation for the Advancement of Teaching, and other groups. Figures for 1920 showed that only 85 institutions had survived the drastic changes. Thus 46 schools had ceased operation during the brief course of a decade. Between 1920 and 1930 several other schools found themselves unable to command the financial support requisite for maintaining necessarily expensive medical training, and so by 1930 the number of schools had been reduced to 76. Ten of the 76, moreover, attempt to give only the first two years of the curriculum, depending upon schools with better clinical facilities to provide the work of the other two years. Since 1930 one new school has been founded, and consequently the number now stands at 77.

It might be expected that the increase since 1900 in the num-

[1] Figures on number of medical schools are from the Journal of the American Medical Association, August 29, 1936, pp. 665, 671. Six institutions, offering a medical curriculum which is not recognized by the American Medical Association or the state board of examiners of nearly all states, are not included. Neither are schools which train persons to be osteopaths, chiropractors, and so on.

[2] See p. 39.

[3] A more detailed description of the reform in medical education which so greatly reduced the number of schools and resulted in a high degree of standardization for remaining institutions, appears in Physicians and Medical Care, by Esther Lucile Brown, Russell Sage Foundation, New York, 1937.

ber of law schools would have occurred mainly in states where schools were either non-existent or few. Such has not been the case. Instead, there has been multiplication in places where schools were already flourishing. Once a school has been established, rivals spring up rapidly. In 1900, two states had 6 degree-conferring schools each, three states had 7, and one had 11. In 1936, 11 states had a total of 110 schools. Pennsylvania and Indiana had 6 each; Massachusetts and Missouri, 8; the District of Columbia and Illinois, 9; New York and Tennessee, 10; Ohio and Texas, 12; and California, 20.

The growth of urban areas has exerted a marked influence upon the number and distribution of schools. Large cities have established their claim to be regarded as the natural home of legal education, because students, practicing lawyers who act as lecturers, and other teachers can be more easily secured in such places. As a result, there are only three cities of more than 200,000 population in the entire United States that have no law school. They are Providence, Rhode Island; Rochester, New York; and Dayton, Ohio. Los Angeles boasts of 8 schools; Chicago, 7; New York City, 6; Boston, 5 (6, if the Harvard Law School situated across the Charles River in Cambridge is included); and San Francisco, 5. On the other hand, in the 6 small or primarily rural states, New Hampshire, Vermont, Rhode Island, Delaware, New Mexico, and Nevada, there are no schools at all.

Law schools differ greatly in size. Of the 190 listed in the Annual Review of Legal Education for 1936, the smallest school had an attendance of 11. There were actually 26 institutions with fewer than 50 students and 80 with fewer than 100. In 91 the number of students ranged from 100 to 500. In 18 there were more than 500, and in 5 more than 1,000. Attendance in the largest school was 1,891. The median size was 120. This was a very different situation from that existing among medical schools in 1936, as will be seen from Table 1.

TABLE 1.—SIZE OF LAW SCHOOLS AND OF MEDICAL SCHOOLS
IN THE UNITED STATES, 1936

Number of students	Number of law schools	Number of medical schools
Under 50	26	2[a]
50 to 99	54	7[a]
100 to 499	91	58
500 to 999	13	10
Over 1,000	5	0
Total	189[b]	77

[a] These schools offer only the first two years of the medical curriculum. There is no school that awards the M.D. degree which has fewer than 100 students.
[b] Attendance was not reported for one law school.

Both very small and very large law schools have been subjected to severe censure by persons acquainted with problems of professional education. The very small school can rarely provide essential physical equipment, an adequate library, a sufficiently broad curriculum, and a well-trained faculty who are paid salaries large enough so that they can be expected to devote a substantial amount of their time to the work of the school. Endowment is generally non-existent, and there is no definite and dependable source of income. Hence, economic insecurity underlies all the problems with which the small school is faced.

In the very large law school the fundamental problem is of a different nature. Numbers are so great as to be troublesome. The school presents the appearance of a factory operating under methods of mass production. In fact, such schools have often been popularly designated "sausage mills."[1] Practically no personal contact exists between teacher and student. Since classes tend to be too large for discussion, instruction is chiefly through lectures. In spite of the fact that this type of institution generally has a large income from fees alone, not all of the income is necessarily devoted to the operation of the school. Often, in the past, a considerable proportion of it was utilized by the parent university to aid other departments or schools which had annual deficits. This problem does not now arise so often as formerly, but many of the university law schools are still unable to exercise control over their own finances.

Although growth in the number of law schools has been very great, it has been exceeded by that of law students. In 1860 the total number of law-school students was about 1,200, or four for each 100,000 of the population. During the next thirty years population increased so rapidly that it had almost precisely doubled by 1890. The number of law students, however, increased nearly fourfold in this period. There were about 4,500 in 1890, or seven for each 100,000 persons. Since then population has increased more slowly, but the number of students has grown at what many members of the legal profession consider to be a dangerous rate. Until 1928–1929, when the peak was reached with almost 49,000 in attendance, there was a continuous tendency for ever greater numbers of students to enter law schools. This tendency was particularly marked during the third decade of the twentieth century when enrolment nearly doubled.

Between 1928–1929 and 1929–1930 a change occurred, and for four years enrolment figures declined. This falling off of

[1] Horack, H. Claude, "Law Schools of To-day and To-morrow." In American Law School Review, March, 1930, p. 655.

matriculants may have been primarily the result of the economic depression. Funds for higher education were not so available as they had been, particularly for that class of students who were largely self-supporting. It is likely, moreover, that the realization that legal positions would be almost impossible to obtain deterred many prospective lawyers from beginning their training.

By the autumn of 1933 the tide changed again, and 500 more students were enrolled than in the fall of 1932. Further gains raised registration in the autumn of 1935 to nearly 42,000, or 33 students for each 100,000 population. Interestingly enough, this recent increase in number of matriculants has not been sustained. Available enrolment figures for the autumn of 1936 showed a total of 40,218 persons attending 190 schools.[1] Although there were five fewer institutions than in the preceding year, the difference in number of schools accounted for less than a third of the decrease in the enrolment figure. Twenty-nine states had fewer students matriculated in 1936, 13 states had more, one remained the same, and 6 states have no schools. This decrease may be attributed in part to the fact that changes have recently been made in bar admission requirements which have resulted in restricting attendance in law schools.[2] Similar changes, now being instituted in additional states, will probably cause further decrease in enrolments. Not until more drastic steps are taken, however, is it likely that the present output of young lawyers will be greatly checked.[3]

---

[1] Matriculation in 1937 showed a still further decline of 2.5 per cent. There were 39,255 students enrolled in the 185 schools.

[2] For further discussion see p. 140.

[3] Unfortunately, it is impossible to present evidence of the growth in the number of graduates from schools of law, important as that subject is. No attempt has ever been made, either by the Carnegie Foundation or the Section of Legal Education of the American Bar Association, to obtain annual

The situation concerning growth in number of law students appears more clearly when comparison is made, as in Table 2, with the number of students in medical schools. Between 1890 and 1905 medical students increased so rapidly that persons interested in the welfare of the medical profession were alarmed. Thereafter, as the reorganization in medical education became effective, numbers declined greatly over a period of fifteen years. After 1920 there was a gradual increase. Growth would have been much greater, however, if requirements for admission to the study of medicine had not been so rigid and if many institutions had not so limited their enrolments that only about one-half of the total number who applied each year were accepted. In spite of the control that medical schools have exercised over admissions, the Council on Medical Education and Hospitals of the American Medical Association has emphatically declared of late that the number of matriculants must be further reduced in those institutions where clinical or other facilities are not entirely adequate. Whether as the result of pressure from the Council or for some other reason, medical school attendance in 1935–1936 was slightly less than for the preceding year.

FULL-TIME VS. PART-TIME SCHOOLS

It is now necessary to inquire in greater detail into the nature of law schools. There are two outstanding types: the full-time

---

figures for number of graduates or degrees conferred. The federal Office of Education publishes information on this subject, but since a considerable and varying number of law schools have failed to report for each of its studies, and since its figures for years subsequent to 1933–1934 are not yet available, the data are of restricted value. The number of graduates appears to have increased roughly in proportion to the increase in students. It is interesting to note that the Office of Education reports 9,308 law-school graduates in 1932, and 8,577 in 1934, for less than the total number of law schools, whereas the numbers of medical school graduates in those years were 4,936 and 5,038.

TABLE 2.—NUMBER OF LAW AND OF MEDICAL SCHOOLS, AND
OF THEIR STUDENTS, 1890 TO 1936[a]

Year	Law[b]		Medicine	
	Schools	Students	Schools	Students
1889–1890	61	4,486	133	15,404
1899–1900	102	12,408	160	25,171
1909–1910	124	19,498	131	21,526
1919–1920	146	24,503	85	13,798
1928–1929	173	48,942	–	–
1929–1930	180	46,751	76	21,597
1931–1932	182	42,165	76	21,135
1932 (Fall)	185	38,260	–	–
1932–1933	185	41,153	77	22,466
1933 (Fall)	190	38,771	–	–
1933–1934	–	–	77	22,799
1934–1935	–	–	77	22,888
1935 (Fall)	195	41,920	–	–
1935–1936	–	–	77	22,564
1936 (Fall)	190	40,218	–	–

[a] Figures for number of law schools and students have been taken from reports of the Annual Review of Legal Education. For sources of information concerning medical schools and students, see Physicians and Medical Care, by Esther Lucile Brown, p. 29.
[b] Figures for law schools are for degree-conferring schools until 1935, for 1935 and 1936 they are for law schools as defined by the Section on Legal Education of the American Bar Association. See p. 32. For some recent years two sets of enrolment figures are available, those for the full year being somewhat larger only than those for the fall quarter.

school and the part-time school. In the former, instruction is given in the morning and early afternoon, and the average student devotes his whole working time to the study of the law. In the latter, sessions generally are conducted in the late afternoon or evening or both, since those hours are most convenient for self-supporting students. In 1936, 83 of the schools listed in the Annual Review of Legal Education were operating only on a full-time basis and 107 were operating wholly on part time or on both full time and part time. Of the 107 schools, 65 gave instruction exclusively in the evening, and 7 both in the afternoon and evening. The remaining 35 schools had morning sessions for full-time students, as well as afternoon or evening courses or both. Alfred Z. Reed has coined the term, "mixed" school, to designate this latter type of institution.

The greater increase in law schools has been in the part-time group. There were about 40 full-time schools in 1890 and only 20 part-time ones, as compared with 83 full-time and 107 part-time or mixed schools at present. Thus, full-time schools have increased at an average rate of about one a year, while those offering part-time courses have increased by two annually. There has also been a tendency in recent years for institutions that began strictly as evening schools to add morning sessions. In 1920 there were only 8 having both morning and evening sessions, as compared with 35 in 1936.

Between 1920 and 1930 enrolments in part-time and mixed schools combined grew much more rapidly than did those in full-time institutions. Figures collected by the Carnegie Foundation show that between 1922 and 1928 matriculation in part-time law schools and part-time divisions of mixed schools increased 43 per cent, while that of full-time schools increased only 17 per cent. During the same period attendance in morning sessions of mixed schools increased 85.5 per cent.[1] Between 1930 and 1936 these trends appear to have been reversed. Full-time institutions gained slightly in the total number of their students, while part-time and mixed schools combined decreased

[1] Reed, Alfred Z., "Autumn Attendance in United States Degree-Conferring Law Schools 1922, 1928, 1931, 1932 and 1933." In Bar Examiner, September, 1934, p. 249.

slightly. In the autumn of 1936 full-time institutions registered 15,375 students; morning sessions of part-time schools, 3,926; and the afternoon and evening sessions of part-time schools, 18,998. There were, in addition, 1,919 students nearly all of whom were matriculated in five mixed schools. They cannot be classified, however, since the five schools failed to report the division between morning and evening sessions.

Several reasons account for the marked growth of part-time schools until the economic depression that began in 1929. Institutions were established, almost without exception, in cities conveniently situated for students who needed to earn a living, and the class periods were arranged to interfere as little as possible with day-time occupations. Fees, in general, were lower than in the full-time schools of the same city. It is true that some state university schools charge a tuition fee smaller than that of most part-time schools, but the frequent situation of such universities in little towns is a handicap to self-supporting students. Requirements for admission to evening schools are usually less severe than those of full-time institutions, and the work required is necessarily less exacting. The evening school, moreover, draws many students who are not prospective lawyers but who are employed in or are preparing for other occupations in which a knowledge of law is an asset.

There has been a great deal of severe criticism of part-time schools. Much of this criticism has come from professors of law in full-time schools, who are convinced that adequate legal training requires the complete attention of students. Even though 69 of the evening schools have recently extended their curriculum from three to four years and 4 have extended it to five years, these professors question whether evening students have sufficient opportunity and energy for thorough preparation in their courses. They point to low admission requirements and show that 54 of the 107 part-time or mixed schools, in comparison with only 3 of the 83 full-time schools, have no academic prerequisites. They are convinced that both the very small enrolments found in some of these schools and the large enrolments and huge classes characteristic of others do not permit of the best type of instruction. They doubt the wisdom of having so high a percentage of practicing lawyers on the faculty as are found in many evening schools.[1] They consider that the teachers are too conservative in formulating curricula, and have continued to use outmoded techniques of instruction. They regret the absence of an experimental approach to problems of legal education, and the lack of research in questions of law. Finally, they object strenuously to that group of part-time schools which are operated for pecuniary profit. They maintain that such institutions have lost sight of any real educational purpose, and, with the minimum of effort and expense, aim only to prepare students to pass bar examinations.[2]

In contrast to criticisms such as these, there is warm praise of evening law schools from some persons, particularly from lawyers who teach on their faculties. A statement made a few years ago by Dean O. C. Snyder of the Columbus [Ohio] College of Law summarized the general attitude of the advocates of part-time schools.[3] He maintained that the full-time law schools had assumed an attitude of superiority, which was due to lack of information and lack of discrimination between strong and weak evening schools. In his estimation the part-time institu-

[1] Lavery, U. S., "Survey of Legal Education in Illinois." In American Bar Association Journal, October, 1926, pp. 713–714.
[2] Horack, H. Claude, "Law Schools of To-day and To-morrow." In American Law School Review, March, 1930, p. 654.
[3] "The Function of the Night Law School." In American Law School Review, May, 1933, pp. 827–832.

tion attracted students of greater maturity and seriousness of purpose than did the morning school; its faculty was composed of members of the bar and bench who were in constant touch with actual legal practice; and the study of law was presented from the functional approach. For these reasons he believed that a good evening school could effectively fulfil its functions, and could meet a need which morning schools were unable to serve.

Mr. Reed, who has devoted a quarter of a century to the examination of legal education and who has attempted to look at part-time law schools objectively, has been their avowed partisan.[1] He has earnestly advocated their continuance, because he believes it essential that there be schools which will keep the legal profession adequately representative of all social and economic groups in the population. Despite everything that full-time schools may do through scholarships and loans for students of restricted means, Mr. Reed feels that such schools draw the great majority of their students only from the more favored classes in society.

Although he has championed the cause of evening law schools, he has not refrained from vigorous criticism of their work. The most serious difficulty into which they have fallen, in his opinion, is that of attempting to copy the program of full-time schools, when they should have created a distinctive sphere of activity that they might occupy with honor to themselves and with profit to the community. They profess with pride to be doing about what full-time law schools do. They give similar

[1] For further details, see Mr. Reed's two books, Training for the Public Profession of the Law, pp. 398–402, and Present-Day Law Schools in the United States and Canada, pp. 287–290, published by the Carnegie Foundation in 1921 and 1928. See also his talk, "Social Desirability of Evening or Part-time Law School," reproduced in American Law School Review, May, 1931, pp. 203–207.

degrees and announce themselves competent to prepare applicants to practice all branches of law. "As a result of these pre-
tensions . . . they necessarily operate as cheapened copies of
the full-time model."[1] Although they have made it possible for
some persons to be admitted to the bar who ought to have been,
and who otherwise could not have been admitted, they have also
permitted young men to enter the practice of law who have injured both themselves and the community.

The inferiority of part-time schools, more than half of which
are not connected with any university, is to some degree the result of lack of financial resources. A few have very large enrolments and an income sufficient to maintain an adequate curriculum and a competent teaching staff. Frequently, however,
stringent economies have to be practiced. When this occurs, as
it does particularly among the proprietary schools, many courses
are offered in alternate years rather than annually; elective
courses are not included in the curriculum; and, aside from the
one man who is the owner or promoter of the school, most of
the teaching is done by practicing lawyers.

Besides the financial difficulty, there is another that is even
more fundamental. It is the problem of how any course of
study to which students devote only a portion of their time may
be made the equal of a soundly conceived and competently administered full-time course. Mr. Reed maintains that it is impossible for part-time schools to offer a student more than two
courses of one hour each in an evening without running the risk
of making the instruction ineffective. Similarly, such schools
cannot wisely conduct sessions oftener than three times a week
if students are to have nearly enough time for preparation. Con-

[1] Reed, Alfred Z., Present-Day Law Schools in the United States and
Canada, pp. 288–289.

44

sequently, he believes that the part-time course would have to be about twice as long as the full-time course were the student to receive anything like a comparable amount of training. So great are the difficulties encountered in attempting to make part-time schools the "equivalent" of full-time schools that Mr. Reed returns to his original thesis: evening schools should cease striving to duplicate the work of morning schools. They should be encouraged to find an appropriate field of instruction to which they, and only they, could do full justice.[1]

APPROVED AND UNAPPROVED SCHOOLS

In 1921 the American Bar Association recommended certain standards that it believed all law schools should strive to meet. Interesting historical developments which resulted in this action will be described in the section on the American Bar Association.[2] That organization, it is sufficient to note here, had finally become convinced that it should assume responsibility for defining minimum standards of legal education, and for withholding its approval from schools failing to meet them.[3] The resolutions establishing these standards read, in part, as follows:

1. The American Bar Association is of the opinion that every candidate for admission to the bar should give evidence of graduation from a law school complying with the following standards:

a. It shall require as a condition of admission at least two years of study in a college.[4]

[1] *Ibid.,* pp. 301–306.
[2] See pp. 136–139.
[3] The resolutions of the American Bar Association, together with the rulings concerning them adopted by the Council on Legal Education of the American Bar Association, appear each year in the Annual Review of Legal Education, published by the Association.
[4] Standards (a) and (b) have been somewhat relaxed as the result of qualifying interpretations. In reference to standard (a) it has been ruled that students not able to meet the requirement of two years of college preparation

b. It shall require its students to pursue a course of three years' duration if they devote substantially all of their working time to their studies, and a longer course, equivalent in the number of working hours, if they devote only a part of their working time to their studies.[1]

c. It shall provide an adequate library available for the use of the students.

d. It shall have among its teachers a sufficient number giving their entire time to the school to ensure actual personal acquaintance and influence with the whole student body.

e. It shall not be operated as a commercial enterprise and the compensation of any officer or member of its teaching staff shall not depend on the number of students or on the fees received.

2. The American Bar Association is of the opinion that graduation from a law school should not confer the right of admission to the bar, and that every candidate should be subjected to an examination by public authority to determine his fitness.

3. The Council on Legal Education and Admissions to the Bar[2] is directed to publish from time to time the names of those law schools which comply with the above standards and of those which do not and to make such publications available so far as possible to intending law students.

The Association's first list of approved schools appeared in 1923. Unfortunately the Council did not have sufficient finan-

---

may be matriculated as special students, providing that the number admitted in any year does not exceed 10 per cent of the average number of beginning law students enrolled during each of the two preceding years. Concerning standard (b) it has been declared, "A part-time course shall cover a period of at least four years of at least thirty-six weeks each and shall be the equivalent of a full-time course." Many persons believe that it is impossible for the part-time school adequately to cover a curriculum even in four years which the full-time school covers in three.

[1] See note 4 on previous page.

[2] The Council on Legal Education and Admissions to the Bar, created in 1920, is the executive body of the Section of Legal Education and Admissions to the Bar. It consists of the chairman, vice-chairman, and secretary of the Section, and of eight members elected by the Section for four-year terms of office.

cial resources or an adequate trained staff at its disposal to make a personal investigation of all schools of law. Upon the basis of such evidence as it was able to obtain, however, it presented the names of 39 institutions which appeared to comply fully with the specified standards.[1] All were connected with a college or university, although the relation of the Hastings College of Law in San Francisco to the University of California is tenuous. In addition to this list of what was called Class A schools, the Council presented a second list of nine Class B schools that were unable to meet all the requirements at the time they submitted their reports to the Council. Since these schools announced their intention of complying with the standards in the near future, however, it was believed that they should be given partial approval.

When the list of approved institutions was submitted in 1926, 64 schools had been given a Class A rating.[2] The Class B list, which had been intended only for temporary use, was then abolished. It was decided, moreover, that no school should receive approval in the future without inspection by a representative of the Council. Since 1926 the number of approved schools has grown slowly but steadily. In 1928 there were 66, 81 in 1931, and 94 in 1936.[3]

The annual publication of the names of approved and unapproved institutions serves a dual purpose. It provides helpful information concerning law schools which the Council recommends. It also tends to improve the status of legal education by influencing schools which are unable to meet the requirements of the Association to raise their standards sufficiently to obtain approval. The list has not been disseminated widely enough,

---

[1] In American Bar Association Journal, November, 1923, p. 728.
[2] In Report of the American Bar Association for 1926, pp. 56–57, 798.
[3] The number increased to 97 during 1937.

TABLE 3.——NUMBER OF LAW SCHOOLS APPROVED AND
UNAPPROVED BY AMERICAN BAR ASSOCIATION IN
1936, BY STATE AND TYPE OF SCHOOL

State	Approved			Unapproved			Total
	Full-time	Mixed	Part-time	Full-time	Mixed	Part-time	
New England							
Maine	—	—	—	1	—	—	1
Massachusetts	2	1	—	—	2	3	8
Connecticut	1	1	—	—	—	—	2
Middle Atlantic							
New York	5	2	—	—	2	1	10
New Jersey	—	—	—	—	2	1	3
Pennsylvania	3	1	—	—	1	1	6
East North Central							
Ohio	3	—	—	1	1	7	12
Indiana	3	1	—	—	1	1	6
Illinois	3	3	—	—	—	3	9
Michigan	1	1	1	—	—	2	5
Wisconsin	2	—	—	—	—	—	2
West North Central							
Minnesota	1	—	—	—	—	3	4
Iowa	2	—	—	—	—	1	3
Missouri	3	1	—	—	—	4	8
North Dakota	1	—	—	—	—	—	1
South Dakota	1	—	—	—	—	—	1
Nebraska	2	—	—	—	—	1	3
Kansas	2	—	—	—	—	—	2
South Atlantic							
Maryland	—	1	—	—	—	2	3
Dist. of Columbia	2	2	—	—	2	3	9
Virginia	4	—	—	—	—	1	5
West Virginia	1	—	—	—	—	—	1
North Carolina	3	—	—	—	—	1	4
South Carolina	1	—	—	—	—	—	1
Georgia	3	—	—	—	—	2	5
Florida	2	—	—	1	—	1	4

TABLE 3.—NUMBER OF LAW SCHOOLS (*Continued*)

State	Approved			Unapproved			Total
	Full-time	Mixed	Part-time	Full-time	Mixed	Part-time	
South Central							
Kentucky	2	–	–	1	–	1	4
Tennessee	2	–	–	1	–	7	10
Alabama	1	–	–	–	–	2	3
Mississippi	1	–	–	–	–	1	2
Arkansas	1	–	–	–	–	1	2
Louisiana	2	1	–	–	–	–	3
Oklahoma	1	–	–	–	–	2	3
Texas	3	–	–	–	–	9	12
Mountain							
Montana	1	–	–	–	–	–	1
Idaho	1	–	–	–	–	–	1
Wyoming	1	–	–	–	–	–	1
Colorado	1	1	–	–	–	1	3
Arizona	1	–	–	–	–	–	1
Utah	1	–	–	–	–	–	1
Pacific							
Washington	1	–	–	–	–	1	2
Oregon	1	–	–	1	–	1	3
California	3	2	–	2	6	7	20
Total	75	18	1	8	17	71	190
	94			96			

however, to exert much pressure upon weak schools. Extensive publicity, fostered by the American Medical Association between 1910 and 1920, so aroused state boards of medical examiners and public opinion in general that large numbers of proprietary medical schools closed their doors. In contrast to such action, the American Bar Association has never attempted to force commercial and other undesirable law schools to discontinue activity. As late as 1936 there were 96 law schools that could not meet the few minimum requirements of the American Bar Association.

It is instructive to examine the approved and unapproved schools in more detail. Of the 94 institutions on the approved list for 1936, 90 are connected with colleges or universities: 37 are part of state universities, 3 are attached to municipal universities, and 50 are privately controlled. Of the last group, 36 are operated by Protestant or non-sectarian institutions of higher learning, and 14 by Catholic colleges and universities. The Hartford College of Law, Chicago-Kent College of Law, Indiana Law School, and Kansas City School of Law are the only institutions having no college or university affiliation.

In contrast to this situation it is found that of the 96 unapproved law schools, only the Hastings College of Law is in any way allied to a state university. Three schools are affiliated with municipal institutions, five with Protestant or non-sectarian institutions, and five with Catholic universities. Fifteen unapproved schools are operated by local units of the Young Men's Christian Association or the Knights of Columbus. The majority of the remaining 67 institutions are entirely independent. Many of them are proprietary institutions, operated primarily for profit. A few are related, although sometimes tenuously, to vocational or business schools.

Of the 94 approved schools, 75 operate on a full-time basis, while 18 give both full-time and part-time work. Only one institution which offers evening courses exclusively has received approval by the Council. Of the unapproved schools, 8 are full-time, 71 are part-time and 17 give both full-time and part-time courses.

Table 3 furnishes information about the location of approved and unapproved schools. There are only 13 states in which all the law schools are approved. Most of these states, moreover, have so sparse a population that the total number of their schools is only 18. The largest number of unapproved institutions is in California, where there are 15; Texas and Ohio have 9 each; and Tennessee, 8. Massachusetts and the District of Columbia have no fewer than 5 schools that do not meet the standards of the American Bar Association.

In 1936, 55 of the 94 approved schools demanded the requisite two years of academic work for admission. The other 39 exceeded the minimum standards of the American Bar Association by demanding three or more years of college preparation. Twelve of the 39 required the baccalaureate degree with certain defined exceptions, and 6 made it an absolute prerequisite. Among the 96 unapproved schools 37 had no requirement of preliminary academic work whatever as late as 1936. On the other hand, 2 schools required three years of college training; 38 required two years; 8 demanded two years of students who wished to receive a degree in law or take the bar examinations; and one demanded one year. In the remaining 10 institutions an undefined amount of college work was either required, or certain academic demands will be made after a specified date.

The length of the course of study in practically all morning law schools is three university years. Seventy-one of the approved schools make this requirement, although about one-half of them permit students who attend summer sessions to complete their course in a shorter calendar period. In the 18 mixed schools that are approved, three years are required of students who attend morning sessions, while evening students are required to take four years for a corresponding course. In the five remaining institutions on the approved list, the curriculum extends over a period of either three or four years depending upon the amount of college preparation that individual students have previously had.

Among the unapproved law schools there is much less uniformity in length of time required to complete the course. Forty schools offer a four-year curriculum and four a five-year one. Twenty-two of the part-time schools and the evening sections of eight of the mixed schools still continue to provide a curriculum of only three years, in spite of the insistence of the American Bar Association that the course of study of evening schools should be longer than three years. The remaining schools in the unapproved group give training of varying duration. There is still one school whose course of study is a single year, and there are five offering only two years.

One further set of figures concerning approved and unapproved schools, which is particularly instructive, deals with the number of students enrolled. In 1936, 22,094 students were matriculated in the 94 approved institutions. They constituted 55 per cent of all students. Although the fact that scarcely more than one-half of all students are connected with approved schools suggests the existence of a very serious problem, encouraging progress has been made recently, for in 1928 only 33 per cent of the matriculants were enrolled in the 66 schools then acceptable to the American Bar Association. The number of students in unapproved institutions in 1936 was 18,124 or nearly 13,000 fewer than in 1928.

The foregoing discussion of approved and unapproved schools has been so statistical in nature that for persons not well acquainted with legal education it probably affords only a confused picture. Concerning most of the unapproved institutions very little is known, even by legal educators, aside from what can be deduced from the few figures appearing in the Annual Review of Legal Education and from the catalogues of the individual schools. Some of these catalogues, moreover, are inadequate in information, while still others are definitely misleading through overstatement of facts. Since most of these schools have never made application to the Section of Legal Education for approval, no investigation has been made of their work. The American Bar Association, the Association of American Law Schools, and the Carnegie Foundation have never undertaken a complete examination and report of all schools of law. Consequently there are no comprehensive studies to which one may turn.

The situation concerning approved institutions is very different. Although more facts might be desired about some of them or about certain problems with which many, or all, are faced, information in general is abundant. They not only tend to publish carefully prepared catalogues annually, but a number also make yearly reports of their work. The investigations that have been conducted by the Section of Legal Education and by the Association of American Law Schools, when they have applied for approval by the former organization or membership in the latter, have greatly enlarged the scope of information. Finally, much has been written about various aspects of the work of a number of these institutions, particularly those that are now carrying on extensive experiments in new forms of legal education.

In California, which has more law schools than any other state in the union, a survey was made in 1933 of the 16 unapproved and the 5 approved schools in existence at the time. This survey, which was conducted at the request of the California bar by Will Shafroth, adviser to the Council on Legal Education, and Dean Claude Horack, of the School of Law of Duke University, is particularly valuable for several reasons. Both men have had long experience in evaluating the work of law schools, and they were able to exercise a degree of objectivity which might have been more difficult for a local committee to attain. Since they examined all the institutions in the state, the report has a uniformity of point of view that would scarcely have characterized a survey made, for example, by a large number of persons or by several committees. Finally and most important of all, law schools in California range from some which are among the best in the United States to others which are among the poorest. Hence the situation in that state would appear to be representative of all types of legal education.[1]

It is impossible to present here even the most condensed résumé of the report of the California survey. A summary of conditions found in two schools in that state, however, will be given, in order to illustrate the contrasts existing among institutions now preparing students for the bar. The first is an approved law school connected with a private non-denominational university. The School of Jurisprudence of the University of California in Berkeley might equally well have been chosen. The second is an unapproved school of a proprietary nature. It was selected because its history exhibits many of the experiences

---

[1] In the autumn of 1937 Mr. Shafroth and Dean Horack made a similar investigation of the 12 law schools of Tennessee, only two of which are on the approved list of the American Bar Association. A summary of this investigation may be found on pp. 311–395 of the Tennessee Law Review, June, 1938, under the title, Report on the Law Schools of Tennessee by the Survey Committee of the American Bar Association. It may be noted that the survey revealed two poorly equipped schools operating in Tennessee in addition to the schools accounted for in the Association's approved and unapproved lists.

and weaknesses through which scores of other evening schools have passed. It is obviously not the best of the unapproved schools; on the other hand, it is not the poorest.

Summary of Report on an Approved School[1]

The School of Law of Stanford University at Palo Alto was established in 1893 and has been in continuous operation since then. It is conducted as a full-time institution, and charges a tuition fee of $100 a quarter or $300 a year for those who do not continue work during the summer. Although the charge for tuition is substantial in amount, it is not high when compared with many other law schools in private universities that provide a comparable type of legal training. The university supplements funds collected from tuition by an appreciable amount.

Although the law school has two buildings at its disposal, the amount of space provided for the library and for offices is inadequate. The library has a collection of 42,000 volumes, which are well selected and are suitable even for advanced legal study. A competent librarian and a staff of several workers devote all their time to the library. The character of instruction offered by the school is such that regular and extended use of the library is necessary.

The customary requirement for admission is the baccalaureate degree from a college or university of recognized standing. The phrase, recognized standing, is interpreted so strictly that the student body is composed of graduates from the best institutions of higher learning in the country. A few years ago the law school initiated an alternative to its former plan of admitting only students with the B.A. or equivalent degree. It now permits students to take what is known as the "combined course." Instead of spending four years in college and three in law school, some students may enter upon the study of law after three years of academic work. When this is done, however, the legal course of study is four years in length. This new arrangement is planned only for students who have attained a high

---

[1] All facts appearing in fine print, unless otherwise indicated, apply to 1933 and are a digest of data from the Report of California Survey Committee, published by the State Bar of California, 1933, pp. 44–50, 101–105.

grade of scholarship, and whose academic subjects have been selected under the direction of a committee of the law faculty. The purpose of the three-four year plan is to integrate academic and legal work more closely.

The average law student spends thirteen hours a week in the classroom. Approximately twelve hundred hours of classroom work are required for graduation. The curriculum of the first year is prescribed. Second- and third-year students have a number of electives from which to choose.

The regular degree awarded is the LL.B. The LL.M. is given for an additional year of work in residence, and the J.S.D. for a year of research after the LL.M. has been received. A thesis showing evidence of productive scholarship is one of the requirements for the doctorate. The number of students working for advanced degrees is small, as is the case in nearly all law schools.

In 1933, when the student enrolment was 183, the faculty consisted of a dean, 11 instructors, a secretary, and other clerical helpers, all of whom devoted their full time to the school. Four or five practicing lawyers usually give lectures without charge, which supplement the instruction provided by the regular faculty. The educational background and the experience of the faculty are excellent. Six or seven hours a week constitutes the classroom schedule of an instructor. Although this teaching load is not heavy in comparison with that of many of the law schools of California, it is as much as the teaching schedule of many of the best schools throughout the United States. Instruction is of excellent quality, and the adequate preparation for it reflects the favorable education, experience, and working conditions of the faculty. Although the case method of teaching is generally used, individual instructors utilize many variations in an effort to make their presentation as effective as possible.

A high standard of accomplishment is insisted upon, and failure to maintain that standard results automatically in the dropping of the student. A careful weeding out of men with an inaptitude or disinclination for law study goes on throughout the first year. As the result of the examinations at the end of the year, another group of students is eliminated. Those allowed to continue, therefore, are fairly uniform in earnestness and in ability. In spite of this fact, about 10 per cent of the class are eliminated during the second year. Third-year students are so carefully selected a group that they subsequently meet with an unusually high degree of success in the California bar examinations.

Summary of Report on an Unapproved School

The Balboa Law College in San Diego is one of several independent schools in the state for the continuation of which Mr. Shafroth and Dean Horack found no justification. It was founded in 1926 as a part of the municipal evening high school under the jurisdiction of the public school system of the city. As has frequently happened elsewhere, it grew out of a course in business law, which was later expanded into a number of courses that purport to cover the main branches of legal study. The school officials of San Diego probably welcomed the inauguration of work in law since a subsidy for each student, which exceeded the cost of instruction by a considerable margin, was paid them by the state.

At first, no plans were made for awarding a degree or diploma, because it was merely part of a program of adult education. After the passage of legislation in California in 1932 which made graduation from high school a prerequisite for admission to the bar examinations of the state, the officials of the public schools declared that the courses no longer properly belonged in the high-school system. Consequently, connection was severed in 1933, and Mr. Leland G. Stanford, who had directed the work since its inception, reorganized it in the form of a law school, privately owned and controlled by him.

Tuition originally was $2.00 for each period of three months, and it remained unchanged for a time after Mr. Stanford became the owner of the school. It later became $100 a year. At the time the Survey Committee visited this school it found that, although fees were very low, a considerable amount of revenue was derived from the sale of "syllabi," prepared by Mr. Stanford and the other two men who taught in the school. There was a syllabus for each course of four weeks and every student was required to purchase a copy. No one was permitted to use a second-hand copy. These syllabi were the only books used during the entire course of study, and the charge for them was $60 a year if paid in advance, or $75 a year if

57

paid in instalments. It was apparent that they were entirely inadequate to give students any comprehensive knowledge of the courses that were supposed to be covered. Although their sale added to Mr. Stanford's income from $2,000 to $4,000 a year, students who bought this material paid as much for it as they would have paid for the best textbooks on the market.

A library, valued at $5,000, had been donated to the school while it was a part of the public school system. Since the books were stored in crates and boxes in the basement of the building, however, they were not available to students and no inspection could be made of their value or usefulness by Mr. Shafroth and Dean Horack.

It was discovered, further, that only one subject was being taught in the school at a time.[1] The topic chosen was presented to all students at two-hour sessions held three evenings a week for a term of four and one-half weeks. Occasionally the subject was continued for two or three terms. The entire curriculum was supposed to cover four years or thirty-six terms. Since the school had no catalogue or printed schedule, the student could not tell in advance what courses would be offered or whether he had already had them. This was apparently not considered of serious importance, however, since he was required to enrol for only a quarter of a year at a time. No definite plan had been formulated concerning an integrated and progressive curriculum. The choice of a particular subject appeared to rest upon a vague determination of the number of students who had not yet had it.

Whereas advertisements of the school had claimed that "Its students with a high-school education have passed the California bar examinations one hundred per cent on the first attempt," the Survey Committee maintained that this statement was misleading. The records of the Board of Bar Examiners showed that of 12 Balboa students who took the bar examinations in 1930, 1931, and 1932, only half were high-school graduates. Of the six who were not, one had failed the examination five times; one, three times; one, twice; and three, once. Of the six high-school graduates, two had failed the examinations during the period and one of the two had failed twice.

[1] Shafroth, Will, "Can the Law Schools Lead Us Out of the Wilderness?" In American Law School Review, April, 1934, p. 1028.

The system of grading was found to be fairly strict. In some courses as many as a third of the students had received less than a passing mark. No one, however, had been asked to withdraw on account of poor scholarship. The dean stated that no formal elimination was necessary as students with poor grades tended to withdraw voluntarily. Only those desiring credit for their work were required to take examinations. As a result nearly half did not attempt the tests.

The school was not only judged entirely inadequate as an institution for preparing men to enter upon the practice of law, but the investigators questioned why business men and others not intending to practice, should spend time and money at such an institution. It has not only continued to exist, however, but in July, 1933 it was incorporated as a degree-conferring institution.

Curriculum

The law "practiced" or applied by a lawyer is that which is in force in a particular jurisdiction. Since there are 48 states, and the District of Columbia, the law of this country is composed of bodies of rules enforced by the courts of 49 independent local jurisdictions. This computation does not take into account Alaska and the insular possessions, nor the laws enforced by the federal courts and the rapidly growing number of quasi-judicial federal bureaus. It follows that the term, American law, though frequently used, is somewhat misleading for there is no one system of law applicable to all the United States.

It is true that powerful forces are at work which encourage increase of uniformity. Pressure exerted by the Constitution of the United States and the federal courts is one such force. Framers of state constitutions and of state legislation, moreover, borrow from other jurisdictions whatever they consider applicable to their local needs. A large part of the law of any state, furthermore, is common law shared with other states. It exists only in the shape of scattered legal principles, stated or implied in judicial decisions as the grounds upon which these decisions rest. Many of the principles of the common law were enunciated by English courts prior to the American Revolution, or have been accepted as authoritative by so many jurisdictions and writers of textbooks since then that they are now regarded, except when modified by statutes, as settled for the entire country. The effect of these influences working toward uniformity cannot, however, do more than mitigate the tendency toward diversity that is inherent in the political structure of the United States.

Because of these numerous legal systems, law schools have been faced with the very serious problem of deciding whether they should teach the law of a particular jurisdiction, or the common law, or both. Many schools long solved the problem by concentrating attention upon the law of the state in which the institution was situated. In this way a student could be given detailed knowledge of the actual law of the jurisdiction in which he was likely to practice. It is obvious, however, that the graduate of a local school is at a disadvantage if he wishes to move to another state or section of the country. Such preparation is too narrow in scope, moreover, to enable him to look at even the law of his own state in perspective.

As early as 1841 Harvard announced in its catalogue that "no public instruction is given in the local or peculiar municipal jurisprudence of any particular state." Thus Harvard was the first of a now considerable list of schools that seek to train lawyers in the "common legal heritage of English speaking peoples." Emphasis is placed, in these institutions, upon fundamental legal principles, which students are taught to view critically. Consequently, if they become judges or legislators at some subsequent time, they are better equipped than are graduates from other schools to convert law into a more efficient instrument of justice.[1]

Institutions offering instruction in the common law are faced, however, with the fact that students must make a living for some years, at least, from the practice of law as it exists in the jurisdictions in which they settle. In order to assist in the solution of this difficulty, these schools began early to add to their regular curricula some local law courses. The practice was pushed to its logical conclusion in the West. In 1891 the law school of the University of Iowa announced that a course in the law of any state would be organized, if at least three seniors applied for it. It is naturally very expensive for a school to offer a number of courses in local law to small groups of students. At present a few of the schools that attract students from a wide geographical area make some attempt to cover the law of those jurisdictions from which the largest number of students come.

Most schools consider it their function to prepare students to practice all branches of the law. Whether this preparation shall consist primarily of training for general legal practice or for practice in the specialties, however, is a question concerning which there is much discussion. The specialties include an important and ever-growing list: admiralty; banking; bankruptcy; collections; corporate business; crime; domestic relations; instalment sales; labor difficulties; management of estates, trust, and investments; mines; negligence and personal injuries; patents, copyrights, and trademarks; probate and surrogate work; public utilities; real estate; receiverships; taxation; workmen's compen-

---

[1] The foregoing paragraphs are a summary of pp. 288–294 of Alfred Z. Reed's Training for the Public Profession of the Law.

sation; and practice before administrative bodies other than courts.

Failure to arrive at some definite conclusion about the relative importance of general legal training and highly specialized subjects has resulted in a chaotic condition that is everywhere noticeable in the curricula of law schools. Many persons interested in legal education believe that the function of a school is to supply the prospective lawyer with a broad general background which will be of use to him in any type of practice, in any specialty, or combination of specialties. Such a background would give him an initial understanding of the legal system and the work of the bar.[1] There are others who believe that law schools should emphasize the specialties. They point to the difficulty of trying to cover the whole field of law, and conclude that it is wiser to focus attention upon a group of legal subjects small enough to be understood.[2] They also point to the increasing importance of the specialties in legal practice.

If any considerable body of students returned to law schools for graduate work, training in the specialties could be reserved for this later period. Because there is little advanced study in law in the United States, however, except in a few schools, such as Harvard, Yale, and Columbia, which train a small number of prospective law teachers or men interested in international law, it is obvious that any formal preparation in the specialties must be included in the regular curriculum.

Since no school can give adequate preparation both in the general field of law and in several specialties, each school emphasizes, according to its financial resources and educational

[1] Wickser, Philip J., "The Law School and the Law." In American Law School Review, April, 1931, p. 135.
[2] Gardner, George K., "Specialization in the Law School Curriculum." In University of Pennsylvania Law Review, April, 1933, p. 686.

philosophy, those features of a theoretically desirable preparation that it deems most important. Mr. Reed once said of such a situation, "It will be many years before any law school faculty . . . can defend its curriculum as an ideal one. All that can be maintained is that it is the best that can be devised under most unfavorable conditions."[1]

It is not surprising that curricula vary widely from institution to institution when there is little agreement among schools regarding what should be taught. Although it is highly desirable that the course of study in each school should be flexible and that standardization of legal education should never be carried too far, planning of programs has generally been a haphazard affair, and fortuitous circumstances have done much to exaggerate differences. Courses have been added to the curriculum of a school, often regardless of their justification, because certain instructors have been particularly interested in them, and highly specialized subjects have been introduced because it was believed that they would meet the peculiar legal demands of the locality. As a result, there are probably no two schools whose curricula are alike even in name, and changes in the program of each school are frequent.

This is very different from the situation in medical education where courses of study resemble each other closely. The Council on Medical Education and Hospitals of the American Medical Association not only prescribes the nine major divisions which constitute the curriculum of every approved medical school, but it defines the approximate amount of work that is required of students in each division.[2] Courses offered in undergraduate medical schools are planned to provide broad, basic

---

[1] Training for the Public Profession of the Law, p. 275.
[2] "Medical Education in the United States and Canada." In Journal of the American Medical Association, August 29, 1936, p. 685.

training, and preparation for the specialties is not encouraged until after physicians have completed their internship.

Similarity is greatest in the first year of law school work when nearly all courses are required and there are few electives. From a survey of 12 current catalogues, chosen as representative of schools approved by the American Bar Association, it was found that all required of their first-year students courses in contracts and in torts. Eleven required a course in real or personal property, or both; 10, in criminal law; 8, in procedure; 5, in agency; and 5, in persons, family relations, or domestic relations. Beyond this point there were marked differences. Four schools offered work in equity which is generally presented to more advanced students; two gave courses in some aspect of constitutional law, and two in sales; one provided instruction in legislation; and so on. The majority of the 12 schools listed one or more general courses designed to give first-year students background for the study of law, or to furnish them with a knowledge of legal ethics and of the history of the legal profession.[1]

Before continuing with a survey of the curriculum of the second and third years, a word must be said about the course in legal ethics that has recently been introduced, under this or some other name, in the majority of schools. A few years ago the American Bar Association officially took cognizance of the numerous criticisms of the moral standards of many lawyers by declaring that more effort ought to be made by law schools to inculcate professional ethics. Instructors were aware of the fact that the moral tone of the bar needed to be raised, but they

[1] See also "Report of the Sub-Committee on the First-Year Curriculum," in American Law School Review, April, 1937, pp. 745–748, for a discussion of changes and trends in the first-year curricula of schools belonging to the Association of American Law Schools.

questioned whether much could be achieved through the teaching of a course in legal ethics. Under pressure from the American Bar Association and the Association of American Law Schools, however, courses have been introduced, and several textbooks have been prepared. In general these courses attempt to point out to the prospective lawyer what is expected of members of a profession whose contribution can be of great importance to the welfare of society.

Since work of the second year is less prescribed than that of the first, the number of courses offered is much greater, and variation from school to school noticeably increases. In the third year, when almost the entire course of study is elective in many schools, and when it is not unusual for an institution to list 20 or more specialized subjects from which students may make selections, dissimilarity of curricula reaches its maximum. More than 75 such courses bearing different names were listed in the catalogues of eight of the leading full-time schools. The only one appearing in all eight catalogues was conflict of laws. Taxation, trusts, municipal corporations, and constitutional law appeared in five catalogues as electives of the third year; equity, evidence, international law, property, business organization, industrial law, insurance, and public utilities were offered by four schools. Four other courses were mentioned by three institutions. There were no fewer than 48 courses, however, which appeared in but one of the eight catalogues.

In addition to training men and women for the practice of law, legal educators are faced with the question of providing supplementary preparation for those other allied vocations which lawyers enter in large numbers. Roscoe Pound, until recently dean of the Harvard Law School, has emphatically stated that, besides producing practitioners and competent business advisers, it should be the function of a law school to train men who will become judges, legislators, teachers of law, and writers on legal subjects; to train those upon whom the public will rely for sound advice and criticism about legislation and the legal aspects of political affairs; and those who can carry on investigations of the problems of legal adjustment of human relations and of how such problems can be solved effectively.[1]

Such a program as Professor Pound visualizes is an ambitious one. Of late years so much attention has been centered upon preparing men to become business advisers, as well as legal practitioners, that the curriculum has already become badly overcrowded. Beyond these two primary aims the average school of law has not accomplished much, and what little has been achieved has not been the result of careful planning. When one considers the problems with which legal education is faced, it does not appear likely that many schools will attempt in the immediate future to train students especially for public service, legal teaching, investigation, writing, and so on. They may come to place more emphasis upon statutory law, legislation, and administrative tribunals and other agencies. There will probably also be a continuation of the present tendency to offer many elective third-year courses from which students may choose work of great value in the public field. But so far as can now be seen, thoughtfully designed preparation for additional goals will rest upon the shoulders of a very few strong and progressive schools.

THE "CASE METHOD"

Regardless of whether schools teach the law of a particular jurisdiction or common law, or both, it has long been their main

[1] "Present Tendencies in Legal Education." In Annual Review of Legal Education for 1935, pp. 7–8.

objective to train students for practice by acquainting them with that great mass of law which is embodied in the decisions of judges. During recent years many institutions, as will be shown later, have been devoting an increasing amount of attention to other subjects besides judicial decisions. In spite of new developments, however, judge-made law is still everywhere the basis of the curriculum.

Judicial decisions were originally taught by textbook and lecture methods. The number and confusion of these decisions, however, became so great that a staggering responsibility was placed upon law schools which attempted to instruct students how to find their way through the vast and unsystematically arranged body of legal source material.[1] It was essential that some method be devised whereby the problem might be simplified. To Langdell belongs the credit for discovering such a method. In 1871 he published a book entitled, A Selection of Cases on the Law of Contracts. It was the first volume of its kind ever prepared, and the method of teaching English common law set forth in it eventually revolutionized legal education. In the preface to the first edition Langdell explained, apparently for the only time, the reason for his innovation which resulted in a struggle that lasted for many years before the case method was generally accepted by law schools. He wrote in part:

Law, considered as a science, consists of certain principles or doctrines. To have such a mastery of these as to be able to apply them with constant facility and certainty to the ever-tangled skein of human affairs, is what constitutes a true lawyer; and hence to acquire

[1] There are now more than 1,800,000 reported judicial decisions, the vast majority of which have been handed down by appellate courts. Any one of these decisions, except in so far as it has become inapplicable through constitutional or legislative process or has been expressly overruled by a court, may be cited as a precedent before any judge.

that mastery should be the business of every earnest student of law. Each of these doctrines has arrived at its present state by slow degrees; in other words, it is a growth, extending in many cases through centuries. This growth is to be traced in the main through a series of cases; and much the shortest and best, if not the only way of mastering the doctrine effectually is by studying the cases in which it is embodied. But the cases which are useful and necessary for this purpose at the present day bear an exceedingly small proportion to all that have been reported. The vast majority are useless and worse than useless for any purpose of systematic study. Moreover, the number of fundamental legal doctrines is much less than is commonly supposed; the many different guises in which the same doctrine is constantly making its appearance, and the great extent to which legal treatises are a repetition of each other, being the cause of much misapprehension. If these doctrines could be so classified and arranged that each should be found in its proper place, and nowhere else, they would cease to be formidable from their number. It seemed to me, therefore, to be possible to take such a branch of the law as Contracts, for example, and, without exceeding comparatively moderate limits, to select, classify, and arrange all the cases which had contributed in any important degree to the growth, development, or establishment of any of its essential doctrines; and that such a work could not fail to be of material service to all who desire to study that branch of law systematically and in its original sources.[1]

In his book on contracts, the author arranged all of the important English cases in chronological form under each topic covered. These were followed by American and Scottish cases. In the course in which the book was used, the principle deduced from the first case was traced chronologically through its developments and its applications in later cases. A colleague, James B. Ames, who later became dean of the school, assiduously prepared case-books in other subjects, as did Langdell himself. It was Ames who really determined the type of case-

---

[1] Langdell, Christopher C., A Selection of Cases on the Law of Contracts. Little, Brown and Co., Boston, 1871, Preface, pp. vi–vii.

book which was subsequently used widely in American law schools. He chose decisions, not for the purpose of tracing the historical development of legal ideas, but for stimulating the thought of the student and for leading the mind on, step by step, until it had become familiar with the fundamental principles of a subject and the reasons for them.[1]

The case method was carried to other law schools, either by members of the Harvard faculty or by men trained there. By the opening of the twentieth century, it was being followed in several of the leading institutions, and case-books in practically every division of civil, criminal, and constitutional law, and the law of procedure had been or were shortly to be prepared for classroom use. Since then the method has been adopted by nearly all of the full-time, and by some of the part-time schools. In the section on Legal Education appearing in the Biennial Survey of Education for 1926–1928 Mr. Reed wrote:

The extent to which the once-derided innovation of the Harvard Law School has established itself as orthodox appears from the following figures. Of 60 law schools, situated in continental United States, that were members of the Association of American Law Schools at the beginning of the academic year 1928–1929, 47 (78 per cent) were certainly genuine case method schools. An additional 6 claimed in their catalogues to be using this method, although the composition of their faculties suggests that they may depart from it to a greater extent than they are themselves aware. In all but one of the remaining 7 schools, at least a minority of the faculty have been trained in this method. Out of the entire group of 60 schools, only 2 explicitly claimed in their printed announcements to be using, as the basis of their system of instruction, something other than the case method.[2]

[1] Centennial History of Harvard Law School, 1817–1917. Published by Harvard Law School Association, 1918, pp. 29–32, 39–40, 46–49, 80–81.
[2] U. S. Department of the Interior, Office of Education, Bulletin 16, 1930, p. 63.

In 1913 when the Carnegie Foundation began its study of legal education in the United States, it decided that a sound and unbiased evaluation of the case method was needed. Dr. Josef Redlich, professor of law at the University of Vienna and for some years a member of the Austrian parliament, was asked to make the survey. Since there is nothing comparable to the case method in Europe, Dr. Redlich was able to view the subject in a fresh and impartial manner. He discovered certain weaknesses, but he believed that they were more than counterbalanced by the essential soundness of the method. He wrote:

As the method was developed, it laid the main emphasis upon precisely that aspect of the training which the older text-book school entirely neglected: the training of the student in intellectual independence, in individual thinking, in digging out the principles through penetrating analysis of the material found within separate cases: material which contains, all mixed in with one another, both the facts, as life creates them, which generate the law, and at the same time rules of the law itself, component parts of the general system. In the fact that . . . it has actually accomplished this purpose, lies the great success of the case method. For it really teaches the pupil to think in the way that any practical lawyer—whether dealing with written or with unwritten law—ought to and has to think. It prepares the student in precisely the way which, in a country of case law, leads to full powers of legal understanding and legal acumen; that is to say, by making the law pupil familiar with the law through incessant practice in the analysis of law cases, where the concepts, principles, and rules of Anglo-American law are recorded not as dry abstractions but as cardinal realities in the inexhaustibly rich, ceaselessly fluctuating social and economic life of man.[1]

[1] The Common Law and the Case Method in American University Law Schools. Carnegie Foundation, Bulletin 8, New York, 1914, pp. 39–40. For a later carefully considered statement of what the case method has achieved and failed to achieve, see Herman Oliphant's "Parallels in the Development of Legal and Medical Education," in Annals of the American Academy of Political and Social Science, May, 1933, p. 160.

During recent years this technique has again been much criticized, especially by teachers of law who are giving constant attention to the curriculum and methods of teaching. Their criticisms are not directed toward its elimination, but against its misuse. The statement may conservatively be made that the principle on which this system rests is now more firmly entrenched than ever before. Many feel, however, that, like numerous other excellent techniques, there has been a tendency to depend upon the case method too exclusively. Attempts have been made, in some instances, to force it to do more than could reasonably be expected. In other instances, failure to understand how to utilize it effectively has minimized its results. A brief review of some of the criticisms follows.

Professor Edson R. Sunderland of the University of Michigan offers a criticism, the implications of which are very disturbing. In his judgment a constant study of cases results in giving a distorted outlook on the purpose of law. When cases are used as the almost exclusive source of legal principles, they tend to accustom students to consider litigation as the normal method by which the law operates upon society. This is a distinctly antisocial point of view. Litigation represents social friction and need for adjustment. The purpose of the law is to enable persons so to direct their affairs that no conflicts will arise. "The more efficient the legal system and the more delicately it is correlated to the needs and conditions of society the more perfectly will it preserve an equilibrium of conflicting interests. In other words the normal function of the law is to prevent law suits, not to decide them."[1]

A second criticism is that the field of statutory law is left

[1] "Law Schools and the Legal Profession." In American Law School Review, April, 1931, p. 97.

largely untouched, because case-books deal almost solely with judicial decisions. Statutes represent an additional source of law which merits far more attention than it has yet received. Some statutes have permanently modified the law, and have become as much a part of the sources of law as the principles of common law which they have replaced or restated. Other statutes have created administrative tribunals whose quasi-judicial rulings constitute a new body of case law which demands equal attention with that promulgated by the regular courts. Statutes, moreover, are nearly always drafted by lawyers, if not conceived by them. As a consequence, the extent to which statutory law is sound and well expressed depends largely upon the ability and training of the legal profession. In spite of these facts, only a few law schools have begun to show interest in teaching the theory and technique of legislation as a fundamental part of professional equipment for the bar.

While on a visit in 1932 to most of the widely known law schools, Leon H. Keyserling, a recent graduate of the Harvard Law School, discovered that little attention was devoted to existing legislation, possible remedial legislation, and the desirability of supplementing common law with statute law.[1] He found few schools that presented relevant legislative materials as a part of each course. Workmen's compensation acts, for example, which have changed fundamentally parts of the law regarding torts, were often not discussed in courses on torts. As the result of such a situation, lawyers have little to contribute in directing the course of social development. They lack the knowledge which is essential to leadership. This lack is a most serious handicap because legislation would enable "improvements

[1] "Social Objectives in Legal Education." In Columbia Law Review, March, 1933, pp. 447–448.

to be made in the most simple, direct and inexpensive way, by rules announced in advance for the guidance of parties. No longer is it deemed necessary to build the procedural system upon the ruined lives or fortunes of litigants, through the slow and painful process of judicial evolution."[1] Unfortunately the legislative method has not been much developed in a constructive way. Where it has been attempted, legislation has often been faulty and ill-considered, or it has come only as a last resort to secure long-delayed relief from injustice.

Albert J. Harno, dean of the University of Illinois Law School, points to the growing conviction that the case method tends to produce lawyers who are too narrowly prepared for the heavy responsibilities which today are laid upon them. It generally fails to give students sufficient perspective for viewing the place and function of law in the social structure. He believes that persons trained through the case method are likely to work entirely within the law, drawing inferences and conclusions here, making refinements there, but never viewing the contours of the law in relief. "Here is the difference between the workman and the architect. The case method tends to train artisans of the law, but not architects of our institutions."[2]

The law consists of a set of precepts and procedures. Precepts exist, as has already been noted, to regulate and control human conduct and to reduce friction. Procedures are the machinery whereby precepts are brought to bear on specific conduct. But precepts, Dean Harno points out, deal with social data which are constantly in a state of ferment and change. A legal system must, therefore, be ever changing if it is to adapt

[1] Sunderland, Edson R., "Law Schools and the Legal Profession." In American Law School Review, April, 1931, p. 98.
[2] Letter to Law Alumni of the University of Illinois, Urbana, Illinois, April, 1937, p. 2.

itself to the evolving social scene. Thus conceived, the law is a form of social and economic expression.

If this be true, "it would seem to follow that those who fashion the law and those who administer it should have a broad understanding of and an insight into the functioning of the whole 'living tissue.' "[1] Unfortunately, under the case system, the prospective lawyer tends to accept consciously or unconsciously the traditional legalistic attitude that a sound system of law must be based on judicial precedent, held together by formal logical reasoning, and applied with unfailing uniformity. Thus he goes out of the law school to perpetuate ideas which have long since lost their social utility.[2]

In his book on Law and Lawyers, Edward S. Robinson, late professor of psychology at Yale and lecturer in the Yale Law School, approached the subject of the case method from another angle.[3] He pointed to the fact that the opinions of judges of higher courts, which students study so carefully, are of great importance, but they rarely give an adequate factual picture of the primary dispute or of the psychological and social forces that gave rise to that dispute. Any form of legal education, Professor Robinson declared, that attempted to gather facts widely would insist in going behind the utterances of the judge to the psychological, sociological, and economic details of the case at the bar.

Thomas I. Parkinson, formerly of the Columbia Law faculty, suggests that any law teacher who has participated in a controversy from its inception to its conclusion in an appellate

---

[1] *Ibid.*, p. 3.
[2] Morse, Wayne L., "Changing Trends in Legal Education," in Oregon Law Review, December, 1931, pp. 43–44. See Dean Young B. Smith's Report of School of Law, Columbia University, 1929, pp. 4–8.
[3] Macmillan Co., New York, 1935, pp. 67–68.

court realizes how inadequate is the report of it which appears in a case-book.[1] The opinion of the judge frequently does not picture the controversy at all. When a case-book is only a series of opinions that are taught as ends in themselves, students are likely, in Mr. Parkinson's estimation, to develop over-confidence and self-satisfaction. The situation has been so simplified that they often feel that they could do better than the court itself. The editor of a case-book should present an accurate condensed statement of the origin of each controversy and the procedure by which it was developed, as an introduction to the opinion by which it was decided.[2]

These comments make explicable a statement written by Dean Horack some years ago about the case method. "While some schools are considering what should be the next step in advance of the case method, a large proportion of the law schools have not yet discovered what it was devised to accomplish nor how it should be used."[3] In many schools, he continued, it is employed merely as a series of illustrative cases; in others as the basis of a lecture course; and in still others as a succession of principles which the student is induced almost to commit to memory on the assumption that in sum total they provide complete knowledge of a subject. He believed that the misuse of the case system is due in part to poorly constructed case-books, hastily put together at the request of a publishing house and adopted by law schools through the persuasion of a book agent. It is also due to the fact that the instructor can more easily tell students

[1] "Are the Law Schools Adequately Training for the Public Service?" In American Law School Review, December, 1935, pp. 292–293.
[2] Frank, Jerome, "Why Not a Clinical Law School?" In University of Pennsylvania Law Review, June, 1933, p. 916.
[3] "Law Schools of To-day and To-morrow." In American Law School Review, March, 1930, p. 659.

about the case than get them to tell him, just as it is easier for him to ask questions than to encourage students to do the asking.

Dean Horack came to the conclusion to which many of his colleagues have also arrived: the case system is the most effective device for teaching law to first-year students, but not necessarily to second-year students, and almost certainly not to those in the third year. After the first year the law of diminishing returns begins to operate. Experience has shown that by the third year students who are required to continue a study of cases become so restless that a different approach to the study of the law is essential. He is of the opinion, therefore, that during the latter part of the course students should be brought into more direct contact with the actual application of the law; they should be introduced to a broader point of view; and they should be stimulated to take a more active interest in the question of how justice may be provided for all social groups.

Sociological Jurisprudence and the Social Sciences

In the preceding section law was spoken of as a form of economic and social expression. Probably no recent legal concept differs more radically from many of the former theories of jurisprudence than does this one, or has a greater potential influence upon professional training. Until the nineteenth century, law was frequently believed to consist of a body of immutable principles. Thus law was "found" by diligent jurists; it was not made. The exact form of this belief changed from time to time in conformity with evolving philosophical ideas. Finally jurists lost faith in metaphysical theories, and many came to conceive of law as consciously created by judges and legislators. Proponents of this new theory busied themselves with analyzing the nature of legal institutions and legal conceptions.

76

Early in the twentieth century emphasis shifted from an analytical investigation of the structure of law to include an interest in its purpose. This was the result of the emergence of a school of thought, known as sociological jurisprudence, that is concerned with a realistic examination of "law in action." This school has attempted to discard old philosophic ideas, and, instead, is making extensive use of the social sciences. Its advocates believe that sociological jurisprudence will bring about enough of a reinterpretation of various fields of law and procedure so that law will be better able to serve socially desirable ends. Roscoe Pound, its leading exponent in this country, has summarized the belief of its disciples as follows:

> They recognize the futility of a detached, self-centered, self-sufficient jurisprudence. Beginning with the proposition that the legal order is a phase of social control and to be understood must be taken in its setting among social phenomena, they urge study of the actual social effects of legal institutions and legal doctrines; sociological study in preparation for lawmaking; study of the means of making legal precepts effective in action; study of the actual methods of juristic thinking, judicial decision and legislative lawmaking; a sociological legal history in which the social background and social effects of legal precepts, legal doctrines and legal institutions in the past shall be investigated; and above all study of how these effects have been brought about.[1]

Sociological jurisprudence is causing some infiltration of the views and findings of the other social sciences into law and legal administration. As illustrative of this infiltration, Professor Sheldon Glueck of the Harvard Law School points to the appellate briefs of a small group of lawyers, of whom Mr. Justice Brandeis and Professor Felix F. Frankfurter were the forerun-

---

[1] "Jurisprudence." In Encyclopaedia of the Social Sciences, 1932, vol. 8, p. 484.

ners.[1] Such men have drawn upon pertinent extra-legal materials to support their arguments before appellate tribunals in cases involving constitutional issues. He also notes the research and writings of creative thinkers in law and judicial administration who insist upon testing philosophical legal dogmas by studies in economics, sociology, psychology, psychiatry, and anthropology. The work of sociological jurists is to be seen in a number of surveys of crime. These were initiated by Dean Pound and Professor Frankfurter in the investigation of criminal justice which they directed in Cleveland, Ohio, and the results of which were published in 1921. It is also to be found in a growing series of functional studies of other branches of law administration, such as the business of trial and appellate courts; the practical administration of divorce laws; the social significance and the legal control of automobiles and various instruments of the machine age.

It is apparent that any philosophy of law which is making itself recognized by both bench and bar, and which is so largely the outgrowth of the thinking of law-school men, as is sociological jurisprudence, is certain to influence legal education. Law teachers are coming to emphasize the fact that "the law cuts across all fields of human endeavor. No interest is solely legal. Social, economic and legal elements are constantly interwoven. The background for law is economic and social but law in turn sanctions the social and economic."[2]

Although this interrelationship of law and the social sciences is acknowledged by a number of law schools, these very institu-

[1] "The Social Sciences and Scientific Method in the Administration of Justice." In Annals of the American Academy of Political and Social Science, May, 1933, pp. 110–115.
[2] Harno, Albert J., Letter to the Law Alumni of the University of Illinois, Urbana, Illinois, June, 1933, p. 2.

tions are faced with the puzzling question of how they shall make their students aware of it. Shall they require that matriculants have some definite amount of instruction in the social sciences before entering law school, shall they introduce the social sciences into the law-school curriculum, or shall they do both? If they offer work in the school, shall they call upon academic professors to give courses in the social studies, even though the professors are not lawyers and hence do not readily know what aspects of their subjects are most valuable to law students? Or shall law teachers themselves, who are without formal training in the social studies, attempt to weave into the law courses as many social data as they can? These are some of the questions which the schools have been asking for several years. As yet they have not been answered with any great degree of satisfaction or unanimity.

One of the easiest, although incomplete, solutions to the problem would be to require that law students should take a considerable amount of prescribed work in the social sciences during their college years. Such a requirement would be comparable to that made by medical schools concerning work in the physical sciences. The Association of American Law Schools has always been opposed to formulating academic requirements in the social studies to which its members would be expected to conform. From questionnaires on pre-legal education which were recently sent by a sub-committee of that Association to the deans of member schools, it was learned that more than half of the 82 institutions belonging to the national association are still opposed to action by that body.[1] Some deans, however, suggested that prerequisites for admission should be established

---

[1] "Report of the Sub-Committee for the Study of Pre-legal Education." In American Law School Review, April, 1937, pp. 743–745.

by the schools individually. The replies to the questionnaire showed that slightly more than half the member schools now recommend pre-law courses, and 14 schools require specific courses. The five subjects which were most frequently recommended or required were English, history, political science, economics, and accounting. Only 17 schools recommended sociology, and only 11, psychology. Many deans frankly stated that they were hesitant about making requirements or even recommendations because of lack of confidence in their own judgment in selecting subjects, and also because of lack of confidence in the effectiveness of college teaching in these fields.

It is difficult to understand why law schools are so hesitant about establishing prerequisites, particularly in the social sciences. Although it is true that such courses in some colleges are so poor as to be almost without value and the contribution of the social sciences is still slight when compared with the achievements of the physical sciences, yet the fact remains that the social studies have gradually evolved significant methods of gathering and interpreting evidence concerning the nature of man and of society. From this evidence has come an insight into human behavior which law schools can scarcely ignore. Yet students in most of these schools are not trained to examine the form or purpose of contemporary society. Their attention, instead, is focused upon situations that are in the past, and upon the "rules of law" that apply to those situations.[1]

A few years ago the faculty of the Columbia Law School pointed to the students' need for a broad knowledge of the structure of society. "The whole life which law affects and which affects law should be viewed comprehensively as an inter-

[1] Britt, Steuart Henderson, "Blood-Grouping Tests and the Law: the Problem of 'Cultural Lag.'" In Minnesota Law Review, May, 1937, pp. 700–701.

relation of processes. This understanding cannot be got today by a 'hit or miss' apprenticeship in life any more than living in our bodies can teach us their structure and functioning."[1] The faculty concluded, "Systematized study deliberately focused toward getting an adequate knowledge of the entire social structure, seen as a functioning, interdependent, and changing mechanism, is a basic prerequisite if law is to be systematically studied as a means to contemporary ends."[2] This comprehensive knowledge of the whole structure must be obtained, in the estimation of these teachers, either before or after the student enters the institution.[3]

At about the time that the Columbia faculty was uttering so unequivocal a statement, John L. Gillin, professor of sociology at the University of Wisconsin, was discussing the relation of sociology to courses in law schools.[4] He found only seven law schools which made sociology a requirement for admission, and nine others that recommended the subject. In commenting on this situation, he suggested that most prospective lawyers probably look upon their future profession as one which does not require special knowledge of the processes by which social life goes forward, any more than they need to understand geology or mathematics.

If, however, the lawyers' and judges' functions are touching social

[1] Summary of Studies in Legal Education by the Faculty of Law of Columbia University, 1928, pp. 80–81.
[2] *Ibid.*
[3] It is interesting to note that an elective undergraduate course on psychology and law is being offered to pre-law and other students at Cornell, and a similar one will be given at George Washington University beginning with 1938–1939. These courses represent an attempt to integrate certain material from law and the social sciences, even on the undergraduate level.
[4] "New Developments in the Departments of Sociology in Relation to Courses in the Law School." In Annals of the American Academy of Political and Social Science, September, 1929, pp. 126–128.

problems at an ever-increasing number of points, and if the law represents organized social endeavor to adjust the legal machinery of society to social needs, future lawyers perhaps ought to get an understanding in some way about the interrelationships of legal machinery and social processes.[1]

Since entrance requirements are so few, it is necessary to examine what training in the social sciences the law schools themselves are furnishing. The majority offer nothing in a planned and purposeful way. Whatever material of this kind may creep into the curriculum generally results from the fact that occasional members of the faculty introduce into their courses such pertinent social facts as they have at their disposal.

In a few schools a sincere effort is being made to present a picture of law in its social setting. Where this occurs, some of the institutions are drawing upon men who are not lawyers to teach certain courses. Other schools are encouraging their lawyer-teachers to utilize the materials of the social sciences in the regular courses. Columbia and Yale have been pioneers in the first method; Harvard and Chicago in the second. According to the current Columbia catalogue, courses in criminal law, family law, and legal factors in economic society are particularly rich in data from sociology and economics. Among the faculty there are academic instructors who teach philosophy, marketing, insurance, and business law. At Yale courses on psychology of modern judicial and legislative institutions, theories of law, psychiatry in law administration, and criminal law and administration all bear evidence of a broad general presentation. Included in the faculty of the Yale Law School are lecturers from the Harvard School of Business Administration, a professor of psychology, a professor of business administration, a physician

[1] *Ibid.*, p. 127.

who is professor of psychiatry and mental hygiene, and a statistician who is director of research in social statistics. A few other law schools offer courses taught by men who are not lawyers. Of these, Louisiana State University lists a professor of philosophy; Minnesota, a professor of political science; Boston University gives a course in psychiatry taught by a physician. The University of Denver also offers a course in psychiatry, which was instituted in 1927 as the pioneer in its field. This course was made possible through the co-operation of the departments of psychiatry and neurology of the University of Colorado School of Medicine and Hospitals and of Dr. Franklin G. Ebaugh, director of the Colorado Psychopathic Hospital. It consists not only of lectures on psychiatry in relation to law, but of evening clinics held at the Hospital.

In schools which do not call upon professors from other disciplines but which are aware of the significance of the social sciences, interpolation of extra-legal material depends upon the experience of the various teachers.[1] At Harvard where sociological jurisprudence is emphasized, for instance, three instructors teaching different sections of the same subject may present the material from three distinct angles. There is no assurance that all of them will include essential social facts. It is exceedingly difficult to find men who are at once lawyers and experts in the social aspects of the division of law they teach. A few instructors, however, like Professor Glueck, who teaches criminology at Harvard, or Professor John S. Bradway, who gives a course in family law at Duke, have become quite as much identified with sociology and social work as with law.

[1] On pp. 94–95 a description is presented of a significant new plan at the University of Chicago Law School, whereby extensive use is being made of the social sciences and other non-legal materials by lawyer members of the faculty.

When all the schools have been canvassed, the results are not very encouraging from the angle of the social studies. As Huntington Cairns has said in the preface to his book, Law and the Social Sciences,[1] "Today there is a persistent demand for the coordination of jurisprudence with the social sciences, but definite suggestions as to how this task is to be accomplished have been few." Only the merest beginning has been made. Several writers, like Mr. Cairns, Professor Jerome Michael,[2] and Professor Mortimer J. Adler,[2] have been discouraged, moreover, by what appears to them the small amount of knowledge that the social sciences yet have to offer law. In contrast to their attitude, Professor Glueck points to writings by lawyers and judges which cover such diverse fields as the relationship of cultural anthropology to family law and concepts of property; of modern psychology and psychiatry to the administration of criminal justice and to the traditional laws of evidence; of psychoanalysis to an understanding of the judicial process; of recent economic studies to judicial interpretation and the constitutional validity of such modern legislation as that dealing with the control of business organization and enterprise, the work of the Interstate Commerce Commission, workmen's compensation, immigration, strikes, lockouts, boycotts, injunctions in labor disputes, and various other legislative interferences with the free exercise of the "right of property."[3]

In all of these and other areas the social studies have a contribution to make. Until they become more exact, however, that contribution is certain to have definite limitations. Hence,

[1] Harcourt, Brace and Co., New York, 1935.
[2] Joint authors of Crime, Law and Social Science, Harcourt, Brace and Co., New York, 1933.
[3] "The Social Sciences and Scientific Method in the Administration of Justice." In Annals of the American Academy of Political and Social Science, May, 1933, p. 112.

for those teachers of law who hope to grasp large bodies of irrefutable facts and solid generalizations, which they can weave whole into the fabric of legal education, the result is likely to be disillusionment. But there is another contribution which the social studies can render that has not been sufficiently emphasized. It is a peculiar point of view or way of looking at social phenomena. From such studies one gains a better understanding of institutions which are so interrelated that alteration in one eventually results in alteration of all the others; of social evolution and cultural change; of the constantly shifting adaptations of society to new conditions; and of the fact that law too is a growth. These sciences, in Professor Wormser's estimation,

. . . have an inspiring and profound significance to one who believes that the law is a reflection of progressing life, and not an unchanging set of words, graven on tablets of stone; that it is a part of life and not apart from life; that it should meet the ever-changing needs of the present hour; and that its life is not embedded in the logic or precise technique of a game of chess, but hinges and depends upon a progressive ability to solve the novel problems continually developing in a rapidly altering economic and social era.[1]

NEW TRENDS IN LEGAL EDUCATION

A few years ago Professor Roscoe Turner Steffen of the Yale Law School wrote, "It may be said without much question that there is more activity in the law school world today than there has been at any time within the last generation or two. Things are in a state of flux."[2] As proof of his statement, he pointed to the fact that new courses are being added to the curriculum,

[1] Wormser, I. Maurice, "Sociology and the Law." In Annual Review of the Law School of New York University, April, 1924, p. 11.
[2] "Changing Objectives in Legal Education." In Yale Law Journal, February, 1931, p. 576.

old courses are being rearranged, integration of subjects is going on, non-legal material is being introduced, and the social sciences are coming to be recognized.

The foregoing pages have discussed this recognition of the social sciences, and have indicated other new trends. More attention, even at the expense of some repetition, must now be given to those efforts to integrate and expand the course of study, which have assumed considerable proportions during the last decade. Before entering upon this discussion, however, a note of caution is necessary. Although the activity of which Professor Steffen spoke is of unquestioned importance, it is, in reality, confined to a small number of the schools.

As one reads the recent literature of legal education, he is impressed with the enthusiasm and labor which are going into the reshaping of curricula. But when he examines the source of this literature, he finds that nearly all of it has been written by a relatively few law professors connected with even fewer schools. After he has gone beyond a possible two dozen institutions that have aligned themselves with new movements in legal education, he begins to wonder whether most of the remaining schools are doing more than adhering to old patterns. He finds practically nothing recorded about new trends in many of the full-time and nearly all of the part-time schools. He recalls the following statement, to which some other institutions would probably subscribe, that appeared in the bulletin of one of the university law schools as late as 1933:

The faculty has in mind no radical experiments in legal education. The subjects offered are found in the course of study of accredited schools. The method of instruction has been in use . . . for many years. We plan to equip our students to practice law in any state where the common law prevails. We stick to fundamentals. No member is inclined to convert his classroom into an expensive laboratory in which to experiment with novel, radical, or untried theories.

The fact that extensive alteration of the method and content of legal education has not yet spread to all schools does not minimize the significance of the reorganization now being effected in some of them. History has demonstrated that continuous experimentation and adaptation to new social trends are necessary if an institution is to be saved from slow decay. The burden of experimentation generally falls, however, upon a relatively small group which has sufficient imagination, zeal, leisure, and financial resources to undertake it. From the ferment at work in recent years in certain law schools, it is not unlikely that there will come results as vital for legal education in the twentieth century as was Langdell's innovation in the nineteenth. It is also probable that when new subject matter and new techniques of instruction have proved their value, they will be taken over gradually by those institutions which are not fertile in experimentation and research but which see the wisdom of following the leadership of more outstanding schools.

Change in Courses and Methods of Instruction

Among the most conspicuous changes of recent years has been the introduction of new subjects. Whole fields of law which were of little importance fifty years ago have become of such moment in our present industrial society, that a great many additional courses have been necessary to meet this need. A substantial part of the curriculum is now devoted to corporation and business law. So closely allied do many lawyers find the practice of law and business that the Yale Law School and the Harvard School of Business Administration offer a joint course. It is designed to train men for law practice in those fields involving contact with or the handling of business problems. The course originally extended over a period of four years, one of which students spent at Harvard and the other three at Yale. Apparently because of the requirement of an additional year, registration was very small. Consequently, beginning with the fall of 1937, the curriculum was reduced to three years.

Louisiana State University and Washington University in St. Louis also provide a similar type of training in both business and law through six-year curricula composed of courses offered in their respective undergraduate schools of commerce or business and public administration and in their law schools. Students spend the first two years in the undergraduate schools. Concerning the amount of work to be taken in business and in law during the remainder of the curricula, the universities make somewhat different requirements. The last three years, however, are devoted predominantly to legal studies. These combined courses lead to a baccalaureate and a law degree.

Business aspects of law are reported to have been sufficiently developed by the average school to afford a fairly satisfactory preparation for commercial law.[1] Development in this field, however, is likely to have been bought at the expense of other necessary subjects. The situation that obtains in reference to the teaching of criminal law, for example, Professor John Hanna believes to be deplorable. With the exception of one or two schools, he finds no institutions that are assuming their obvious responsibility of training students not only in criminal law but in criminology and penology, and then of placing such students in executive positions dealing with criminal and penal administration.

[1] Hanna, John, "The Law School as a Function of the University." In North Carolina Law Review, December, 1931, pp. 151–152.

Recent social trends are forcing law schools to offer more courses in statutory law, and more preparation for practice before governmental agencies. The New Deal, that grew out of the economic depression, has been responsible for two developments which are likely to have important results for legal training.[1] It has become apparent, first, that legislation rather than the judicial process is increasingly employed as the method of accommodating legal rules to rapid social change. As a consequence, it is necessary that the lawyer appreciate the role of statute law and master the technique of legislation. Second, lawyers are being drawn into governmental service or are practicing before official agencies, other than the courts, in large numbers. This fact requires that they be trained for a type of work distinctly different from that of private law.

In his open letter of April, 1937, to the law alumni of the University of Illinois, Dean Harno wrote of the phenomenal growth of public law and its implications for legal education. With sales tax laws being enacted almost everywhere, and the scope of estate, inheritance, and income taxes being expanded, the lawyer must be trained to cope with the legal problems raised through these developments. According to Dean Harno, taxation gives indication of becoming a major subject in the law curriculum. The growth of administrative law, he insists, must also be given a place in the course of study. So must the legal aspect of government regulation of business, not only with reference to public utilities, as formerly, but in relation to the broader expanse of trade regulation. Constitutional law, which is today almost a recapitulation of current events, must likewise be included. How these subjects can be incorporated into an

[1] Handler, Milton, "What, If Anything, Should Be Done by the Law Schools to Acquaint Law Students with the So-called New Deal Legislation and Its Working." In American Law School Review, April, 1935, p. 164.

already overcrowded curriculum is a problem with which many administrators are struggling.

Lloyd K. Garrison, dean of the University of Wisconsin Law School and president in 1936–1937 of the Association of American Law Schools, reports, after a recent visit to six of the leading schools in the Middle West, that the increased emphasis upon public law courses is already clearly noticeable in these institutions.[1] Constitutional law, which only a few years ago was rarely a prescribed subject, is now required by four of the six schools. Courses in judicial administration that stress development, organization, and functions of courts, selection of judges, and simplification of court procedure are offered in the six institutions, and are required in all except Chicago. Work in legislation is announced at four of the institutions; courses in jurisprudence are offered at four and required at two of the four. Administrative law is assuming a new importance and other public law courses, such as taxation, labor law, and trade regulation are also receiving more attention. Most of these courses are elective, however, and are taken by a mere handful of students.

A second change of note in legal education is the rearrangement of courses.[2] In place of the former patchwork pattern of courses, alignment of related subjects is going on. Combination courses, which stress the function that legal devices play in modern life are being substituted for a large number of indi-

---

[1] "Developments in Legal Education at Michigan, Illinois, Chicago, Northwestern, Minnesota and Wisconsin." In Annual Review of Legal Education for 1936, pp. 12–14.

[2] For a description of the reorganized and otherwise extensively altered curriculum that will be introduced in the Harvard Law School in the fall of 1938, see Professor Sidney Post Simpson's contribution to the symposium on "Law School Objectives and Methods," in American Law School Review, April, 1938, pp. 1038–1044.

vidual subjects.[1] Courses in business organization frequently replace the older topics of agency, partnership, and corporations. Under the heading of security or credit transactions appears the former material in bankruptcy, mortgages, and suretyship. A course in procedure may draw upon facts taken from common law, pleading and trial practice, and equity.

Together with the introduction of new material in the curriculum and the realignment of courses, there have been changes in teaching techniques and methods of approach to subject matter. It is apparent that large classes do not lend themselves to discussion in which everyone can freely participate. Consequently, there is a tendency to substitute small discussion groups for formal lectures. Graduate seminars have also been made available to competent third-year students, and in some instances to exceptional second-year men. Students are being expected to assume a greater degree of responsibility than formerly for individual investigation and research. In some schools where the elective system is widely utilized, they are required to select a particular field in which to carry on intensive study. Through these means the schools employing them believe that initiative, intellectual curiosity, and a greater maturity of judgment will be developed and students will come to be well acquainted with at least one field of law.

This type of training appears to be excellent for the capable and independent student. It is not, however, well adapted to those who are unable to assume a considerable degree of individual responsibility. As a result, a school must either select only students who show marked ability, or it must supplement this new type of work with the customary formal classes. Small

[1] Kinnane, C. H., "Changing Materials in Teaching Law." In American Bar Association Journal, April, 1933, pp. 240–244.

discussion groups and individual attention, furthermore, are expensive, inasmuch as they require an enlarged faculty or a small student body. Consequently, for schools without endowment, this system is difficult to introduce even if the dean approves of it.[1]

The Four-Year Curriculum

One further trend in legal education must be noted—that of extending the full-time school curriculum to four years. Now only the law schools of the universities of Minnesota, Chicago, and Louisiana are reported to have students enrolled in such a course, and even in those institutions it is elective.[2] Other institutions, however, are giving the subject careful consideration, and some of them are arranging to lengthen their course of study in the near future. In 1938 the plan will be made compulsory at Minnesota, and the University of Washington in Seattle will put its entire curriculum on a four-year basis. A year later Washington University in St. Louis intends to initiate a similar program on an optional basis.

The mere extension of the course of study to cover an additional year is, in itself, a matter of secondary importance, particularly when it is achieved by requiring only two, instead of three or four, years of academic preparation. But the reasons for this change, as they have been evolved at Minnesota and

[1] For further details, see "Report of Committee on Curriculum," in American Law School Review, April, 1932, pp. 440–441; Green, Leon, "A New Program in Legal Education," in American Law School Review, May, 1931, pp. 193–197; Report of Dean of Law School of University of Wisconsin, 1932–1933; Clark, Charles E., "Educational and Scientific Objectives of the Yale School of Law," in Annals of the American Academy of Political and Social Science, May, 1933, pp. 167–168.

[2] The writer is indebted to Professor Alfred Harsch of the University of Washington School of Law for permission to use material from his manuscript entitled, The Four-Year Law Course in American University Schools.

Chicago, are of marked significance in the light of current criticisms of the curricula of law schools. It may be said that the general purpose of the four-year course is to provide opportunity to introduce more non-legal material on the one hand, and more legal material of a broadly professional rather than vocational nature on the other. Attempts are also being made to integrate further the legal course of study, and to relate the work of the undergraduate preparatory years to that in the law school.

The efforts of Dean Everett Fraser and his colleagues at the University of Minnesota, begun in 1931, to broaden and unify the curriculum are receiving so much attention from law-school teachers that future undertakings are likely to be devised in terms of their likeness to or their difference from what is popularly known as "the Minnesota plan." A brief description of it, consequently, will be given. The well-defined and somewhat different program at Chicago will then be contrasted with it.

Pre-law students at Minnesota are organized separately within the College of Arts and 70 per cent of their work, during a required two-year period, is prescribed. Freshmen are obliged to study English literature and composition; philosophy, including logic and ethics; the theory of government and comparative government. Either English or American history is recommended. In the sophomore year English constitutional history, principles of economics, and psychology are required. A natural science; half-year courses in sociology and public speaking; and other courses in economics, government, and philosophy are recommended.

No work in a foreign language or in the arts is suggested; sociology is not required; and no course, such as anthropology or zoology, which would provide some insight into the theory of evolution and the development of man, is mentioned. In view of the need for cultural background and broad outlook on the part of lawyers, this undergraduate curriculum appears too limited in scope. Its great virtue lies in the fact that it furnishes more preparation in

93

the social sciences than do many four-year courses of study where students are largely free to elect whatever they wish.

The first two years in the law school are devoted wholly to the study of prescribed work in substantive law. The courses are those that would normally be offered in the subject under an elective system. In the third year seven weekly hours of adjective law—consisting of courses in practice, evidence and pleading, and legal-aid work —are required. The remainder of the student's time may be filled with elective courses.

Emphasis in the fourth year is placed upon a program that is essentially professional rather than vocational, and that stresses training for public service rather than learning to care for the interests of clients. Courses in jurisprudence, judicial administration, legislation, and either administrative law or labor law and trade regulation are required. During the four remaining hours a week, work in the law school or some other division of the University may be elected.

Under this plan there appears to be little essential difference, other than some reorganization of courses, between the work of the first three years and that offered in other approved schools. Standard case-books are used, and the catalogue does not indicate any attempt to introduce non-legal material. In the fourth year, however, courses that are more generally offered on the graduate level and hence are taken by very few students, are required. Thus areas of law of particular current significance are surveyed, the important subject of judicial administration is not neglected, and opportunity is provided the student for some investigation of non-legal but related subjects.[1]

The University of Chicago, in the fall of 1937, introduced its four-year curriculum for which two years of academic work are a prerequisite, as an alternative to the established three-year course, based upon a complete college education.[2] There are three outstanding features in this plan. First, the social sciences and other non-

---

[1] For further details of "the Minnesota plan" see Everett Fraser's "An Integrated Course of Training for Lawyers," in American Law School Review, April, 1937, pp. 714–718.

[2] This plan is described by Professor Malcolm P. Sharp in the symposium, "Law School Objectives and Methods," appearing in American Law School Review, April, 1938, pp. 1044–1049.

legal materials are being utilized extensively, not only by drawing upon them in law courses, but by offering specific courses in them. Psychology and English constitutional history are being presented in the first year; economic theory, accounting, and political theory are to be given in the second; and ethics in the third. These courses are deemed essential to the intellectual equipment of the modern lawyer. They will be taught by members of the law faculty who have been trained in law and the specific subject, and presented in such a fashion that the student can apply the knowledge gained therein to law courses taken either prior to or simultaneously with them.

The second distinct feature of the Chicago plan is the investigation of the relationship between law and society, and the ends that law should serve. The student will be encouraged to consider the social desirability of legal and judicial behavior, and will be provided with the materials—psychological and economic as well as legal—for formulating such judgments.

Finally, the entire curriculum is to be standardized, except for a limited degree of specialization. About three-fourths of the work in law will be required and must be taken in a designated sequence. A small part of the student's time during his third year and about half of the fourth year will be devoted to research and the preparation of reports dealing with one or two broad fields of concentration. Examinations in specific subjects have been abolished, and comprehensive annual examinations have been substituted.

Because this course of study has been so recently initiated, the success with which it will meet is still unknown. If it later seems to be a distinct improvement over the more traditional curriculum, it may serve as a pattern for other institutions that favor the extensive introduction of non-legal materials and that desire to emphasize the social aspects of law.

SUPERVISED PRACTICE AS PART OF LEGAL TRAINING

For some years it has become increasingly clear to legal educators that the training generally offered in law schools does not fit students for the actual practice of law. In contrast to the old form of apprenticeship training through which men learned from observation and daily routine how to act as lawyers but acquired only an insufficient knowledge of the law itself, the modern school has emphasized the scientific and scholarly approach to legal subjects and has neglected preparation in the techniques of practice.

As a result of the present situation, the graduate is likely to find the transition from law school to law office a difficult one. Justin Miller, now a judge of the Court of Appeals of the District of Columbia, recalls the tradition still extant in the legal profession that there should normally be a starvation period during which the young lawyer should serve as a briefing clerk, or, if he opens an office for himself, should expect few and impecunious clients.[1] During this time he is expected to work out an adjustment for himself. It is a period, in Judge Miller's estimation, however, of disillusionment as well as of starvation. Economic necessity not infrequently strips him of his ideals and social point of view, and tempts him to engage in ethically undesirable forms of practice.

Because many schools are aware of the student's difficulties in entering upon the practice of law, there has been much discussion of how the process might be made easier. In 1933 Jerome Frank wrote an article that has attracted much attention, in which he advocated the reorganization of the curricula of law schools so that they would become clinical institutions.[2] He suggested that students be brought into closer contact with the every-day activities of practice by a study of complete records of appellate

[1] "New Developments in Law Schools." In Annals of the American Academy of Political and Social Science, September, 1929, p. 118.
[2] "Why Not a Clinical Law School?" In University of Pennsylvania Law Review, June, 1933, pp. 908–923. See also George K. Gardner's "Why Not a Clinical Lawyer's School? Some Reflections," in University of Pennsylvania Law Review, June, 1934, pp. 785–804.

cases, by frequent visits with their instructors to the courts, by working as supervised apprentices in law offices during their law course, and by participating in the operation of a legal clinic connected with the law school. He suggested, furthermore, that the social sciences be correlated with formal instruction in law. In order that there might be time for the program outlined, he recommended that most of the present case-book method of instruction be omitted. He recommended also that the faculty be recruited largely, not from legal scholars, but from experienced practitioners and from teachers of the social sciences.

All the changes advocated by Mr. Frank had been advocated by others also. Rarely before, however, had any one person suggested so large a number of alterations or so drastic a reorganization of the curriculum. His concept of supervised apprenticeship training is coming to be discussed with increasing frequency, and some persons insist that there is imperative need for preparation of this sort. In the five states, Delaware, New Jersey, Pennsylvania, Rhode Island, and Vermont, legislation already exists which makes some office work a prerequisite for admission to the bar.[1] Except for New Jersey, where the student is obliged to spend a year in an office, the required period is six months. Pennsylvania demands that four of the six months be served after completion of the regular course. Elsewhere the office work may be done during vacations. An occasional law school also requires an office apprenticeship. At the University of Wisconsin nearly all students are expected to spend three months during each of two summers in offices approved by the school. Dean Garrison favors this plan, particularly in states like Wisconsin where many law graduates begin private practice immediately after receiving their degrees. Were

[1] Annual Review of Legal Education for 1936, Table opposite p. 36.

97

it not for such apprenticeships, they would open their offices without any training at all under an older man.[1]

Valuable as apprenticeship undoubtedly is in theory, the very practical question arises of the manner in which it can be organized effectively.[2] If the training forms part of the law course, the period allotted to it is short and the work which students can do that is of value to the office is necessarily simple and routine. If apprenticeship follows graduation from a law school, as a few law teachers believe it should, the problem is even more complex. It is true that there are some law offices, particularly among the smaller ones, where young lawyers are given widely diversified work and where they receive personal attention and counsel. In the large offices of urban areas, law-school graduates are generally engaged to perform duties which are highly specialized and are repeated so often that they soon cease to learn anything new. Seldom do they have a chance to engage in several fields of work or to come in contact with clients, and almost never are there supervisors to guide their progress from simple to more complicated and responsible tasks. Whatever training these young lawyers receive is a by-product of the contribution they make to their employers; it is not apprenticeship in any true sense of the word.

The suggestion has been made that a system might be devised whereby the law schools would provide supervisors to direct the work of students or graduates employed in private offices during a period of apprenticeship. Such a system has been developed effectively in social work education, where training through

---

[1] "Character Training of Law Students from the Point of View of the Law Schools and the Bar." In American Law School Review, December, 1936, p. 595.

[2] For recent suggestions regarding apprenticeship in governmental agencies, see Dean Garrison's "The House of Law in a Time of Change," in American Law School Review, April, 1938, pp. 1029–1030.

field work is frequently carried on in social agencies under supervision of a faculty member of a school of social work and under direction of a member of the staff of the particular agency. The establishing of a co-operative system of this kind in legal training is likely to be so difficult, however, that it scarcely seems to furnish any immediate solution for law graduates in need of practical experience and guidance in the early stages of their careers.

An alternative method for giving students some practical training, which has been tried with success in a few schools and which many believe to be superior to apprentice work in a private law office, is the use of the legal clinic. Strictly speaking a legal clinic is a law office operated for teaching purposes. Its clients are poor persons, who apply for assistance. Students handle their cases, at least in the initial stages, with the assistance of the director. Sometimes the legal clinic is part of a law school or under its immediate control. The majority of schools, however, which are interested in providing clinical experience for students, have not attempted to operate clinics of their own but have arranged that local legal aid societies should furnish the training. These societies, which will be described in a later section, are of significance here only to the extent that some of them are a factor in legal education. In the following discussion the term, legal clinic, will be used to mean an agency operated primarily for the training of students in law practice either by a law school or a legal aid society.

The first legal clinic made its appearance in 1893 at the University of Pennsylvania, where some students of the law school opened what they called a legal dispensary. The enterprise was soon discontinued. Aside from a clinic established at the University of Denver in 1904, there was no further progress until

1908. During the next eight years several schools made provision for offering clinical training. Then followed a decade when not one new clinic was established and training was continued only at Northwestern, Minnesota, and Harvard. By 1927 the pre-war momentum and creative interest began to be recovered. Since then several law schools have either opened clinics of their own, or have entered into co-operative relationships with legal aid societies whereby their students may gain practical experience.

Although the legal clinic has as yet found a place in very few schools, several law teachers are its ardent proponents. They maintain that it gives the student an opportunity to synthesize what he has learned in theory in many different courses; it teaches him how to plan and conduct a campaign in a legal case; by bringing him in contact with clients it helps him to learn to deal with the human factors involved in every legal proceeding; and it provides the instructor with an opportunity of determining a student's dependability, judgment, initiative, and other characteristics.[1]

Many of the schools that are without clinics have stated reasons for not undertaking this kind of instruction: some say that they are not situated where they can readily obtain clients; others feel that they cannot assume the financial and administrative responsibility; still others find their curricula so overcrowded that they do not wish to add anything more. Another group of schools is definitely of the opinion that its function is the laying of a sound, theoretical foundation and that nothing should deter it from so important a task. And finally, there are schools which do not regard clinical work with poor clients favorably,

[1] For a discussion of legal clinics see Reginald H. Smith and John S. Bradway's Growth of Legal-Aid Work in the United States, U. S. Department of Labor, Bulletin 607, 1936, pp. 156–163.

since they maintain that their students will enter a very different type of practice, for which legal aid experience would be of little assistance.

Because of the youth of the legal clinic movement and the little that is generally known about it, this section ends with a description of the clinical work that has been developed by Northwestern University and the Legal Aid Bureau of the United Charities of Chicago. The following account is summarized from articles by Dean Leon Green[1] and Miss Nellie Mac-Namara, a lawyer who is on the staff both of the law school and of the Bureau,[2] and from the bulletin of the school for 1937–1938:

Clinical training was begun at Northwestern in 1908 through a co-operative arrangement with the Legal Aid Bureau. In 1926 the Raymond Foundation was established to finance the Bureau's legal service for the poor under the superintendence of a joint committee of the Northwestern School of Law, the United Charities of Chicago, and the Chicago Bar Association. Further gifts have been sufficient to sustain civil and industrial branches of service. These branches are under the direction of attorneys of the law school, aided by the staff of the Legal Aid Bureau. Indigent claimants and defendants in every type of case are represented. Claims successfully prosecuted aggregate thousands of dollars annually, and the legitimate defenses afforded the poor are equally valuable.

This work, from the angle of student instruction, is considered so important that all third-year men and women, except those who are members of the Legal Publications Board, are required to spend a generous amount of their time for eight weeks at one of the branches. Even the members of the Board are encouraged to enrol for clinical practice if possible. When a student reports for training, he is given

[1] "Integrating Law School and Community." In American Law School Review, May, 1933, pp. 822–825.
[2] "Teaching Legal Ethics by the Clinical Method." In American Law School Review, May, 1935, pp. 241–245.

a definite undertaking. This is changed as frequently as his experience and the needs of the office warrant it. No hypothetical cases are assigned; students participate in the actual problems of the clinic. These problems include questions relating to wage claims, wage assignments, garnishments, small loans, collections, contracts, landlord and tenant relationships, conversion and recovery of personal property, insurance, domestic relations, probate of estates of the deceased, minors, and insane persons, and numerous miscellaneous matters.

The student is given an opportunity to interview clients not only when they first come to one of the clinics but at subsequent visits. From these interviews he attempts to diagnose the legal problems presented and to give sound advice. This advice is reviewed, corrected, or supplemented before the client is permitted to leave the office. In cases involving social aspects, the student learns to make contacts with the various social agencies which co-operate with the courts. He is also instructed in the keeping of accurate records of all cases to which he is assigned. Thus the results of his work are available for use by the attorney and social worker who are, in the final analysis, responsible to the client. He is allowed, under supervision, to draft pleadings, legal instruments, and letters. Students who exhibit more than an academic interest in the difficulties of a client are permitted to conduct the adjustment of the case from the initial interview to the final settlement, or, in event of suit, to prepare and file the necessary pleadings and assist the lawyer in the actual preparation and trial of the case. Only those licensed to practice, however, are permitted by state law to assume responsibility for conducting the trial.

Immediately before beginning clinical training, students are given a short intensive lecture course by a member of the faculty of the school on civil practice and procedure. During the period of field work further classes are held, and problems arising from practical experience are analyzed and discussed. The organization of courts, of county and city office, and records; the existence and function of social agencies and their relation to the practice of law; the filing of suits and other pleadings; questions of practice and rules of court; methods of procedure; and drafting of legal documents are subjects which furnish much class discussion. The facts of actual cases arising in the legal aid office are also submitted to the group for their consideration. Thus an attempt is made to enhance the value of the training gained in the clinic.

LAW-SCHOOL FACULTIES

For many years there was vigorous discussion of the question of whether instruction in law schools should be provided primarily by teachers who devote their entire time to the work of the school, or by practicing lawyers who can spare only a limited amount of time for teaching, or by both. Even recently the question has been raised more than once. We have already noted that in his proposal for a clinical law school, Jerome Frank suggested that teachers be recruited largely from experienced practitioners. In 1930 G. L. Archer, dean of the Suffolk Law School in Boston, aroused a storm of discussion when he offered a resolution at the annual meeting of the Section of Legal Education of the American Bar Association to the effect that one-half of all law teachers be practicing lawyers or men who had had at least ten years' active experience.[1] Although many of those present spoke in favor of having a much larger proportion of practitioners on law faculties than there were at the time, Dean Archer's resolution was lost by an overwhelming majority.

It is evident that the professional teacher and the practicing lawyer have distinct and widely different contributions to make to legal education. A teacher has sufficient time to devote to the efficient organization and operation of a law school; he is able to have more intimate contacts with students; he can more easily make adequate preparation for classroom instruction, and engage in research and writing; and finally he has a better op-

[1] "Proceedings of the Section of Legal Education of the American Bar Association." In American Law School Review, December, 1930, pp. 37-43.

portunity to view both legal education and the legal profession with some quiet objectivity. The criticism is often made, however, that such teachers have had so little actual legal practice or have been so long removed from practice that they tend to over-emphasize the approach to law as a science rather than as an art. It is also said that they are even unaware at times of new developments in law which need to be introduced into the cur-riculum. The system of instruction by full-time teachers, more-over, is a very expensive one.

A practicing lawyer or judge who is engaged in teaching ob-viously does not have enough time to devote to tasks requiring long preparation and careful consideration. Dean Garrison aptly remarked not long ago: "As one who joined the teaching profession after ten years of practice I can testify to the heart-rending labors necessary to the facing of a class for a single hour—labors which most practicing lawyers simply do not have the time to undertake."[1] A practitioner does, however, bring into the classroom the spirit of the law office and the court. He is more likely to center his attention upon the application of law to specific cases than upon a search for general principles of law. His concern with concrete situations is frequently very stimulating to students. A further advantage of the system of part-time teachers is that of greater economy for the school.

The question of the full-time versus the part-time teacher has confronted almost every type of professional education. Profes-sional training was founded by practitioners in the several fields, and, although they still play an important role in some divi-sions, there has been a steadily growing tendency toward requir-ing full-time services of instructors. Increasingly it is being

[1] "Character Training of Law Students from the Point of View of the Law Schools and the Bar." In American Law School Review, December, 1936, p. 595.

emphasized that responsibility for maintaining a professional school should rest with those who can give the institution all their attention. It is believed, however, that practitioners should be called upon, as conditions permit, to supplement and enrich the curriculum with their experience.

This trend toward emphasis on full-time teaching is clearly evident in legal education, but it has not progressed so rapidly as in some other fields. In 1892 the American Bar Association expressed the opinion that there should be in every school at least one instructor who devoted himself to the study and teaching of law as a science. This was deemed essential if students were to understand and profit by the instruction provided by practitioners.[1] In 1916 the Association of American Law Schools ruled that not later than 1919 all members of that body should have faculties consisting of at least three instructors who devoted substantially all of their time to the work of the school.[2] The pronouncement of the American Bar Association in 1921 concerning standards of legal education, which have already been noted, declared that a school should have a sufficient number of full-time teachers to insure actual personal acquaintance and influence with the whole student body. The interpretation of this statement was left to the Council on Legal Education.[3] In 1924, in spite of considerable opposition, the Association of American Law Schools made the requirement that in no case should the number of full-time instructors be fewer than one for each 100 students or major fraction thereof.[4] In 1930 this body raised its requirements once again by ruling that after the

[1] Annual Report of the American Bar Association, 1892, pp. 9, 20.

[2] Handbook of the Association of American Law Schools, 1916, pp. 67–80.

[3] The Council now rules that there shall be at least one full-time instructor for each 100 students, and in no instance shall the number be fewer than three.

[4] Handbook of the Association of American Law Schools, 1924, pp. 51–64.

fall of 1932 all member schools should employ at least four instructors who would devote substantially all their time to the work of the school.[1]

William Draper Lewis, who had long been a professor of law and subsequently dean at the University of Pennsylvania, once made the statement that the rise of law teaching as a distinct career was the most important institutional change which had occurred in the legal profession in forty years.[2] He believed that it had already produced profound changes in ideas concerning adequate preparation for the bar. At a later time Dean Herbert F. Goodrich of the same university spoke of the rapidly growing prestige of law teachers and of the influence they were exerting not only in the classroom but through legal writings, as counselors in legislation, and so on.[3] Although no informed person either within or without the legal profession would question the significance of these remarks, the fact remains that the Association of American Law Schools, and the American Bar Association have been far less insistent in their demands concerning full-time teachers than has the American Medical Association.

For a medical school to be acceptable to the Council on Medical Education and Hospitals, it must have at least 10 full-time persons of the rank of assistant professor or above in the preclinical sciences alone.[4] It is expected that these men will have been appointed on the basis of thorough training, successful teaching experience, ability in research, and willingness to pur-

---

[1] *Ibid.*, 1930, pp. 24–25.
[2] "The Law Teaching Branch of the Profession." In American Law School Review, March, 1925, p. 447.
[3] "Address of President Goodrich." In Handbook of the Association of American Law Schools, 1931, pp. 34–44.
[4] "Essentials of an Acceptable Medical School." In American Medical Directory, 1936, p. 84.

sue an academic career. The Council has recommended, furthermore, that for every 25 students in a class there should be at least one full-time assistant in each of the pre-clinical departments. Teaching in the clinical subjects may be done by physicians in active practice. So highly specialized has medical education become that there were no fewer than *15,243* teachers of all grades in the 77 medical schools in 1935–1936. If only the teachers of pre-clinical subjects are considered, since they represent the great body of full-time instructors, there were 2,594, or an average of 34 per school.[1]

Regarding the number of law-school teachers information is not readily available. From the Directory of Teachers in Membership Schools,[2] however, it is possible to obtain figures for the number of instructors in the 81 schools in continental United States that belong to the Association of American Law Schools. In 1936–1937 there were 989, including deans, or an average of 12 per school. The number ranged from 4 in the School of Law of the University of Utah to 35 at New York University. Thirty-eight schools had fewer than 10 faculty members. How many of the 989 men taught only on a part-time basis is not known. It is safe to assume, however, that by far the greater proportion of teaching in this group of schools is done by those holding full-time positions.

For the number of teachers in the other 114 law schools there are no figures available. A few of the best evening schools have a considerable staff of teachers who are on a full-time basis, but, in general, evening schools are manned by practi-

[1] Zapffe, Fred C., "Number of Physicians and Others Connected with the Faculties of the Medical Schools of the United States and Canada." In Journal of the Association of American Medical Colleges, November, 1936, p. 350.
[2] Issued annually by West Publishing Co., St. Paul.

tioners. In the proprietary institutions practically all of the teaching which the dean cannot undertake is done by such men.

Even less is known about the salaries of law teachers than about their number. The statement has been made that teachers of law in universities are among the best paid members of the faculty.[1] Apparently it is often necessary, as in the case of medical schools, to offer salaries somewhat above the general level for the university in order to attract able men. The very writers, however, who mention the relative advantage of teachers of law over other teachers declare that law faculties have smaller incomes than have practicing lawyers of equal training and ability. Hence law instructors are not able to maintain a standard of living comparable to that of their colleagues at the bar. Some full-time teachers augment their income by private practice in varying degrees. Law educators question whether time and energy spent in this way should not be devoted to teaching, research, writing, and the advancement of professional standards. Until salaries are raised substantially, however, many teachers are likely to feel obliged to continue their remunerative efforts.

If a university is an aggregation of scholars, as Dr. Alan Gregg of the Rockefeller Foundation once characterized it, the importance of the faculty is paramount. Regardless of the exact degree of the influence that professors exert, their role is so significant that it appears somewhat inexplicable that the two national associations interested in legal education have made no significant surveys of teachers and teaching in law schools. Although many schools exercise deliberation and care in choosing their faculty, and although the dean of one of the best schools

[1] Hanna, John, "The Law School as a Function of the University." In North Carolina Law Review, December, 1931, p. 122.

in the country declared to the writer that every other question pertaining to legal education is relatively of little importance, there has never been a comprehensive report of such subjects as adequacy of the number of teachers, their training and experience, salaries, and so on. The evaluation of the competence of any teaching staff is naturally a difficult task. If there is truth, however, in the statement of a distinguished law teacher that there are not nearly enough able teachers to staff all of the law schools and if the generally accepted opinion is valid that much of the present teaching is poor in quality, it would seem essential that there be investigations which might become the basis for improvement of the situation.

Postgraduate Training for Practicing Lawyers

Discussion up to this point has centered around professional training for prospective lawyers. Nothing has been said, except in connection with apprenticeship, about further training for attorneys who have already begun the practice of law. Until recently it was taken for granted that once a lawyer had been admitted to the bar, his professional preparation through formal means was at an end. Of late there has been a slowly growing realization that a system of legal preparation which does not go beyond graduation from a law school is inadequate. Emphasis is coming to be placed on the fact that young attorneys are in need of practical assistance during their early years, and that men who wish to enter a specialty require more background than that provided by a few courses that they may or may not have elected while in law school. There is also the dawning recognition that lawyers generally are in need of information concerning the new fields of law and legal practice which are continually appearing. One of the reasons for the slowness with which the bar has adjusted itself to emerging trends has undoubtedly been the result of the lack of facilities whereby the busy practitioner might keep abreast of such trends.

It is for these reasons that attention is beginning to be directed toward initial forms of postgraduate work, or, to use the term preferred by the Council of the Section of Legal Education, post-admission legal education. When that body made its report to the annual meeting of the American Bar Association in September, 1937, it took cognizance of the fact that various communities have begun to provide means for furnishing practicing lawyers with the opportunity to inform themselves of current developments in law.[1] Since it believed that there is a demand among lawyers for such supplementary legal education and that systematic measures should be taken to satisfy that demand, it recommended that the American Bar Association sponsor and encourage a nationwide program of post-admission legal education for the benefit of the legal profession.

To those who might logically expect law schools to assume responsibility for postgraduate instruction, the recommendation of sponsorship by the national association must come as a surprise. As a matter of fact most law schools have not attempted to provide courses designed expressly for practicing attorneys. We have already noted that few of them have succeeded in creating successful departments of advanced study, and such efforts as have been made to expand the curriculum beyond the lower level have generally been directed toward courses primarily of interest to prospective law teachers rather than to practitioners. In the opinion of the Council the occasional postgraduate course

---

[1] "Report of the Council to the Section of Legal Education and Admissions to the Bar." In Advance Program of meeting of American Bar Association at Kansas City, September 27–October 1, 1937, p. 321. See also Harold P. Seligson's "Post Admission Education for Lawyers," in American Bar Association Journal, April, 1938, p. 231.

that has been offered has not been of great importance and, aside from a few instances of schools situated in large cities, has been poorly attended.

The proper function of the law school in relation to postgraduate work has been much discussed by legal educators and members of the bar. Many are agreed that these institutions should confine themselves to instruction in substantive law and legal analysis, and that they should not dissipate their energy and finances by attempting to offer work for practicing lawyers. Others believe that law teachers are too far removed from the field of practice to present the type of instruction that is most needed. Still others are of the opinion that it is the definite duty of law schools to extend their activities into this field. Whatever opinions may be held, the schools offer slight promise of cultivating this new area in the near future.

One contribution to postgraduate instruction that the schools are making, although it must be regarded as an indirect contribution, is the publication of law reviews. There are some 56 of these reviews, and the Council to the Section of Legal Education has recently characterized them as the most important medium there is at present for keeping attorneys abreast of contemporary trends. Without underestimating the significance of these reviews, it may well be asked whether such a large number of publications, edited usually by able but busy students, serves an educational function as adequately as would a much smaller number that had larger financial resources, salaried full-time editorial staffs, and a distribution much greater than the present restricted circulation of most of these journals.

Next in importance to the law reviews, as a means of enabling attorneys to supplement their formal law-school preparation, are the programs of local, state, and national bar associations. Many of these organizations hold meetings devoted to topics relating to the practical work of lawyers, and more than 50 have periodicals that go to their members. The recent introduction of numerous small sections, as a substitute for some of the general meetings of the state associations, has provided more adequate means for discussion of the law on such subjects as insurance, real estate, taxation, public utilities, and aviation. Short series of lectures, known as institutes, have been conducted by local associations in recent years in Cleveland, Cincinnati, Toledo, Detroit, and on the Pacific coast. The adequacy of such plans is limited by the fact that state bar associations generally meet but once a year, and that institutes consist of only a few lectures held in a handful of places. Some of the local bar associations do much better. The New York Chapter of the National Lawyers Guild, for example, is now offering a series of lectures on labor law and another on taxation extending over several weeks, and the Chicago Chapter has a similar series on labor law.

Having canvassed the work of the various agencies that might be considered the logical ones to promote postgraduate training, mention must be made of the pioneer endeavors of an individual attorney, Harold P. Seligson of New York City, and his advisory council.[1] Since 1933 Mr. Seligson has been experimenting, first with a general introductory course, and later with courses in the legal specialties. The introductory course, consisting of 30 lectures of two hours each, is designed to orient the young lawyer in the field of general practice by furnishing the background and the essential information ordinarily acquired only after years of experience. For those who have completed the

---

[1] "What the Law Schools Can Do for the Practicing Profession," in American Law School Review, December, 1937, pp. 926–929; "Practicing Law Courses," in American Bar Association Journal, March, 1938, pp. 200–203.

introductory course and for older members of the bar, who desire a more detailed presentation of the specialists' methods of handling matters in particular fields, some 12 specialized courses are offered, each of which consists of from 10 to 16 two-hour lectures.

Although there is little formal organization, more than 100 attorneys, who have been graduated from law schools on an average of two years, usually matriculate for the introductory course. The fee charged is $35, and it is offered twice a year. Registration varies widely in the courses dealing with the specialties. A course on real estate law may have 60 members, while one on negligence may have only 20. Between September, 1937, and January, 1938, it is reported, the total registration exceeded 400.

Mr. Seligson's undertaking has met with warm approval by others besides those who have taken the courses which his staff offers. The Association of the Bar of the City of New York adopted a report in November, 1936, recommending the establishment of an independent institution with a modest endowment to carry on the work that has been begun. Mr. Seligson hopes that such a postgraduate school will be chartered in the near future.

His general plan was adopted in 1937 by the Stanford Law Society of San Francisco, which announced a series of 15 weekly lectures on the technique of law practice. About 450 attorneys registered for the course, for which a fee of $5.00 was charged. Since it was impossible to accommodate so large a number, only 300 were finally admitted. Because of the success of this course, plans were made for similar ones to be given at regular intervals. Shortly afterward arrangements were begun in Los Angeles for establishing comparable work. Courses have also been initiated in Philadelphia and Toledo, and the Illinois State Bar Association is endeavoring to stimulate such instruction by providing local groups with lectures on practical topics.

The foregoing pages reveal in how embryonic a stage is postgraduate instruction. Not a single formal institution exists, as yet, for the primary purpose of aiding lawyers to continue their education throughout their professional careers. Definition of the scope and nature of such work is still rudimentary, and plans for the future are few and hazy. The very fact that the bar has begun to exhibit interest and activity, however, is distinctly encouraging.

Some of the other professions are now busily promoting postgraduate work in their respective fields. The medical profession, in particular, is placing much emphasis upon its importance. Although physicians have progressed much farther than has the bar, they recognize that they have made but a mere beginning.[1] The teaching profession, on the other hand, has devised an extensive and elaborate system, often in the face of serious obstacles, for acquainting its personnel with new knowledge and techniques of practice.

EXAMINATIONS FOR ADMISSION TO THE BAR

Graduation from a law school does not generally confer the right of admission to the bar. It is necessary, therefore, to examine the method whereby prospective lawyers are inducted into their profession.

In every jurisdiction in the United States there is a central official body, most often known as the board of bar examiners, whose duty it is to determine through examination the fitness of

---

[1] For facts concerning developments in postgraduate medicine see Physicians and Medical Care by Esther Lucile Brown, pp. 84–88.

candidates who seek to become members of the bar.[1] Boards
had appeared in four states before 1890, but it was not until
the middle of that decade that there was any general inclination
on the part of most states to create such bodies. Afterward the
movement spread rapidly.

It should not be inferred that an official board of bar examiners always has the right to examine all applicants for state
licenses. Graduates of certain law schools, usually those connected with state universities, were long exempt from the regular bar examinations in a large number of jurisdictions and still
are in nine. Although the American Bar Association has emphatically condemned the use of the "diploma privilege" for
forty-five years, many states have been hesitant to renounce it.
Hence the number permitting it has only slowly decreased. A
great victory was achieved in June, 1937, when Texas, which
had formerly extended the privilege to a considerable number
of schools outside the state, as well as to several local schools,
abolished it. Nebraska discontinued the practice in 1938.

Bar examiners are not appointed in a uniform way in all the
jurisdictions; they reflect the evolution of legislative, judicial,
and bar activities in the several states. In general the highest
appellate tribunal has the right of appointment, although in nine
states the recent movement to replace judicial by professional
control, through the establishment of a "self-governing bar,"
has succeeded in making the bar itself responsible for the appointment of examiners. In Florida appointment is by the governor of the state.

Boards of examiners vary in number from three to 15; the
length of their term varies from one to seven years. Appoint-

[1] In South Dakota the law faculty of the state university fulfils this
function.

ments are frequently arranged so that only a portion of the board will be renewed at any one time. Compensation is inadequate in all but a very few states, and in 14 no provision is made for paying even for the reading of examination papers. Consequently, these boards are obliged to carry on the functions of examiners as best they can in addition to their regular professional duties. A few states, however, have a salaried secretary who is himself a member of the bar. In a recent report made to the Association of American Law Schools by Professor Harold Shepherd, chairman of a special committee of law-school teachers that had been asked to study bar admissions, the statement was made that

. . . neither the method of selection, term of office nor compensation is designed to select and retain a group of experts in the art of conducting examinations, nor a group that can devote any major part of its time and energy to a task comparable in character and importance to that of the law teacher.[1]

Bar examiners are faced with very different problems from state to state. In New York, for example, there are more than 4,000 candidates annually, while Montana and South Dakota generally do not have even 10. Seven states had fewer than 25 in 1936, while six states had more than 800.

When the results of bar examinations are scrutinized, one finds wide variation in the proportion of students passed. For the year 1936 the percentage of students who successfully completed their tests ranged from 22 in Arkansas to 94 in North Dakota. It should be borne in mind, however, that graduates of the School of Law of the University of Arkansas are granted the "diploma privilege." Had they taken the examination, it is likely that the total percentage of those passing would have

---

[1] "Report of the Committee on Bar Admissions." In Handbook of the Association of American Law Schools, 1936, p. 100.

been considerably higher. Only 33 registered for the North Dakota examination, of whom 31 were successful. New York State, with 4,299 registrants, passed 44 per cent. The percentage of success for all states combined was 46.5.

If the percentage of those passing the examinations in 1936 is plotted in comparison with the number examined for the jurisdictions not granting the "diploma privilege," an interesting picture presents itself. In nine states with over 450 applicants there was relatively slight variation in the percentage admitted to the bar. Massachusetts and Ohio passed only 38 per cent of their candidates; California passed 51 per cent. The others were between these limits. Such uniformity did not characterize the states with fewer than 450 applicants. With some exceptions, however, these states passed more than half and several more than three-fourths of those examined.

The foregoing discussion should not be interpreted to mean that fewer than 50 per cent of all prospective lawyers, the country over, are admitted to the bar. The figures that have been presented apply only to the applicants of a given year. Mortality at any one examination is great, but a large proportion of law students who fail the first time repeat the tests until they pass. The number of old applicants accumulates from examination to examination until in New York State, at least, repeaters about equal the new examinees each year. Although the percentage of students who fail increases with each succeeding test which they attempt, probably well over 80 per cent finally achieve a passing grade, and in New York, Ohio, and Pennsylvania, where large numbers of applicants are registered, the percentage exceeds 90.[1]

[1] Collins, J. C., "Address of the Chairman to the National Conference of Bar Examiners." In American Law School Review, December, 1933, pp. 911–912.

Philip J. Wickser states that of 22,827 students who applied in New York between 1922 and the end of 1931, 87 per cent had passed before December, 1932. It is significant to note that of those who had first applied in 1922 and 1923, 96.5 per cent had passed by 1932; of those making new applications between 1925 and 1928, 92.5 per cent had been successful by 1932; while 83.5 per cent of the candidates of 1929 and 1930, and 76 per cent of those in 1931 had passed.[1]

There has been much criticism of the validity of a system which passes a relatively small proportion of its applicants at their first attempt, but eventually passes nearly all of them. If examinations are planned for the elimination of the unfit, is this goal achieved when applicants are permitted an unlimited number of repetitions? Many agree with Mr. Wickser in believing that the system, whether of unlimited or of several repeated examinations, allows to enter the ranks of lawyers large numbers of inadequately trained men against whom the examinations were designed to afford protection.[2] There are others, however, who believe that it is so nearly impossible to prepare examinations which will fairly test students' knowledge of law, that they should be given an opportunity to repeat an examination at least several times.

The question of how many repetitions should be permitted an applicant has received considerable attention of late, and a few jurisdictions have restricted the number, generally to from three to five. The observations of the Board of Law Examiners of Pennsylvania, as set forth by George F. B. Appel in 1933,

[1] "Law Schools, Bar Examiners, and Bar Associations." In American Law School Review, April, 1933, pp. 726, 730.
[2] "Ideals and Problems for a National Conference of Bar Examiners." In American Law School Review, December, 1931, p. 289.

show how experience has modified practice in that state. Until October, 1928, candidates were permitted to take the examinations as often as they chose. It was then decided to limit the number of repetitions to five. Statistics for the years from 1928 to 1931 indicated that only 26 out of 1,531 candidates needed more than three attempts to pass. It seemed reasonable to the Pennsylvania Board to conclude, therefore, that three examinations should be sufficient. Consequently, that number has been fixed for the present. In the opinion of Mr. Appel the Board is providing a service to the state of Pennsylvania when it excludes from the bar the 1.7 per cent of the applicants who need more than three trials. He notes, however, that points of view differ from state to state, and he cites the case of one jurisdiction where public opinion was so aroused that it was necessary to suspend the regulation which would have limited examinations to four.[1]

Something must now be said of the nature of these bar examinations which have come to be deemed highly important but which have been subjected to much criticism. The report made to the Association of American Law Schools by Professor Shepherd and his Committee on Bar Admissions, which has already been mentioned, is of particular significance in this connection, since it provided general information about the methods and content of examinations in all the jurisdictions. The Committee found that the number of questions asked applicants in the various states ranges from 25 to 100. Although an examination generally extends over two or three days occupying an average of about eighteen hours, the time available for answering each question is usually only about eighteen minutes. This is

[1] "Pennsylvania System." In American Law School Review, December, 1933, p. 932.

considerably less than the time to which students have been accustomed in law schools.

Except for an occasional state, examiners do not attempt to cover "the whole field of the law," but concentrate on specific subjects, generally publicly announced in advance of the test. The average examination covers some 19 subjects. In comparison with the number of courses offered in the modern law school, the scope of the examination in many states appeared to the Committee to be too limited and optional questions too few. What it considered far more significant, however, than the number of subjects in which an applicant is tested, is that examinations do not reflect recent vital trends in legal education. Subjects resemble those taught in law schools a quarter of a century ago, rather than those listed in current catalogues. More than half the examiners admitted that they did not attempt to check their questions in the light of the contents of modern text- and case-books.

For the drafting of questions, decisions of the local supreme court provide the favorite source of material. When used as the basis for factual questions rather than for principles of law, the Committee asserted that such questions become a test of memorizing decisions rather than a test of reasoning ability. Questions drawn from problem case-books or from law school and bar examinations of other states are not used so extensively as might be expected.

In a few states individual examiners prepare more questions than will be used, and the board then makes a selection. More often, however, an examination is the composite of the contributions of the several members, each of whom is responsible for devising questions on the subjects assigned him. Rarely does a board ask for assistance from a committee of lawyers or of law teachers or both. In two states all grading is done by paid readers, and in two others readers are sometimes employed. Otherwise, the task falls upon the examiners themselves. The majority of examiners prepare in advance an outline of what they consider a correct analysis and answer, and usually each paper is read in part by more than one examiner.

The Committee concluded its report with an affirmation of its belief that the work of bar examiners is a continuation of the process of legal education, and that the establishment of sound legal training and adequate tests for admission to practice are common objectives for which bar examiners and law schools should assume joint responsibility. It recommended, therefore, that a joint advisory committee, composed of representatives of the two groups, be created in each state. Such committees should serve as a clearing house for the exchange of information about the practice, policies, and objectives of each group in matters affecting legal education. The Committee recommended further that these new bodies should give special consideration to the following problems:[1]

1. The scope of the bar examination and the desirability of a redistribution of emphasis on the subjects or fields covered, in light of existing curricula in approved law schools.

2. The source and methods of drafting examination questions, the methods of grading and determination of the passing grade.

3. Advisability of the wider use of optional questions to accommodate the "elective system."

4. Length of time allowed for the whole examination and for answering individual questions.

[1] "Report of Committee on Bar Admissions." In Handbook of the Association of American Law Schools, 1936, p. 108. For a discussion of what has already been accomplished in California and Ohio, see John H. Riordan's "The National Conference of Bar Examiners" and H. W. Arant's "The Relationship of the Law School and the Bar Examiners," in American Law School Review, December, 1937, pp. 941 and 951–952 respectively.

5. Desirability and practicability of taking into account other factors than the examination grade [college and law school records, for example] in determining the right to practice.

Suggestions, such as those made by the Committee on Bar Admissions, are designed to improve the present system of examinations. Note must be made of the fact that some informed persons consider bar examinations so inadequate a method for testing preparation for admission to the bar, that they believe it essential that a totally different system be instituted. Dean Leon Green is one of these persons. According to the plan he has proposed, a board of admissions would replace the present board of bar examiners.[1] This new board would be an administrative agency, under the control of the courts and the state bar, charged with responsibility for supervising legal training and all methods pertaining to admission to the bar. It would formulate policies concerning requirements for admission to law schools, curricula, techniques of instruction, quality of teaching, and so on. If legal education were greatly improved in the weak schools and all the institutions of a given state were required to maintain certain standards of excellence, Dean Green believes that a board of admissions could then, except in marginal cases, admit an applicant to a probationary period of practice on the basis of his college and law-school record, without requiring a bar examination. At the end of the probationary period the board of admissions would again review his history, including the record of several years' practice. As a result of this review, it would grant or withhold a permanent license. By instituting some such scheme, law schools would be so strength-

[1] For a complete statement of Dean Green's proposal, see his articles, "Bar Examinations and the Integrated Bar" and "Development of an Adequate Bar Admission Agency," in Bar Examiner, June, 1932, pp. 213–219, and November, 1934, pp. 291–297 respectively.

ened that there would be no considerable number of poorly qualified men, and hence little need for examinations. Thus bar examiners would be relieved of a task that has proved too difficult for them. There would be substituted an administrative function, which they could successfully undertake, in Dean Green's estimation, provided they had sufficient financial assistance and the unwavering support of an integrated bar.

Although bar examinations are still far from satisfactory, it is generally admitted that some degree of real progress has been achieved in testing professional training. Eligibility for admission to the bar, however, supposedly rests not only upon the successful passing of the bar examination but upon the "good moral character" of the candidate. So important has the "moral character" of a lawyer always been considered in this country that great stress was placed upon ethical integrity as a requisite for admission to the profession long before training in a law school was emphasized. In spite of all the insistence upon it, however, the fact remains that the obtaining of adequate information about the character of prospective lawyers is still an unsolved problem. Even those states that have sought most vigilantly to devise methods for ascertaining whether candidates have the desired moral qualifications and have created special character committees declare that they have achieved relatively little.[1]

A method which has been and still is most frequently employed for obtaining information about candidates, although it is the least effective, is that of requiring that the applicant reply

[1] Character committees should be able to profit from observation of the thorough methods used by the National Conference of Bar Examiners in investigating the character and record of attorneys who, after having been admitted to the bar of one state, seek permission to practice in another state. A description of this aspect of the work of the National Conference appears on pp. 160–161.

to a questionnaire and that letters be submitted by those "character witnesses" whose names he has listed. If the letters are satisfactory and the replies to the questionnaire do not suggest the necessity of further investigation, it is assumed that the candidate has a good moral character. The following severe criticism has been made about such a method.

> This procedure is no safeguard whatsoever to the public. It is not even a real and genuine attempt to find out what the man's character is. It is common knowledge that anyone, no matter how dishonest or unscrupulous he may be, can supply as references the names of three persons who will vouch for him.[1]

In nearly half the states names of applicants are either published or lists are sent to members of the bar. This device was originated on the supposition that information would be provided examiners by those who were acquainted with particular applicants. Oscar G. Haugland, secretary of the Minnesota State Board of Law Examiners, has pointed to the weakness of this plan in the following words:

> In Minnesota, we are commanded to publish the name of each applicant in a newspaper of the county in which the applicant resides more than twenty days prior to our report upon him to the Supreme Court. . . . In the eight years during which those published notices have invited the transmission of information concerning the applicants to my office, the total of the information thereby elicited has been zero. Our files disclose no better record prior to that period.[2]

Such a plan might have worked satisfactorily in the early period of American history when population was slight and all the

---

[1] Shafroth, Will, and Horack, H. Claude, Report of California Survey Committee, 1933, p. 7.
[2] "Psychology Points Way to New Character Tests." In American Law School Review, December, 1936, p. 617.

members of a community were well acquainted with each other. It is obviously outmoded now.

A more successful method which is being utilized by at least 13 states is that of entrusting to a committee, other than the board of bar examiners, the work of investigating applications. In these states it is recognized that the examiners are so busy with testing the professional training that the task of determining character should rest in other hands. In many instances the committee on investigation has subcommittees located in the various sections of the state.

Mr. Shafroth concluded in 1934, when he made a study of character examinations throughout the United States, that 11 states provide adequate methods for giving a thorough and conscientious examination to all candidates.[1] Pennsylvania has done more than any other state in attempting to evolve a system whereby undesirable applicants may be kept from admission to the bar.[2] As the result of a rule of its Supreme Court which became effective in 1928, there is a county board in each of the 67 counties in the state whose function it is to pass on an applicant's general fitness for the profession of law as well as on his character. Before beginning his law course, each student is required to register with the board in his county. After he has filled out the requisite questionnaire, two members of the board interview him and the three citizens whom he has asked to stand sponsor for him. Boards are encouraged to make independent inquiry about applicants, and in some of the larger counties a private investigator is employed.

[1] "A Study of Character Examination Methods in Forty-Nine Commonwealths." In Bar Examiner, July–August, 1934, p. 199.
[2] English, Charles H., "Impressions of Ten Years," in American Law School Review, December, 1935, pp. 315–319; Shafroth, Will, "The Next Step in the Improvement of Bar Admission Standards," in Annual Review of Legal Education for 1935, pp. 16–17.

But Pennsylvania goes still farther. At the time of registration the applicant must name a lawyer who has practiced for five years in the state who will serve as his preceptor. Both preceptor and applicant must be approved by the board. During his period of law study, the candidate is required to report at stated intervals to his preceptor, and the latter must agree to give him a clerkship of six months in his own law office before the candidate takes the bar examination. Again at the end of his professional training he must be examined by the county board and receive its certification as to his moral character. The decision of the board and the recommendation of the preceptor are then reviewed by the State Board of Examiners and, on appeal, by the Supreme Court. During the eight years from 1928 to 1936 the Philadelphia County Board interviewed 2,217 applicants for registration. Of these 51 were rejected and 97 withdrew, making together about 7 per cent. In the same years, of the 1,600 applicants examined for final admission, 13 were rejected and 6 withdrew, or about one per cent.

The Pennsylvania plan has aroused much interest and has received warm praise from many, both within and outside the state. Its achievements have probably been due in part to the enthusiastic support which members of the bar of that jurisdiction have given it. In any such system, however, it is the preceptor who plays the most important role, by aiding the candidate to understand the ethics, duties, responsibilities, and temptations of the profession and by endeavoring to develop in him a high ethical standard. Whether busy lawyers could or should be expected generally to assume so important a task is an unanswered question.

A method for ascertaining character which has been much discussed of late is that of establishing a probationary period of from three to five years during which a young lawyer would be permitted to practice on the basis of a temporary license. At the expiration of probation, a further investigation of his moral integrity would be made before he was entitled to receive a permanent license. The only state experimenting with this plan is New Mexico, which began in 1934 to require a probationary period of one year. Because most candidates for admission to the bar are too young and have had too little experience for any character committee to judge effectively of their probable subsequent conduct in legal practice, the awarding of a temporary license might prove valuable. The chief objection to this plan lies in the fact that an applicant should be rejected, if it is in any way possible to discover his undesirability, before he has spent three years in training and a further period in practice.

NATIONAL ASSOCIATIONS

Associations that are nationwide in the scope of their program and membership are spoken of generically as national associations. Organizations of this type which have been created by the bar are relatively few in number when compared with those representing the medical, engineering, and teaching professions. There are, nevertheless, more of these bodies than can be discussed in so small a volume. Consequently, attention will be centered in this section upon the American Bar Association, National Lawyers Guild, Association of American Law Schools, and National Conference of Bar Examiners. These four organizations exist primarily for the purpose of raising professional standards and improving professional training. Consideration will also be given to the American Judicature Society, because of its long and courageous efforts in behalf of the promotion of justice. In later sections devoted to surveys of methods for extending legal service and for making needed modifications in the law and the administration of justice, brief mention will be made of further national agencies.

AMERICAN BAR ASSOCIATION

In 1878, 75 attorneys from 21 states met in Saratoga, New York, and formed the American Bar Association.[1] According to the constitution that was adopted, the new body had five objects: to uphold the honor of the profession, encourage cordial intercourse, promote the administration of justice, advance the science of jurisprudence, and promote uniform legislation throughout the United States.

The following year saw over 500 persons enrolled in the organization. Growth for some time afterward, however, was slow, except for the number of jurisdictions represented. At the beginning of its second decade, the Association had only 750 members and had achieved little. Even "cordial intercourse" had not always characterized its sessions. There had been both internal difficulties and friction with state and county or city bar associations.

In the medical profession such friction between national and local bodies has rarely existed because of the difference in form of organization. When a physician joins a county medical society, he automatically becomes a member of the state society and of the American Medical Association. Each county society

---

[1] For details of the history of the American Bar Association between 1878 and 1920 and for a critical analysis of its organization and its accomplishments, see pp. 203–239 of Alfred Z. Reed's Training for the Public Profession of the Law. See also the article by Philip J. Wickser entitled "Bar Associations," in Cornell Law Quarterly, April, 1930, pp. 391–413; and M. Louise Rutherford's study, The Influence of the American Bar Association on Public Opinion and Legislation, Foundation Press, Chicago, 1937.

elects delegates to represent it in the state association, and each state society, in turn, chooses delegates who form the governing body of the national organization. Thus a completely integrated system is attained.

Although the advisability of creating a similar structure within the legal profession was early discussed, little was done. Local bar associations continued to be independent of state associations, and state groups of the national group. The Association resembled, therefore, what Mr. Reed has designated as a self-perpetuating clique, with little in its record to justify a claim to leadership of the American bar. It was a national organization only by virtue of the fact that its constituency came from many jurisdictions; in reality it was but one of many independent organizations of the bar and it competed with them for membership. As the result, it numbered in 1910 fewer than 3,700, or only 3 per cent of all the lawyers in the United States. Attendance at the annual meeting of that year was 326.

In 1912 a new membership committee began a concerted drive which met with considerable success. By 1920 the Association had nearly 12,000 names on its books. In 1930, some 27,000 persons, or 17 per cent of all lawyers and judges enumerated by the federal census of that year, belonged to it. Thus it found itself in the anomalous position of being too large to be a compact, carefully selected, and homogeneous body, but still composed of only a small minority of the legal profession. In spite of the fact that it had been in existence for over half a century, it had exerted relatively little effective control over professional matters. It had never been able to wield more than a fraction of the power exercised by the American Medical Association or some of the national engineering bodies, such as the American Society of Civil Engineers, within their respective professions. To those, however, who view the degree of control vested in the American Medical Association critically, this difference may not seem wholly unfortunate.

In an attempt to establish relations with other organizations of lawyers, the American Bar Association, in 1916, created the Conference of Bar Association Delegates, composed of representatives of all bodies that were interested in some co-operative effort. Since the Conference had no authority to speak officially or to act for the organizations from which its members came, it was much restricted in what it could do. It evolved, therefore, into a forum that served as an educational agency to bring to the attention of the many bar associations vital questions in which it believed they should be interested. At various times it fostered movements, such as co-ordination of the bar, judicial councils, improvement in state bar organizations, reform in procedure and the administration of justice, better judicial selection, and higher standards of legal ethics and of admission to the bar. It also attacked the illegal practice of law. Its special meetings held in Washington in 1922 and 1926 to discuss legal education and incorporation of the bar, both of which will be discussed later, are generally considered its finest achievements.[1]

Although the Conference made a contribution to the legal profession through its attempt to form opinion, it did not result in making the American Bar Association representative of all the lawyers of the United States. Further attempts at changing the structure of the national body in order to accomplish this purpose did not appear likely to achieve appreciable results, and so in 1933 a movement known as the National Bar Program

[1] Wickser, Philip J., "Representative Government in the American Bar Association." In American Bar Association Journal, January, 1933, pp. 17–20.

was instituted. The primary purpose of the Program, which the Carnegie Corporation offered to subsidize in part, was to enlarge co-operation between the American Bar Association and state and local associations. It was believed that if these groups could be persuaded to work together in behalf of certain specific projects, a degree of unification which had failed to be accomplished through altering the structural form of the Association might actually be accomplished.

Four subjects of general interest and importance to the profession and the public were chosen for study during the first year. They were: criminal law and its enforcement, unauthorized practice of the law, legal education and admission to the bar, and judicial selection. The American Bar Association offered to provide a field representative who would confer with the various associations; to establish a bureau at headquarters for exchange of data; to provide opportunity for discussion at the annual meeting; and to record and publicize the sentiment of the profession in connection with proposals for improvement in the administration of justice. Will Shafroth was made director of the Program.

In her book on the influence of the Association, Dr. Rutherford has recorded the fact that the plan not only received vigorous prosecution by the central bureau during its first year, but met with wide acceptance by state and local associations throughout the country.[1] Over 300 such organizations answered questionnaires, and held meetings for study and action on National Bar Program subjects. As a result of this accomplishment, the Association committed itself to continuation of the Program for a three-year period. The four subjects were retained for fur-

[1] The Influence of the American Bar Association on Public Opinion and Legislation, pp. 27–29.

ther study, and a fifth on enforcement of professional ethics was added.

In 1935, among several official proposals made to the national body concerning its future structure, was one suggesting the creation of a federation composed of the Association, state, and local organizations. This proposal was accepted with the understanding that the National Bar Program should be continued, and plans were once more laid to provide for an organic connection between it and other bar associations. Many lawyers hoped that the changes instituted would at last result in making the national body a representative organization, similar in form to that of the American Medical Association.[1] State and local associations, however, insisted that they be allowed to handle all matters that were not nationwide in scope, without fear of being dominated by the American Bar Association. They wished to preserve their integrity, but were willing to have representation in a larger unit that could express the opinion of the bar as a whole upon certain broad subjects. At the same time the Association was unwilling to delegate full control to constituent state and local units. When the constitution was revised, therefore, the government of the Association was not entirely vested in delegates from state and local bar associations, but they were given substantial representation in the House of Delegates.

According to the constitution adopted in August, 1936, any person who is a member in good standing of the bar of any state or territory of the United States is eligible for membership in the national body, on endorsement, nomination, and election as provided in the by-laws. Members of the Association who are present at the annual meeting compose what is known as the

[1] Chandler, Jefferson P., "Proceedings of Assembly." In American Bar Association Journal, October, 1936, p. 673.

Assembly. The Assembly has the right to present to the Resolutions Committee for action resolutions pertinent to the legal profession, or to the aims and work of the Association.

Control and administration of the Association is vested in a House of Delegates. The House is composed of delegates representing each jurisdiction, each state bar association, and a few large county and city associations. Officers of the Association, members of the Board of Governors, representatives from the Assembly and the various sections, and the Attorney General and the Solicitor General of the United States are also members of the House. Provision is made for representation from the American Law Institute, the American Judicature Society, the National Conference of Commissioners on Uniform State Laws, the National Conference of Bar Examiners, the National Conference of Judicial Councils, the Association of American Law Schools, and the National Association of Attorneys General. There are at present about 160 members.

In the interval between meetings of the House of Delegates, authority is vested in the Board of Governors to perform all functions which the House would perform were it in session. This Board consists of the president, last retiring president, secretary, and treasurer of the Association; the chairman of the House of Delegates; and one elected member from each federal judicial circuit.

Work of the Association is carried on by 12 sections and 14 standing committees. Members of these units transmit to the House of Delegates annually written reports of what they have accomplished during the preceding year and such recommendations as they choose to make. The following list of these units will give the reader some idea of the nature and scope of the activities of the national body.

Sections

Legal Education and Admissions to the Bar
Patent, Trade-Mark, and Copyright Law
Judicial Administration
Public Utility Law
Bar Organization Activities
Criminal Law
Mineral Law
Municipal Law
Insurance Law
International and Comparative Law
Junior Bar Conference
Real Property, Probate and Trust Law

Standing Committees

Admiralty and Maritime Law
Aeronautical Law
American Citizenship
Commerce
Commercial Law and Bankruptcy
Communications
Federal Taxation
Jurisprudence and Law Reform
Labor, Employment, and Social Security
Legal Aid Work
Noteworthy Changes in Statute Law
Professional Ethics and Grievances
State Legislation
Unauthorized Practice of the Law

It is obviously impossible, within the brief compass of this volume, to describe the work of the many sections and standing committees. The Section of Legal Education and Admissions to the Bar, to which frequent reference has already been made, must, however, receive attention. At the first meeting of the American Bar Association in 1878, a Committee on Legal Education and Admissions to the Bar was appointed. In 1879 it presented several progressive resolutions to the effect that state and local bar associations be requested to recommend the maintenance by public authority of law schools with at least four "well-paid and efficient teachers." It further resolved that the various bar associations should recommend that the diploma of such schools be an essential qualification for admission to the bar, and that the course of study in these schools prior to the bar examinations should be three years. These resolutions were rejected by the American Bar Association, although several others pertaining to legal education and admission to the bar, which were submitted subsequently, were accepted.

In 1893 a group of men interested in professional training was instrumental in forming the Section of Legal Education and Admissions to the Bar. It was the object of this Section to discuss methods of legal education and make suggestions to the Committee on Legal Education. The suggestions covered such topics as the lengthening of the law-school course, the raising of requirements for admission to professional schools, disapproval of the diploma privilege, establishment of boards of bar examiners, the necessity for character examinations, and so on.[1] Although recommendations were numerous, they were frequently futile. The unfortunate rivalry that existed between the Section of Legal Education and the Committee on Legal Education, as well as the general apathy of the American Bar Association, made accomplishment negligible. The record of the proceedings of the meetings from 1893 to 1920 is one of

[1] For further details concerning the history of the Section of Legal Education and Admissions to the Bar, see George H. Smith's "History of the Activity of the American Bar Association in Relation to Legal Education and Admission to the Bar," in American Law School Review, December, 1930, pp. 1–6.

lengthy controversy and little action. Just before the end of those years of inertia Justice Harlan F. Stone, then dean of the Columbia Law School, spoke excoriatingly of the failure of the Section to accomplish anything.[1] He maintained that it had not in twenty years proposed any constructive program for the improvement of legal education which had met with approval or endorsement of the American Bar Association. In 1917 the Committee was abolished, and the organization of the Section was strengthened. Thus the way was cleared for more constructive work, and for the appointment, in 1927, of a salaried executive secretary, known as adviser to the Section.

As the first two decades of the twentieth century are viewed in retrospect, one is inclined to believe that the two most important acts in connection with legal education were, first, the creation, under the auspices of the Section, of the Association of American Law Schools, and, second, the request by the Committee on Legal Education and by the Association of Schools that the Carnegie Foundation conduct an investigation of legal education similar to its earlier study of medical education. As the result of that request, four bulletins and a long list of annual reviews and reports were published during the next twenty years that have been of inestimable value to the legal profession. Aside from the importance of the factual data presented in these thoughtful and carefully studied publications, they have been of particular significance because Mr. Reed, the author of all but two of the publications, took a courageous and by no means generally accepted position in discussing certain controversial questions.

The year 1920 witnessed the turning-point in the attitude of

[1] "Address of President." In American Law School Review, April, 1920, p. 488.

the American Bar Association toward professional training. The Section of Legal Education voted that a committee be appointed to present recommendations for the improvement of legal education at the next annual meeting. This committee consisted of Elihu Root, as chairman, and a group of outstanding attorneys, whose reputations were unimpeachable and whose judgment could be trusted to carry weight with the Association. It sent questionnaires to the deans of all law schools; to every committee on legal education of state and local bar associations; to all state boards of bar examiners; and to many individual members of the bar. In addition, it held a hearing in New York City in May, 1921, at which the points of view of part-time and of full-time schools, of the great universities, and of the Carnegie Foundation were presented. A report was then prepared, which was sent to all members of the American Bar Association.

When the Association convened for its annual meeting in Cincinnati late in 1921, the recommendations which have already been presented in the discussion of approved and unapproved schools[1] were submitted to the Section of Legal Education by Mr. Root, who spoke eloquently in behalf of them. At the three sessions in which they were discussed, were ardent protagonists, like William H. Taft, and also excited and vigorous antagonists. Attempts were made both to amend the recommendations and to lay them over until the following year, but they were finally passed by an overwhelming majority. Mr. Root then presented them before the Association as a whole. Again they were vociferously attacked, but when the vote was taken they were passed.[2]

[1] See pp. 45–46.
[2] For further details see, "Report of Special Committee to the Section of

The next step was the calling together by the American Bar Association of the Conference of Bar Association Delegates and other representatives in Washington, D. C., in February, 1922. Three hundred and thirty-one persons were present representing the national association, 44 state bar associations, 116 local and foreign associations, and 27 law schools. The professional standing of the delegates and the invited guests, among whom were the Chief Justice and the Attorney General of the United States, made it not only the largest but the most distinguished gathering of lawyers which had ever met in this country for the purpose of discussing the problems of legal education and admission to the bar.

The result of the Washington Conference was the publication of resolutions which incorporated and expanded the recommendations already passed in Cincinnati the preceding year. The Conference noted the fact that a form of training which had been fairly adequate under simpler economic conditions had become outmoded, and consequently higher standards were necessary. It maintained that law schools should not be operated as commercial enterprises, and that the compensation of the faculty should not depend on the number of students or the fees received. It reiterated the idea so often expressed that, since public officials are frequently chosen from among lawyers, the legal profession should not be the monopoly of any economic class. It did not believe that the proposed requirement of two years of college work plus study in a law school would militate against a bar open to all social classes. It urged that courts and bar associations charge themselves with the duty of devising

Legal Education of the American Bar Association," and "Proceedings of the Section of Legal Education Held at Cincinnati, August 30–31, 1921." Both of these reports appear in the American Law School Review for November, 1921, pp. 671–692.

means for bringing law students into contact with members of the bar from whom prospective lawyers might learn "that admission to the Bar is not a mere license to carry on a trade, but that it is an entrance into a profession with honorable traditions of service which they are bound to maintain."[1]

Since acceptance of the recommendations concerning approved standards of legal education, a considerable part of the work of the American Bar Association has been directed toward their adoption by the law schools and by the several states. The degree of success which the Association has met in connection with the schools has already been reviewed. Something should also be said about the states and what they have done.

So long as the general attitude persisted in America that the practice of law was a natural right of which no one of sound moral character should be deprived, there was little attempt on the part of state supreme courts or legislatures to make requirements concerning academic education or training in a law school. Only in 1933 did Indiana succeed in repealing a provision written into its constitution in 1851 which allowed any voter twenty-one years of age of good moral character to be admitted to the bar.[2] It is not surprising, therefore, that in 1921, when the resolutions of the American Bar Association were adopted, only 14 states had any requirements of preliminary general education, and only 10 required the equivalent of graduation from high school.[3] Kansas was then the one state in the Union that demanded two years of college training, and it is the only state

---

[1] Reed, Alfred Z., "Progress of Legal Education." In Seventeenth Annual Report of Carnegie Foundation, pp. 72–74.

[2] "Proceedings of the Section of Legal Education of the American Bar Association." In American Law School Review, December, 1936, pp. 631–632.

[3] Clark, Charles E., and Douglas, William O., "Law and Legal Institutions." In Recent Social Trends in the United States, McGraw-Hill Book Co., New York, 1933, vol. 2, p. 1485.

at present whose Supreme Court has ruled that every applicant for admission to the bar, subsequent to 1940, must either have had four years of academic work followed by three years spent in a law school or three academic years followed by four years in a professional school.

Recently there has been a steadily growing realization that the public must take steps to protect itself against the misuse of power by badly educated, badly trained, and unscrupulous lawyers, just as it had earlier protected itself against malpractice in medicine. This realization, which the American Bar Association has done much to effect, has expressed itself during the last decade in rulings by one jurisdiction after another that have appreciably raised the amount of general education and of law-school training required of prospective lawyers. There are now 32 states that require or will shortly require at least two years of college preparation or its equivalent before matriculation in a law school. Seven other states require two years of college before admission to the bar, but not necessarily before law study. Fourteen states have made rulings concerning the necessity of a high-school education or its equivalent. Only Arkansas and Georgia have no educational requirements.

In regard to demanding that professional training be obtained in a law school, the states have not yet been so urgent. Although 40 states require a minimum of three years of legal preparation and 6 require at least two years, there are only 6 states that definitely refuse to recognize study in a law office. Something of the old tradition of "reading law" in an office still lingers and exerts a restraining influence over state courts and legislatures. In spite of this fact, the number of men admitted to the bar on the basis of such apprenticeship training is small.

Thus far only the states of New Mexico and Arizona and

the territory of Hawaii have adopted the standards of the American Bar Association in full. Nebraska conforms to them except for still permitting study in an office. Four other states—West Virginia, Alabama, Ohio, and Oregon—approach compliance by demanding a minimum of three years of law-school study. Omitting Alabama, this study must be taken in a school approved by the Section of Legal Education. It is likely that under continuing pressure from the Association and other groups who believe in the desirability of official control, further states will move in the direction of incorporating the standards of the national body or comparable ones. As this occurs, unapproved schools will find their future more precarious. They will probably be forced ultimately to close their doors or greatly improve the training they offer. When that day arrives, it will not be possible for a man to enter upon the practice of law without at least some fundamental academic preparation and some training of a truly professional nature.

Returning again to consideration of the American Bar Association as a whole, a final word should be said concerning the position that it occupies in the United States and what it has accomplished. It has frequently been criticized, both by lawyers and the public, on the ground that it is composed chiefly of the financially more successful lawyers and that it is lacking in social vision. Some of these criticisms have been as scathing as one recently appearing in the Nation, where the Association was spoken of editorially as typifying "to the full the blindness of a ruling class" and as "the most reactionary wing of a reactionary profession."[1] In 1935, William L. Ransom, then president of the Association, reviewed the defects and inadequacies for which the national body had been attacked in the following words:

[1] October 9, 1937, p. 366.

141

It is often charged that in membership and leadership, the American Bar Association does not represent the majority of lawyers, the great rank and file of the profession engaged in the practice of law; that too few lawyers engage actively in its work and decide its policies; that its structure of organization provides no adequate means for ascertaining the real views and wishes of the whole profession; that the work of the Association is sub-divided into many phases, not a few of which seem unimportant to the average practicing lawyer; that the emphasis on the matters of paramount importance is often blurred and indistinct; and that the Association has never attained or realized fully the ideals and aspirations of American lawyers devoted to maintaining the traditions of an honorable profession.[1]

Reorganization of the Association in the following year was designed to remedy some of these shortcomings. That it did not succeed in enlisting the support of a considerable group of attorneys will be seen when we later discuss the new National Lawyers Guild, that was created for the purpose of achieving professional and social objectives with which it believed the Association to be insufficiently concerned.

Two generalizations must be borne in mind in connection with the American Bar Association. First, all organizations, as they attain maturity and large numbers, tend to become conservative. This fact is so well known that, when the National Lawyers Guild was being formed, someone suggested that it be dissolved at the end of ten years before signs of reaction had had opportunity to appear. That the older national body has entirely escaped the inertia of age can scarcely be expected. Second, the public is often unjust in its criticisms. This is likely to be particularly true of such an organization as the Associa-

---

[1] Ransom, William L., "Constructive Work of the American Bar Association." In American Bar Association Journal, November, 1935, p. 701.

tion, whose annual meetings receive extensive publicity in the press. Because resolutions opposing certain types of social legislation, for example, have been adopted at various times, some have readily conceived the idea that such action is typical of the entire program of the body. An unbiased evaluation of the Association should rest not so much on the basis of a few resolutions passed under the emotional strain of crowded conventions as on that of the work done year after year by the central office and by the numerous sections and committees of the Association.

When we examine this work, we find a full-time salaried staff of between 20 and 30 persons, besides more than a thousand practicing lawyers or law teachers who give some portion of their time to planning and executing the program of the organization. The American Bar Association Journal appears monthly, and a year book and an extensive advance program of the annual meeting are published. Some of the sections also issue publications, and data about such subjects as legal education, the unauthorized practice of the law, and judicial recall have been prepared and circulated widely.

Achievements of the Association in connection with raising standards of legal education have already been reviewed. Although many persons believe that the action taken in 1921 should have come earlier and have been prosecuted more vigorously, and that standards should be still higher than they are, no one can deny the importance of accomplishments in this field. The Association of American Law Schools and the National Conference of Bar Examiners, which are doing much to improve professional training, owe their inception to the Association.

Much emphasis has been placed by the national body upon the promulgation of the Canons of Ethics, originally adopted in

1908 and supplemented and changed since then.[1] Thousands
of copies of these Canons have been distributed, as well as a
handbook of disciplinary procedures, and the official opinions
of the Committee on Professional Ethics and Grievances. In
1921 the Conference of Bar Association Delegates recommended
that the Canons be adopted in those states that had not yet
adopted them, and that each state and local bar association be
urged to aid in the maintenance of high standards of professional conduct. The action of the Association in connection
with the teaching of legal ethics in the law schools was noted in
a preceding section.

The subject of the unauthorized practice of law was discussed
by the Conference of Bar Association Delegates as early as 1919.
In 1930 the Committee on Unauthorized Practice was created
to make an investigation of the practice of law by corporations
and by lay persons, and of the relations existing between such
corporations and individuals and the lawyers associated with or
employed by them. Investigation showed that unauthorized
practice was general and increasing on the one hand, while state
laws prohibiting such practice were sometimes lacking and more
often unenforced on the other. The Committee has, therefore,
attempted to stimulate state bar associations to secure appropriate legislation, and has sought to guide the work of both
state and local organizations through conferences, addresses,
radio talks, monthly pamphlets, and other literature.[2]

Some question the wisdom of certain attitudes expressed by
this Committee. They believe that it is possible for well-estab-

---

[1] For a detailed statement of the Association's efforts in the field of legal
ethics, see Dr. Rutherford's The Influence of the American Bar Association
on Public Opinion and Legislation, pp. 86–93.

[2] Dr. Rutherford presents an account of work in this area in pp. 93–100 of
her book.

lished corporations, specializing in particular phases of activity, to render service in some easily standardized types of legal work more efficiently than can the individual lawyer.[1] They are aware of the problem that occasionally exists when the corporation attorney must divide his allegiance between employer and client. But they are inclined to feel that, in general, advantages of economy and convenience may outweigh any disadvantages encountered.[2] They are of the opinion, moreover, that a great deal of legal work has been lost to the profession that probably can never be recovered. Consequently, they wonder why the Association does not direct its time and energy to investigating and developing new fields of legal service, such as will be described later, of which the public is in need.

In connection with the administration of justice the Association has advocated better methods for the selection of justices, and for their security and independence of tenure. It has also been active in behalf of raising and maintaining the salaries of federal judges. Besides scrutinizing all proposed legislation that would affect the promotion of justice, it has sponsored and partially financed the National Conference of Commissioners on Uniform State Laws.[3] Through the Section of Municipal Law it is beginning the task of improving local self-government. It has participated in the making of laws and rules of procedure pertaining to new subjects, such as aviation and communications. It has sent representatives to conferences on crime called by the Attorney General and by governors of various states, and has been interested generally in the administration and enforcement of the criminal law. The Committee on Legal Aid Work

[1] Ashley, Paul P., "The Unauthorized Practice of Law." In American Bar Association Journal, September, 1930, p. 559.
[2] "Notes." In Harvard Law Review, May, 1931, p. 1114.
[3] See pp. 224–226.

is assuming increasingly larger responsibility for sponsoring legal service for the poor.

During the current year a far-reaching program has been launched by the Section of Judicial Administration for the purpose of improving certain aspects of judicial administration.[1] Committees composed of outstanding judges, lawyers, and law teachers have been appointed to study and recommend standards pertaining to: selection of juries, simplification of appellate procedure, control of state administrative agencies, and improvement of pre-trial procedure, of trial practice, of the law of evidence, and of judicial organization and administration. Just as state and local bar associations have sponsored the standards relating to legal education that were issued by the national body, so it is hoped that they will assume responsibility for attempting to have these standards put into effect as soon as possible after promulgation.

These are only a few of the activities which the Association has undertaken. Perhaps one of the most important parts of its program is the opportunity it provides lawyers to meet and exchange ideas. In a country so vast and new as is the United States, provincialism offers a constant threat to the development of broad and informed points of view. To the extent that annual meetings and the work of the organization bring together lawyers from all parts of the country, the Association indirectly promotes the growth of a wider understanding of what constitutes the nature and functions of the profession of the law.

NATIONAL LAWYERS GUILD

The National Lawyers Guild, the newest of the nationwide

[1] Vanderbilt, Arthur T., "Section of Judicial Administration Launches Program on Wide Front." In American Bar Association Journal, January, 1938, pp. 5–6, 78–82.

bar associations, was established by a group of attorneys who maintain that "recent and developing social and economic changes are profoundly disturbing our nation and make new legal attitudes imperative."[1] They were of the opinion, as has been noted, that the American Bar Association was not primarily interested in the legal attitudes they had in mind; and that too little would be achieved if they attempted to work through that body. They decided, therefore, to form another group for the purpose of bringing together

. . . all lawyers who regard adjustments to new conditions as more important than the veneration of precedent, who recognize the importance of safeguarding and extending the rights of workers and farmers upon whom the welfare of the entire nation depends, of maintaining our civil rights and liberties and our democratic institutions, and who look upon the law as a living and flexible instrument which must be adapted to the needs of the people.[2]

The Guild had its inception at a dinner meeting in New York City in December, 1936, when 14 members of the bar, bench, and law schools met for the purpose of discussing the desirability of an organization of lawyers which should interest itself in social and economic questions of general purport and in the plight of thousands of attorneys unable to secure enough law practice to earn a living. Shortly afterward a meeting was called which was attended by some 600 attorneys. A statement of the purpose of the Guild was distributed, and speeches were made by Frank P. Walsh and Morris Ernst, New York attorneys; Professor Karl N. Llewellyn of the Columbia Law School; Henry T. Hunt, formerly mayor of Cincinnati; and others. Enthusiasm was so intense and suggestions concerning the form

[1] Taken from the preamble to the constitution of the Guild.
[2] *Ibid.*

and function of the Guild so numerous that at this and subsequent meetings progress was retarded by the continuous attempts of many lawyers to gain the recognition of the chair.

The work of organization was also begun almost immediately
in Philadelphia, Chicago, Minneapolis, Boston, Newark, San
Francisco, Washington, D. C., and other cities. Temporary
officers, with Mr. Walsh as president, and a National Executive
Committee were informally chosen.

In February, 1937, the Guild held its first annual convention
in Washington, D. C. The program fell roughly into three
parts: general sessions addressed by members of Congress, the
bench, the bar, and the laity; the drafting and adoption of a
constitution; and the acceptance of 21 resolutions. The general
sessions were characterized by excoriating statements of the
failure of the legal profession to assume progressive leadership
in matters pertaining to the social welfare of the country, and
to be as much interested in civil as in property rights. A statement issued subsequently by the newly elected president, Judge
John P. Devaney, may be taken as a summation of the general
attitude expressed at the convention. He said, in part:[1]

In recent years there has been an alarming growth of non-con-
fidence in law and in the administration of law. In the mind of the
average man the legal profession has failed to make democracy work
in the court house and if democratic government should fail in this
country, the lawyer who is given the primary place in all its branches,
legislative, executive and judicial, will not be able to escape responsibility. We need not go far to find the reason for the mistrust of
lawyers as a group. On almost every public question of major importance the organized Bar and its leaders invariably representing
but a small minority of the lawyers, assume to speak for the profession as a whole, thereby leading the public who have little if any

[1] Why the Guild? Pamphlet distributed by the Guild.

personal contact with lawyers, into the belief that the anti-social attitude of the few is representative of the attitude of all members of the Bar. . . . The National Lawyers Guild has as its prime objective, the task of convincing the ordinary citizen that all the members of the Bar are not working to defeat the legitimate demands and aims of the great masses of people, for a better and a fuller life.

The constitution provides that any person who is a member of the bar in good standing may be admitted to the Guild regardless of sex, race, color, or religious or political beliefs. Wherever a local chapter exists, membership in the national body must be obtained through joining the chapter. In places where there are no local units, attorneys may affiliate themselves directly with the Guild. In February, 1938, 26 chapters were in existence. The total membership of the organization was then 3,774, comprised of attorneys from 45 states and Puerto Rico.

The highest governing body is the National Convention. Each chapter is entitled to representation in this Convention of one delegate for every 15 of its members. Other members of the Guild attending the annual meeting have all the privileges of delegates except the right to vote. Officers, consisting of president, 10 vice-presidents, secretary, and treasurer, are elected at the Convention. The vice-presidents are chosen from the 10 federal judicial circuits and the District of Columbia. A National Executive Board, made up of the officers and 63 elected members, is required to meet twice yearly when the Convention is not in session. In this Board is vested all the power and authority of the larger body. The president, secretary, and five or more members of the Board constitute, in turn, the National Executive Committee, which meets at least once every three months to transact such business and plan such work as the Board delegates to it.

The by-laws provide for 22 standing committees. In some instances the committees are similar in name, at least, to the sections or committees of the American Bar Association; in others, they represent interests with which the older organization is unconcerned. They are as follows:

Administrative Law and Agencies
American Citizenship, Immigration and Naturalization
Civil Rights and Liberties
Civil Service
Constitution and Judicial Review
Consumers and Co-operative Organizations
Criminal Law and Criminology
Economic Welfare of the Legal Profession
Farm Problems
International Law
Judiciary
Labor Law
Legal Research and Legal Education
Legal Service
Professional Ethics
Public Utilities
Publications and Public Relations
Relation of Government to Business
Research on Relation of Law and Economics
Social Legislation
Taxation
Unauthorized Practice of the Law

Some of the resolutions adopted at the first annual meeting and later endorsed by a mail vote of the membership provide an excellent indication of the major interests of the Guild. Around their philosophical content has centered much of the subsequent work of the national body and its chapters. Both President Roosevelt's proposal for increasing the number of justices of the Supreme Court and the federal Child Labor

Amendment, which were subjects of current interest at the time, were endorsed. It was agreed that the federal Social Security Act should be enlarged and extended to assure a minimum standard of health and decency to all workers, including farmers, and that the cost of such a program should not be financed by a tax upon employes but by further taxation of incomes, gifts, and inheritances. It was resolved that the federal public works and relief program should be continued, and that socially useful governmental work projects for unemployed lawyers and other professional persons should be provided without the requirement of a "needs test."

In behalf of the preservation of civil liberties, the Guild at its first convention adopted no fewer than nine recommendations. A resolution on labor relations upheld the right of labor to organize free from interference by employers, to bargain collectively, to strike, to picket, and to boycott. Another favored the extension of the civil service system to all persons in governmental service, including attorneys, except those holding elective or policy-making positions. The unauthorized practice of the law was condemned; but the services of the public defender, of legal aid bureaus, and of similar bureaus for persons of small means were endorsed.

In the year that intervened between the first and second conventions, an office was opened in Washington, D. C., and a full-time secretary employed. The various standing committees were appointed. A monthly news-letter made its appearance in June, and the first issue of the dignified appearing and finely printed National Lawyers Guild Quarterly was issued in December. It is of interest to note that the editorial policy of the Quarterly provides for articles dealing with broad current issues, contributed by representatives of political and academic life as well as of the legal profession. One of the tasks to which much time was given was the planning and conducting of a conference on labor relations, held in Washington for a period of three days in December, 1937.

During the past year the chapters, that have almost complete autonomy, have been individually devising programs. Groups in New York, Boston, Philadelphia, Chicago, and Washington have been particularly active. The Civil Rights Committee of the Eastern Massachusetts Chapter investigated and wrote a report on legal aspects of the injunction and contempt proceedings resulting from the shoe strike in Lewiston and Auburn, Maine. The Chicago Chapter, jointly with the Chicago Citizens Rights Committee and the Citizens Emergency Committee on Industrial Relations, examined witnesses, conducted hearings, and prepared a report on the activities of the police in connection with the Memorial Day fatalities in South Chicago. This same chapter is offering a course on labor law for practicing lawyers and is working on a plan for legal service bureaus that would provide legal service to low income groups. In Philadelphia attention has been given to the formulation of professional standards that should be met by law offices assisting persons of small means.[1] In New York City courses are being given to practitioners,[2] and recommendations have been prepared designed to end the evils of judicial patronage and the appointment of referees and guardians by political preference.

At the second national convention the secretary reported on what had been accomplished by the various chapters, and raised the question of the function of the national office. Should it undertake a program of its own, or should it serve as a clearing-

[1] See pp. 281–282. [2] See p. 112.

house and an agency for co-ordinating the work of a federation of chapters? This important question has not yet been answered.

The annual meeting of 1938 resembled that of the preceding year in essential respects. In addition to general sessions addressed by Dean Lloyd K. Garrison, Senator LaFollette, Representative Maverick, Solicitor General Jackson, Judge Devaney, and Judge Ferdinand Pecora, a series of conferences was held under the auspices of the several committees of the Guild. These included such subjects as a legislative program for the farmer, international law, labor law, legal service and professional economics, civil rights and liberties, public utilities, social security, relief, and taxation. From these conferences, as well as from other meetings, came a large number of resolutions which showed a considerable broadening of interest over those submitted a year earlier.

It is still too soon to forecast the future of the Guild. Its program is envisaged as one that should extend beyond the narrower limitations of problems directly pertaining to the bar and bench. Much of the emphasis of the Guild, therefore, is definitely centered upon what is popularly known as social reform or social action, and it functions as a social pressure group. The task it has undertaken is an exceedingly difficult one, and success will probably depend in very large part upon the leadership that the national office is able to exert.

ASSOCIATION OF AMERICAN LAW SCHOOLS

Upon the founding of the American Bar Association in 1878, law-school teachers took an active part in the work of the Committee on Legal Education and in the subsequent Section of Legal Education. By the close of the century, however, there was a widespread feeling that law schools were faced with many problems peculiarly their own, which would not be solved by groups within that national organization. Consequently, the Association of American Law Schools was established in 1900, under the auspices of the Section of Legal Education, for "the improvement of legal education in America, especially in the Law Schools."[1]

During the early years of its existence the new body held its annual meeting at the same place and time as did the American Bar Association. This procedure resulted in frequent question about the line of demarcation between the work of the Section of Legal Education and that of the Association of Schools. Lack of harmony and close co-operation weakened the effectiveness of both groups. In 1914, when the American Bar Association met at a time inconvenient for law-school instructors, the latter gathered by themselves in Chicago during their Christmas recess. The separate convention was so successful that it was repeated the following year. Since then, except for one special meeting, the schools have held their annual sessions entirely apart from those of the older association.

The Association of American Law Schools early adopted the principle that only reputable law schools which met certain objective standards might belong to it.[2] It decided, furthermore, to advance these standards as rapidly as possible. In its original Articles of Association, it decreed that any school which wished to become a member should conform to the following four requirements. Candidates for a degree must have received (not necessarily prior to admission) a high-school education or its equivalent. The course must cover at least two years of thirty

[1] "Articles of Association." Published annually in Handbook of the Association of American Law Schools.
[2] Reed, Alfred Z., Present-Day Law Schools in the United States and Canada, pp. 24–30.

weeks each, with a minimum average of ten hours of classroom work weekly. Examinations for the degree must be given. Students must have access to a library containing the reports of local courts and of the United States Supreme Court.

Since the promulgation of these first standards, requirements for membership have been amended frequently until they are now far more severe than were the original ones. Inasmuch as they are similar to those formulated by the American Bar Association which have already been listed, they will not be enumerated here.[1] It is essential to note, however, that amendments made by the school men have been more continuous, and interpretations more numerous and detailed than those by the bar. As a consequence the Association of Schools tends to maintain a more advanced position. This is seen in such action as the requirement that each member school have four full-time instructors and a library of 10,000 volumes, while the American Bar Association has ruled that approved schools have three instructors each and libraries of 7,500 volumes.

The raising of requirements to their present level has not been achieved easily. The Association has been so crippled by lack of financial resources that it has never been able to engage the services of an executive secretary or a paid staff. Neither has it been able to publish a journal, which might have done much to promote progress in legal education. It prepares an annual Handbook, however, and the American Law School Review summarizes the proceedings of its yearly meetings and reproduces some of the papers. Many law-school journals also print articles and papers by members of the Association.

Because of insufficient funds, schools applying for membership in the early years were frequently admitted without ade-

[1] See pp. 45–46.

quate investigation of their eligibility. The Association often did not know, moreover, whether schools, once accepted, continued to adhere to requisite standards or not. Both of these situations have been greatly improved of late. The Association is now more exacting about admissions. It has succeeded in obtaining the voluntary services of experienced law teachers, who visit schools that wish to become members. They also visit each year, in rotation, a certain number of member schools. Although power is delegated to them to recommend that schools whose standards are found unsatisfactory be dropped, they conceive of their task primarily as that of offering advice. Thus they attempt to aid constructively in the improvement of legal education rather than in merely making certain that the few formal standards of the Association are being met.

Perhaps the most troublesome problem with which the organization was faced for many years concerned the admission of part-time schools. When the Association was founded in 1900, it made no distinction between full-time and part-time schools. As already stated, it demanded from all at least ten hours of weekly classroom work. In 1909, however, the minimum standard for part-time schools was reduced from ten to eight hours, and the curriculum lengthened from three to four years. Since no evening school was willing at that time to add an additional year to the course of study, the Association lost its last representative of the part-time system. In 1912 it formally resolved that since "the maintenance of regular courses of instruction in law at night, parallel to courses in the day, tends inevitably to lower education standards, the policy of the Association shall be not to admit to membership hereafter any law school pursuing this course."[1]

[1] One of several resolutions listed under article 6, sec. 3 of Articles of Association.

This and subsequent action in 1919 raised a storm of protest from various part-time schools. The phrase, "the *narrow* and *petty* attitude of the Association," used in conversation with the writer by a teacher in a New York evening school, probably well characterizes the feeling that many instructors of part-time schools long had for that body. In 1922, after extended controversy, the national organization reversed its position, making evening schools eligible for membership if a course of resident study was required that, in the opinion of the Executive Committee of the Association, was equivalent to the requirements for a full-time school. By 1937, 11 of the schools with both morning and evening sessions had been admitted. No school providing evening work exclusively, however, had membership in it.

The Association has had a slow but steady growth. It began with 27 member schools in 1900; reached 43 in 1914; 71 in 1930; and 84, including the University of the Philippines College of Law, at the beginning of 1937. There are still 106 schools in the United States that do not belong to the Association. It has done much to stimulate greater activity among members. Unfortunately, its proceedings have been given little consideration by the legal profession in general, and the large number of schools that are not affiliated with it have benefited only indirectly, although they are the very institutions most in need of its services. Visitors from these non-member schools are now invited to attend the annual meetings, in the hope that they may become interested in what it is attempting to accomplish.

A contribution which has perhaps been of more importance than the creation of standards or the inspection of schools has been the providing of a forum for discussion of questions pertaining to all phases of professional training. In the early years it devoted much time to a consideration of the case method of teaching; later it turned to the functional approach to the study of law. It has considered such topics as the introduction of new subjects, rearrangement of courses and material, new methods of instruction, pre-law curricula, degrees, nature of examinations, graduate work, and preparation of law teachers. Much of the discussion at the round-table councils, which are held at each annual meeting, centers around the subject of the content of the various courses of the curricula. There is also consideration from time to time of aspects of legal history, jurisprudence, law reform, co-operation with bench and bar, requirements for admission to practice, and comparative law.[1]

One further type of work in which the Association has engaged should be mentioned—that of enlarging and making more readily available the literature of law.[2] As early as 1905, at the suggestion of John H. Wigmore, then dean of Northwestern University Law School, it investigated the advisability of publishing translations of foreign books on law and studies in legal history and bibliography. The result was the appearance, between 1907 and 1909, of three volumes of Select Essays in Anglo-American Legal History. There followed a series of 10 volumes of Continental Legal History, and another of 12 volumes of Modern Legal Philosophy. In 1922 the Association created a Committee on Reprinting Leading Articles. After an extensive review of significant articles appearing in legal periodicals, the Committee decided to publish first a volume on contracts. A four-volume collection of articles on constitutional

[1] Kirkwood, Marion R., "A Retrospect." In American Law School Review, April, 1935, p. 104.
[2] Ibid., pp. 107–109.

law is now being made. In considering future work mention has been made of the need for a compendium or an index of American statute law, a reference book on social science literature useful to law teachers, a source book of business materials, and a volume evaluating contemporary textbooks in law.[1]

The Association has aided other agencies such as the Social Science Research Council and the Encyclopaedia of the Social Sciences in the preparation of useful material. Its outstanding achievement in this field has been its participation in the founding and program of the American Law Institute. In 1914 it began advocating the need of a "juristic center" which would "direct the attention of law schools toward the improvement of the law."[2] A special committee was later appointed which decided that the co-operation of courts, bar associations, law schools, and learned societies was desirable. In 1922, 40 judges, practicing lawyers, and law teachers, under the leadership of Elihu Root, met to formulate the initial plans which resulted in the establishment of the American Law Institute. The subsequent program of the Institute in restatement of the substantive law and in making a model code of criminal procedure will be discussed in a later section.

NATIONAL CONFERENCE OF BAR EXAMINERS

The National Conference of Bar Examiners was formed in 1931 for the purpose of increasing "the efficiency of local boards of law examiners and character committees in admitting to the bar only those who are adequately equipped." It was also designed as a medium for co-operation with those other branches

---

[1] Bogert, George G., "The Future Work of the Association." In Handbook of the Association of American Law Schools, 1936, pp. 20–24.

[2] Pound, Roscoe, "American Law Institute." In Encyclopaedia of the Social Sciences, 1930, vol. 2, p. 30.

of the profession that deal with problems of legal education and admissions to the bar. All members of the boards of the various jurisdictions belong to it ex officio. Although state bodies which license lawyers have exercised a role in law that has been far more important than that of comparable bodies in engineering or even in medicine, the national association representing law examiners did not appear until relatively late. A federation of examining boards was established for the medical profession in 1892, and for engineers in 1920.

In order to assist the National Conference of Bar Examiners to open a central office and initiate its program, the Carnegie Foundation contributed funds annually for five years. The Conference now finances its work through fees collected from investigations that will presently be described. The central office serves as a clearing house for information of interest to the state boards of bar examiners. Statistics are collected annually for the number of candidates at each examination, the number passing the examination, and the number admitted to the bar by virtue of the "diploma privilege." These figures enable each state board to compare its record with that of other boards, and also to examine trends over a period of years in the percentage of applicants passed. The Bar Examiner, the official monthly magazine, is used for the distribution of these statistics and other material of interest to bar examiners. An annual convention and round-table meetings provide opportunity for the discussion of all matters pertaining to the function of examiners, while bar examination "clinics" which have recently been held in various states give those present an opportunity to see a board of examiners actually engaged in conducting its work.

In 1934 the National Conference extended the scope of its functions by inaugurating, through its central office, a service of investigating the character and record of attorneys who seek admission to the bar of one state by virtue of having already practiced law in another state. It had long been known that some of these "migrant" or "foreign" attorneys, as they are called, were professionally unscrupulous and even disreputable men who found it advisable to move to a distant part of the country. State boards of bar examiners frequently did not have adequate facilities for making investigations that revealed the true facts about them. The National Conference, therefore, decided to offer this service to its constituency for a fee of $25 for each investigation. California, which had been overrun with migrant lawyers and was unable to cope with the situation, was the first state to make use of the service. A year later the California Board of Examiners stated officially, "This service is a very valuable one and has brought to light a number of cases of flagrant misconduct on the part of some of these applicants, as a consequence of which their admission has been denied."[1] The American Bar Association has also approved the plan and recommends it to the several states. In September, 1937, there were 22 jurisdictions using it.

It is reported that the National Conference has contributed materially to raising standards of admission to the bar, to improving the quality of the examinations given, and to establishing beneficial relations with law schools, courts, and bar associations.[2] A resolution was passed in 1936 to the effect that joint advisory committees consisting of representatives of the bar examiners, law schools, bar, and bench be set up in each state to give consideration to questions relating to legal education and

[1] Riordan, John H., "Address of the Chairman." In Bar Examiner, September, 1936, p. 151.
[2] "Proceedings of the Section of Legal Education of the American Bar Association." In American Law School Review, December, 1935, p. 325.

bar admissions. Most of the boards have signified their willingness to co-operate, and some have already acted on the resolution.[1] Since the Association of American Law Schools has sponsored a similar recommendation, substantial assistance may be expected from many of the schools.[2] Such committees should prove instrumental in solving some of the intricate problems pertaining to the admission of lawyers to the bar.

AMERICAN JUDICATURE SOCIETY

The American Judicature Society was established in 1913, largely through the efforts of Herbert Harley and Charles F. Ruggles, for the purpose of promoting the efficient administration of justice.[3] The incorporators and directors—men such as Chief Justice Harry Olson, Dean James Parker Hall, Albert M. Kales, Dean Pound, Dean Wigmore, and Mr. Harley, the secretary—believed that much could be done to improve the deplorable administration of justice in this country, if means were provided for co-ordinating the efforts of those groups within the bar that were already concerned with reforming the situation.

The Society decided that its efforts should be directed toward the legal profession rather than the public. Although there was recognition of the fact that the laity was sadly misinformed, or uninformed, about the administration of justice, the organization doubted how effective public education could be in so technical a field. And even if the public were aware of what reforms should be instituted, it questioned whether changes could

[1] Riordan, John H., "The National Conference of Bar Examiners—Its Accomplishments and Service." In American Law School Review, December, 1937, p. 940.

[2] See pp. 121–122.

[3] For a more detailed account of the organization see Herbert Harley's "Concerning the American Judicature Society," in Journal of the American Judicature Society, June, 1936, pp. 9–18.

be made while an unconcerned bar controlled the judiciary committees in every legislature.

The program of the Society has centered around research and preparation of material, published in bulletins and the bimonthly Journal, concerning needed reforms in the entire field of judicial administration. As early as 1914, it presented studies on the selection, retirement, and disciplining of judges and members of the bar; organization of judges; selection of the jury and its guidance; rules of practice and procedure; selection of court officials; and organization of the legal profession. Its subsequent draft of a model Metropolitan Court Act was aimed at unification of the entire jurisdiction of a populous district in a single court, to be governed by a judicial council and presided over by a chief justice. The model State-Wide Judicature Act described a method for the unification of all judicial agencies in a given state, from the office of chief justice to that of justice of the peace. In its model rules of civil procedure appeared recommendations concerning the entire subject except that of pre-trial procedure. Finally, in its long advocacy of the integrated bar, judicial councils, and other potentially desirable agencies, it has suggested ways whereby the bench and bar could serve both the professional and the public need for a better administration of justice.

Elihu Root once said, "The Society has done directly many admirable things and it has served as a guide and model for a great amount of thorough research and effective effort in the field of administration of justice and in the kindred fields of substantive law and jurisprudence now undertaken by newly created organizations."[1] Unfortunately, it has always been financially handicapped, and consequently limited in what it

[1] *Ibid.*

could achieve. Until 1925 its program was supported entirely by Mr. Ruggles. When he was no longer able to continue his contributions, it seemed advisable to open the Society to individual membership with an annual fee of $5.00. At the beginning of 1937 there were about 1,500 members. From their dues, a gift from the Carnegie Corporation, and some contributions from other sources, including the Northwestern University Law School and the Law School of the University of Michigan, some expansion of program is being undertaken.

The bar as a whole long showed scant interest in the Society. Often the recommendations of the latter were so many years in advance of professional thought, that lawyers have only slowly come to see the wisdom of the ideas promulgated. It is, therefore, an encouraging indication of progress that the Society has been given a representative in the House of Delegates of the American Bar Association. Further co-operative action has recently resulted in a plan for sending copies of the Journal of the Society to all members of the Association for a period of twelve months, and in the appointment of Will Shafroth to the newly created office of assistant secretary-treasurer.[1]

NUMBER OF LAWYERS AND DEMAND
FOR THEIR SERVICES

During the last few years there have been persistent rumors that the bar is badly overcrowded. Similar rumors have been heard from time to time since the days when John Adams lamented the fact that every county of the Province of Massachusetts swarmed with students and young practitioners of law, and John Jay was almost excluded from law study because New

---

[1] Mr. Shafroth continues to serve as adviser to the Section of Legal Education, as director of the National Bar Program, and secretary-treasurer of the National Conference of Bar Examiners.

York lawyers had agreed among themselves to admit as clerks no more prospective members of the profession.[1] In recent years, however, the reports of overcrowding have become much more widespread and emphatic.

The question of the number of lawyers is one of vital importance, not only from the point of view of the profession but from that of the welfare of society. It is one of the most difficult questions, unfortunately, with which to deal. Attorneys have done much talking about the congested condition of the bar, but they have made few factual studies. Hence, there are not enough available data on which to base a discussion of the demand for and supply of legal service. Most of the statistical information in existence has been collected by the United States Bureau of the Census. From this source comparative figures can be obtained for the number of lawyers at decennial intervals in the country as a whole, in each state, and in individual cities of more than 25,000 population. Figures are also presented showing the age, sex, color, and nativity of all lawyers.

The first difficulty, therefore, in drawing any conclusions about the adequacy or inadequacy of the numbers of lawyers arises from a lack of sufficiently detailed information concerning supply. A second difficulty grows out of the fact that the legal profession has little knowledge of the extent of the demand for legal service, either in the entire United States or in various localities. Consequently, it has no definite standard for judging whether the 160,000 lawyers reported by the census for 1930 were too few or too many. Generally when members of the profession have talked about an overcrowded bar, they have compared the ratio of lawyers to population in one census year

---

[1] Jay, William, The Life of John Jay. J. and J. Harper, New York, 1833, vol. 1, p. 13.

with that of another year. In drawing inferences they have frequently gone on the assumption that the number for the earlier period selected was probably adequate to meet the demand for service. The possible fallacy of this conclusion is at once apparent.

Furthermore, it would be difficult to determine, even on the basis of more data than exist, whether there are too many lawyers or not, because the question of supply and demand is so interwoven with several other questions which are themselves unresolved. Supply and demand can be discussed only in the light of numerous factors in our economic and social system, and only in terms of specific localities. A consideration of whether there are too many or too few lawyers in general is academic and somewhat futile. Lawyers are not licensed to practice anywhere within the boundaries of the United States but within a specific state, and migration from state to state is relatively slight. Numbers in each jurisdiction, and in the cities and rural areas of which that jurisdiction is composed, ought, therefore, to be considered. The adequacy of these numbers, moreover, should be determined in terms of the economic structure of an area, the density of population, the level of income, the extent of the use of legal service, and so on.

Aside from the significant surveys of the Wisconsin and California bars that will be reviewed later, there has been no extensive study on the basis of several such considerations. One criterion that has been occasionally used for attempting to determine the potential demand for legal service has been that of per capita wealth. Ratios of wealth to lawyers should give some indication, so it has been believed, of what areas were oversupplied and what ones were undersupplied with attorneys. Dean Garrison has pointed to the inherent weakness of this theory and its limited usefulness.[1] Much of the wealth, such as real estate and industry, may be dormant in one locality and active elsewhere. The utilization of mineral resources which swell the per capita wealth of a particular state, may be supervised by lawyers a thousand miles away. Agricultural states with their relatively small populations, moreover, tend to have a higher per capita wealth than do the densely populated industrial states, although the latter obviously furnish a more productive field for lawyers. When one considers that the per capita wealth of Nevada is twice that of Illinois, it is apparent that such wealth furnishes slight indication of the supply of lawyers needed in a given state.

Even if we were able to speak authoritatively of the sufficiency of the number of lawyers at a given moment, there is no assurance that a similar situation would exist in the future. The determination of the number needed annually to maintain a given ratio to population, therefore, would not provide a sound statistical basis for increasing or decreasing admissions to the bar.[2] Economic and social factors are constantly shifting, and new conditions may appear at any time which will create a new demand for lawyers or render the existing supply too great. The extension of legislation and the functions of government, introduction of new corporate undertakings, establishment of agencies competing with the legal profession, development of great real estate projects, changes in divorce laws—these and other

[1] "A Survey of the Wisconsin Bar." In Wisconsin Law Review, February, 1935, p. 139.
[2] Mr. Shafroth reported in 1931, in Notes on Legal Education, March 16, 1931, pp. 6–7 (published by the Section of Legal Education and Admissions to the Bar of the American Bar Association), that some 9,500 lawyers were being admitted to the bar annually. Of the 9,500, he estimated that about 7,200 entered practice. The latter figure appeared, however, to be nearly 60 per cent higher than was needed to keep the number of lawyers constant.

social changes may very suddenly increase or decrease requirements for legal service. Fluctuations in business activity, moreover, have so marked an effect upon the demand for legal services that they need to be considered in any examination of the extent to which the bar is overcrowded.

The foregoing discussion has briefly suggested how complicated is the question of demand and supply. In this connection a survey of such factual information as exists will be helpful. Although studies have been too few and too fragmentary, they cast some light upon a very important subject, which warrants more careful investigation.

Census figures showing the number of lawyers in the United States were first compiled in 1850. During the next half-century the number reported increased in relation to population at each decennial interval, except in 1870; in that year an apparent decrease, which was more than made up in 1880, may have been due merely to the acknowledged deficiencies of enumeration. In 1910, and again in 1920, there was a pronounced decrease in the number of lawyers reported, and the proportion to population was below that of 1880. Although the 1930 enumeration showed a sharp increase, the number of lawyers relative to the population was still well below the peak attained in 1900. Meanwhile, the progressive shift of the working population from agricultural to industrial and commercial pursuits, has presumably increased the demand for lawyers.[1]

This general trend seems clear, despite the fact that a change in the census classification of occupations makes it difficult to tabulate the development with precision. Before 1910 the census gave merely the number of "lawyers." In that year and in sub-

[1] Reed, Alfred Z., Annual Review of Legal Education, 1933, p. 60.

sequent enumerations, figures were given both for "lawyers, judges, and justices," and a semi-professional group described as "abstractors, notaries, and justices of the peace." While this change increases the significance of recent figures, it complicates comparison with previous years. Fortunately, the second

TABLE 4.—NUMBER OF LAWYERS COMPARED WITH
POPULATION, 1850 TO 1930[a]

Year	Population	Lawyers, judges, and justices	Abstractors, notaries, and justices of the peace	Per 100,000 population	
				Lawyers, judges, and justices	Abstractors, notaries, and justices of the peace
1850	23,191,876	23,939[b]		103	
1860	31,443,321	34,839[b]		111	
1870	38,558,371	40,736[b]		105	
1880	50,155,783	60,626[c]	3,511[c]	121	7
1890	62,947,714	85,224[c]	4,406[c]	135	7
1900	75,994,575	109,140[c]	5,320[c]	144	7
1910	91,972,266	114,704	7,445	125	8
1920	105,710,620	122,519	10,071	116	9½
1930	122,775,046	160,605	11,756	131	9½

[a] Based upon federal census figures and adapted from table in A. Z. Reed's Annual Review of Education, 1933, p. 60. It is assumed that notaries and justices of the peace, who had other occupations to which they devoted more of their time, were not included, since the census classification is by principal occupation.
[b] Census figure for "lawyers."
[c] Estimated from census figure for "lawyers."

group which was probably included formerly with "lawyers" is a small one—between 8 and 9.5 to each hundred thousand of the population in the last three census reports. If it be assumed, arbitrarily, that in each of the three preceding enumerations 7 per hundred thousand of the population fell within this semi-professional classification, the comparison shown in Table 4 may be made.

The census figures indicate that the number of lawyers increased by 31 per cent between 1920 and 1930, while population gained by only 16 per cent. Seven small or sparsely populated states showed some decrease in the actual number of lawyers during the decade, while in 11 other states the bar did not increase so rapidly as did population. In 31 states, however, the legal profession outstripped population in rate of growth, often to a marked degree. The following figures reveal the situation in nine jurisdictions in which lawyers increased during this decade by at least 40 per cent. Only in the instance of California did growth in population exceed that of attorneys.

	Per cent increase in lawyers	Per cent increase in population
Massachusetts	40	10
Connecticut	41	16
District of Columbia	44	11
Michigan	48	32
New York	49	21
California	50	66
North Carolina	51	24
New Jersey	69	28
Florida	130	52

Although a gain of 31 per cent in the number of lawyers during the brief period of ten years has alarmed many members of the legal profession, the fact must be borne in mind that between 1900 and 1910 population increased about four times as rapidly as did lawyers, and between 1910 and 1920 it increased twice as rapidly. As a consequence, the ratio of population to lawyers in 1920—863 to 1—was higher than at any time subsequent to 1870. When the rapid growth of lawyers during the last decade is viewed in the light of these facts, Dean Garrison has concluded that it is scarcely disturbing.[1]

This generalization does not necessarily apply, however, to all states or to all cities. In six of the nine states enumerated above the ratio of population to lawyers had been lower in 1920 than was the average for the country as a whole. It would be desirable to know whether the bars of these six states had been appreciably understaffed in the earlier year. Or did an extension of the use of legal service between 1920 and 1930 warrant the marked growth, or were their bars definitely overcrowded in 1930? These are questions which imperatively need to be answered. Philip J. Wickser, who has given much attention to the problem of overcrowding, believes that on the basis both of population and per capita wealth three of the states already mentioned—New York, California, and Florida—and also Oklahoma and Maryland were seriously congested with attorneys in 1930.[2]

Since lawyers have a tendency to concentrate in urban areas, it is instructive to note what had been happening during the ten-year period in the 66 cities which had more than 120,000 population by 1930. In 20, lawyers had not increased so fast as had population; in the remaining 46 the bar had gained over population. In nearly one-half of the 46 the gain had been less than 10 per cent, but in 11 cities—Newark, Jersey City, Paterson, Akron, New Haven, Trenton, Boston, Washington, D. C., New York, Springfield (Massachusetts), and Toledo—the increase in ratio of lawyers to population had ranged from 20 to

[1] "A Survey of the Wisconsin Bar." In Wisconsin Law Review, February, 1935, p. 136.
[2] "Law Schools, Bar Examiners, and Bar Associations." In American Law School Review, April, 1933, p. 734.

171

39 per cent. Except in Boston, Washington, and New York the relative numbers of lawyers in these 11 cities had been low in 1920 as compared with the average for urban areas of similar size. The pronounced growth may, therefore, have occurred in considerable part because the bar had been understaffed in the earlier year. By 1930, 6 of the 11 were still below the average for large cities, but the differences had appreciably decreased.[1]

The foregoing discussion of changes occurring during the last decade fails to reveal one fact of particular significance. Although the average ratio of population to lawyers in 1930 was 746 to one for the entire country and 556 to one for cities of more than 120,000 persons, 17 of the 66 large cities had fewer than 400 persons per lawyer. The situation in Washington, D. C., which is included in the list, is not characteristic of other cities, since the majority of lawyers there are probably connected directly or indirectly with the federal government. New York and Chicago are also not representative, even of the large cities, because they handle a vast volume of national and international legal business. Some of the other cities are state capitals, which afford unusual opportunities for legal service. In spite of such facts, however, there are so many lawyers in these centers that only extraordinary circumstances would appear to justify their presence in anything like present numbers. Although there is need of much more factual information about the volume of legal work, it seems safe to conclude that the bar is badly overcrowded in many if not all of these 17 cities. Their 1930 ratios of population to lawyers computed from census figures were:

[1] In this and following discussion the fact has not been overlooked that lawyers frequently live outside the political limits of the cities in which they practice, and that hence the census figures may not provide an accurate picture of the number actively engaged in legal work in a given area.

City	Population per resident lawyer in 1930
Washington	140
Tulsa	215
Oklahoma City	280
Kansas City, Mo.	287
Denver	321
Des Moines	323
Albany	323
Portland, Ore.	351
Seattle	359
Fort Worth	360
Yonkers	363
San Francisco	371
Houston	378
New York	379
Salt Lake City	383
Los Angeles	383
Omaha	386

The concentration of lawyers that has already been noted characterizes only in more marked fashion the situation existing generally in urban centers. The census of 1930 showed that the 93 cities of over 100,000 persons accounted for only 29 per cent of the total population but 48 per cent of the lawyers. In contrast to this situation, communities of fewer than 25,000, which include all rural areas, constituted 60 per cent of the population but had only 38 per cent of all lawyers. In these latter places, Table 5 shows that there was an average of 1,216 persons to each attorney, and in these communities in South Carolina, Alabama, and Louisiana there were more than 2,000 persons per lawyer.

TABLE 5.—NUMBER OF LAWYERS AND POPULATION PER LAWYER IN 1930, BY STATE AND SIZE OF COMMUNITY[a]

GEOGRAPHIC DIVISION AND STATE	NUMBER OF LAWYERS IN STATE	POPU-LATION PER LAWYER	PLACES OF FEWER THAN 25,000 POPULATION			CITIES OF FROM 25,000 TO 100,000 POPULATION			CITIES OF OVER 100,000 POPULATION		
			Lawyers, per cent of total in state	Popu-lation, per cent of total in state	Popu-lation per lawyer	Lawyers, per cent of total in state	Popu-lation, per cent of total in state	Popu-lation per lawyer	Lawyers, per cent of total in state	Popu-lation, per cent of total in state	Popu-lation per lawyer
New England											
Maine	763	1,045	67	83	1,290	33	17	540	—	—	—
New Hampshire	363	1,282	56	71	1,626	44	29	840	—	—	—
Vermont	331	1,086	100	100	1,086	—	—	—	—	—	—
Massachusetts	6,940	612	25	34	821	29	24	522	46	42	554
Rhode Island	675	1,019	17	26	1,607	27	37	1,405	56	37	662
Connecticut	1,886	852	38	46	1,013	24	25	880	38	29	669
Middle Atlantic											
New York	27,593	456	17	27	725	6	6	467	77	67	396
New Jersey	6,633	609	41	46	676	27	23	529	32	31	591
Pennsylvania	8,093	1,190	40	57	1,698	15	12	931	45	31	821
East North Central											
Ohio	8,886	748	33	49	1,117	19	11	427	48	40	626
Indiana	3,818	848	45	61	1,161	16	15	752	39	24	530
Illinois	11,770	648	26	41	1,028	17	13	509	57	46	517
Michigan	4,507	1,074	28	46	1,761	16	15	984	56	39	754
Wisconsin	2,600	1,130	46	64	1,572	24	16	783	30	20	732
West North Central											
Minnesota	3,145	815	36	67	1,531	—	—	—	64	33	415
Iowa	2,634	938	59	78	1,236	24	16	637	17	6	323
Missouri	5,560	653	39	61	1,023	9	5	397	52	34	421
North Dakota	600	1,135	88	96	1,231	12	4	409	—	—	—
South Dakota	743	933	86	95	1,032	14	5	321	—	—	—
Nebraska	1,751	787	54	79	1,137	14	5	318	32	16	386
Kansas	1,832	1,027	67	83	1,281	12	5	402	21	12	597

174

South Atlantic										
Delaware	207	1,152	38	55	1,690	—	—	—	62	45	826
Maryland	2,782	586	39	47	705	4	4	653	57	49	502
Dist. of Col.	3,477	140	—	—	—	—	—	—	100	100	140
Virginia	2,419	1,001	60	78	1,300	13	9	700	27	13	479
West Virginia	1,554	1,113	59	85	1,599	41	15	405	—	—	—
North Carolina	2,389	1,327	68	87	1,699	32	13	546	—	—	—
South Carolina	1,135	1,532	66	90	2,078	34	10	451	—	—	—
Georgia	2,813	1,034	66	83	1,297	13	9	755	22	8	399
Florida	2,615	561	51	68	754	15	9	326	34	23	378
East South Central										
Kentucky	2,639	991	66	80	1,217	12	8	620	22	12	528
Tennessee	2,484	1,053	53	75	1,500	2	1	440	45	24	564
Alabama	1,598	1,656	62	85	2,291	12	10	1,325	26	5	320
Mississippi	1,249	1,609	82	96	1,883	18	4	358	—	—	—
West South Central										
Arkansas	1,512	1,227	73	94	1,576	27	6	299	—	—	—
Louisiana	1,632	1,288	38	72	2,431	17	6	473	45	22	629
Oklahoma	3,514	682	57	84	1,009	6	2	288	37	14	248
Texas	6,591	884	48	74	1,365	14	8	483	38	18	423
Mountain										
Montana	714	753	75	87	871	25	13	391	—	—	—
Idaho	580	767	100	100	767	—	—	—	—	—	—
Wyoming	300	752	100	100	752	—	—	—	—	—	—
Colorado	1,563	663	34	64	1,247	9	8	627	57	28	321
New Mexico	350	1,209	79	94	1,443	21	6	354	—	—	—
Arizona	542	804	52	81	1,268	48	19	308	—	—	383
Utah	603	842	31	64	1,750	8	8	805	61	28	—
Nevada	231	394	100	100	394	—	—	—	—	—	—
Pacific										
Washington	2,285	684	34	58	1,189	4	4	590	62	38	416
Oregon	1,595	598	41	65	954	5	3	332	54	32	351
California	10,109	562	25	43	989	16	13	458	59	43	411
All states	160,605	764	38	60	1,216	14	11	561	48	29	471

ª Figures compiled from federal census data for 1930; lawyers include "lawyers, judges and justices."

Unfortunately the census does not provide helpful information concerning legal service in strictly rural areas, since it does not subdivide its category of lawyers in communities having fewer than 25,000 population. If the distribution in places of 2,500 persons and under could be determined, it would probably be found that the majority of lawyers were located in county-seats, and that almost none was in the open country. In C. Luther Fry's study of 177 incorporated villages of fewer than 2,500 persons, which he considered representative of villages in the entire United States, he discovered that 403 of a total of 600 lawyers lived in the 56 villages that were county-seats.[1] Of the 121 villages that were not county-seats, 41 did not have a single resident lawyer. If his facts are applicable to the country as a whole, they indicate that for the rural population living close to local governmental centers legal service, although probably only of the general practitioner type, is readily available. In the open country, by contrast, there are few opportunities for people to obtain assistance. They must either go to a county-seat or to a still larger center of population.

We turn now to an examination of the few studies that have been made by the legal profession which deal with the subject of the number of lawyers and the crowding of the bar. The most helpful of these is the survey of the Wisconsin bar undertaken in 1934 by Dean Garrison. As a preliminary step in this survey, his research workers attempted to ascertain as nearly as possible (using original sources and not census data) the exact number of lawyers actively engaged in practice in each year from 1848, when Wisconsin became a state, to 1932. The resulting figures were then compared with those collected by the

---

[1] American Villagers. George H. Doran Co., New York, 1926, pp. 119–120.

Bureau of the Census at the decennial periods. It is interesting to note that only in 1890 and 1900 were the two sets of figures in substantial agreement. In 1930 there were 16 per cent more lawyers actively engaged in practice, according to the Wisconsin study, than were recorded by the census. While this part of the survey concerns itself only indirectly with the question of overcrowding, it is of particular value to those who wish to test the probable validity of census data.

Having traced the growth of the Wisconsin bar, Dean Garrison and his assistants began to trace the growth from 1880 to 1933 of those activities or factors that would necessitate or be reflected in legal business. For 15 legal indices, as they were designated, information was collected in each of the counties of the state. The indices selected were as follows:

Number of papers filed in the office of Register of Deeds
Number of civil and criminal suits commenced in circuit courts
Similar data for county courts
Similar data for municipal courts
Amount of suit tax paid
Number of estates probated
Amount of inheritance tax paid
Number of divorces granted
Number of cases arising (subsequent to 1910) under the
    Workmen's Compensation Act
Suits commenced in United States district courts
Appeals taken to Supreme Court of Wisconsin
Number of business failures
Number of bankruptcy cases concluded
Amount of fees paid to lawyers, including referees, in bankruptcy proceedings
Number of automobiles registered

Further information was collected for five economic indices. Although it was recognized that the relation between these economic factors and legal activity was indirect, they at least indicated the relative state of the prosperity of Wisconsin. It seemed a reasonable assumption that in periods of increasing productivity and wealth, there would not only be more legal business but more money with which to pay for it. These indices were:

Value of manufactured goods
Number of workers in manufacturing establishments
Value of all farm property
Amount in dollars of farm mortgages
Value of all farm crops

As a final index population was used. Trends in these 21 indices between 1880 and 1933 were then compared, county by county, with the growth of the bar during the same period.[1] It was found upon examination of the results that with only two exceptions all of the index numbers for 1933 (or for 1932, if figures were not available for the later year) were higher than the index number for the lawyers of the same year. Some were many times larger than the lawyer index. The majority, in fact, had been higher than that for lawyers in each year subsequent to 1890. The legal indices revealed, furthermore, that the volume of legal business apparently kept on increasing through 1932. But in 1933, they showed that the depression had begun to result in a contraction of legal activity.

The survey had certain weaknesses and omissions, which Dean Garrison noted. The material presented did not weigh qualitative factors, and mere increase in transactions or in suits filed, for example, did not necessarily involve more money or

---

[1] For information concerning the method used in this comparison, see Lloyd K. Garrison's "A Survey of the Wisconsin Bar," in Wisconsin Law Review, February, 1935, pp. 145–146.

more fees. No measurement was made of the various kinds of office work done by lawyers which might or might not have increased. The great growth in the number and activity of administrative tribunals was omitted, as was all reference to the rapid multiplication of federal and state laws affecting business, which had undoubtedly resulted in augmenting the need for legal advice.

In spite of such shortcomings, however, the conclusion seemed clear that the volume of legal business and opportunities for lawyers had increased in Wisconsin since 1880 more rapidly than had either lawyers or population.[1] Even allowing for contraction of legal business in 1933, the position of the lawyer appeared to be more favorable than at any time prior to 1932. Dean Garrison was convinced that his conclusions would be received with skepticism, especially by those lawyers whose incomes had dwindled since the beginning of the depression. The indices did not reflect what the community could afford to pay for lawyers; they indicated rather how much the community needed and used legal services.

A second survey was conducted in 1935 by Professor James E. Brenner of the Stanford University Law School for the purpose of ascertaining facts concerning the demand for legal service in California.[2] The study consisted of an examination of the number of attorneys admitted to practice over a series of years, and a comparison for the years 1910, 1920, 1930, and

---

[1] It must be borne in mind that Wisconsin had but one law school before the second decade of this century. Since then it has had only two, both of which are approved by the American Bar Association. Consequently, the situation regarding oversupply of lawyers is probably not typical of states that have long graduated large numbers of law students, many of whom have been trained in poor institutions.

[2] "Trends in Lawyer Population and the Amount of Legal Business." In Los Angeles Bar Association Bulletin, November, 1935, pp. 53–67.

1933 of the growth of the bar relative to the growth of population, of other professions, and of legal business as reflected by statistics for manufacturing, commercial failures, savings deposits, automobiles, farming, and suits commenced in the various courts. Special figures for Los Angeles County included post-office receipts, bank clearings, and building permits. This examination of the relationship between the growth of the bar and the growth of factors presumably reflecting legal business was similar to the more detailed Wisconsin survey. Like its predecessor, it showed that with occasional exceptions the indices of legal business subsequent to 1910 had increased more rapidly than had the index for lawyers. Professor Brenner concluded, therefore, that it was impossible to state whether or not the California bar was overcrowded. The data seemed clearly to indicate, however, that there should have been more business in 1930 for each attorney than in 1910.

Another survey was that begun late in 1934 and published in 1936 by the Committee on Professional Economics of the New York County Lawyers Association. Since this study was concerned primarily with the earnings of lawyers, it will be reviewed in a later section.[1] We need only to note here that the Committee discovered that the median income of lawyers in New York County (Manhattan) in 1933 was very low. It believed that overcrowding of the bar was largely responsible for so serious an economic situation, and declared that "overcrowding is clearly indicated by the comparison with actual and changing population and business figures."[2] Although the facts presented in support of this statement are entirely inadequate to prove that overcrowding resulted in low incomes, the data on

[1] See pp. 188–191.
[2] Survey of the Legal Profession in New York County, pp. 56–57.

lawyers' earnings seem to provide partial but substantial evidence of the existence of overcrowding of the bar in Manhattan.

A survey which was conducted in 1935 in Connecticut, under the auspices of the Yale Law School, throws some light upon the important question of latent demand for legal service. The survey attempted to ascertain the extent to which the ordinary citizen performs acts or executes documents without legal advice when such advice ought normally to be had; the extent to which litigation and other difficulties arise from failure to consult an attorney; the way in which the public selects its attorneys, and so on.[1] The study was carried on through interviews by the field staff with a cross-section of Connecticut's business men, retail merchants, white-collar workers, and householders. While the results are not conclusive, they are said to indicate the existence of a large amount of potential legal service not being sought or rendered, which would both benefit the legal profession and save trouble and litigation for the public.

Because of the increasingly prevalent belief that the bar is overcrowded, many suggestions have been made for limiting the number of lawyers. Some persons have recommended that enrolments of law schools be drastically reduced, and a few have even suggested that no students be admitted to study law in those states which seem to be definitely congested until there is an active demand for more lawyers. Many have proposed that the educational requirements for admission to law schools be raised, that the professional course be more difficult, and that the bar examinations and character tests be more rigid. Others have maintained that there should be definite limitation in the

---

[1] Information obtained by the Connecticut investigation has been published since the foregoing section was written. It may be found in Charles E. Clark and Emma Corstvet's, "The Lawyer and the Public," in Yale Law Journal, June, 1938, pp. 1272–1293.

number of applicants admitted to bar examinations in any one year. Still others have insisted that there should be absolute denial of new admissions for a limited period, or until the number of lawyers engaged in practice has fallen below an arbitrary figure.[1]

To each of these and other suggestions there appear to be many valid criticisms. First of all, facts are still so inadequate that, with the possible exception of a few jurisdictions, any immediate attempt to limit admissions to the bar would seem premature. The American Bar Association is aware of the need for more information concerning what it has designated as "the economic condition of the bar," and a special committee, of which Dean Garrison was chairman, has now issued a manual showing what data are available, what methods were used in collecting them, and what studies are urgently needed.[2] Any comprehensive plans for limitation of the bar, however, must presuppose the continuation of studies of the demand for and supply of lawyers in each jurisdiction under consideration. As has been stated earlier in this section, political, economic, and social changes may occur so rapidly that the number of lawyers adequate for the needs of the present moment may be too small or too large to meet the exigencies of the future.

Next, there arise philosophical considerations concerning the justification for arbitrary reduction of numbers. Some persons have questioned whether there should be a reduction of lawyers to the number actually needed unless there is a generally planned society. Robert F. Maguire has emphatically said:

[1] See Sidney Teiser's "A Proposal for a Limited Bar" and Robert F. Maguire's "Is There Overcrowding of the Bar?" in American Bar Association Journal, January, 1935, p. 45, and February, 1937, pp. 85–87, respectively.

[2] The Economics of the Legal Profession. American Bar Association, Chicago, 1938.

"There is, and should be, no excuse for limiting the number of lawyers purely for the purpose of benefiting the members of the profession. We have no right to close the doors to new men, who may be better prepared and better able in the long run to render the service which we render, simply that we may be assured of a competency."[1] Dean Harno, who has weighed the merits of this question, has similarly concluded that if numbers in the legal profession are to be restricted "we must find a public concern other than that incident to mere conditions of overcrowding." Because the lawyer deals with the problems of other people—problems involving matters of trust and confidence—Dean Harno believes that what is to the public interest, therefore, is not "a restricted Bar to benefit members of the profession, but a Bar personnel which is qualified through demonstrated mental capacity and through attributes of character to accept commissions of trust and confidence and to undertake the responsibilities of leadership in public affairs."[2]

Concerning the specific suggestions noted for limiting numbers, there are further cogent criticisms. The recommendations that in congested areas law schools admit no students for designated periods of time would almost certainly arouse strenuous opposition, for the schools represent large capital investments that must be kept in operation. Recommendations for restricting admission to the bar would likewise meet with violent objection from students who had completed their law course, and from those political forces that would be rallied for the attack. Any such proposal for limitation of numbers would be decried on the ground that it was at variance with democratic traditions

[1] "Is There Overcrowding of the Bar?" In American Bar Association Journal, February, 1937, p. 85.
[2] Letter to the Law Alumni of the University of Illinois, Urbana, June, 1933, pp. 1–2.

and theories of equal opportunity. Finally, several of the suggestions are merely palliative rather than preventive in nature, and therein lies perhaps the most serious cause of their weakness. Is it necessary to wait until prospective lawyers have spent at least two years in college and three in a law school before determining whether there is a place for them?

If further study reveals that there should be limitation, it would be generally agreed that the facts should be put into the hands of all persons in the secondary schools and the colleges who are concerned with vocational counseling. They should be impressed and seek to impress their students with the fact that, for the welfare both of society and the individual lawyer, only those of exceptional ability should enter upon the study of law. As a next step, many would agree with Mr. Shafroth that state regulations should be raised and strengthened.[1] If the several jurisdictions forbade any person to present himself for admission to the bar unless he were a graduate of a school approved by the American Bar Association, the number of such applicants would be greatly reduced and their educational and vocational qualifications would be much higher. If the number of prospective lawyers were still too large, the period of academic and professional training could be further lengthened, as has often been proposed; law schools could be discouraged by the national associations from taking more students than facilities permit; and students could be chosen in fewer numbers and on the basis of more careful selection than at present. If regulation by legislative acts and by pressure exerted by the American Medical Association and the medical schools has resulted in reducing the

---

[1] "The Next Step in the Improvement of Bar Admission Standards." In Annual Review of Legal Education for 1935, pp. 21–22.

number of medical students to scarcely more than one-half the number of law students, similar attempts should substantially reduce applications for admission to the bar.

INCOME OF LAWYERS

Until a few years ago almost no attempt had been made either by the legal profession or by other agencies to discover what attorneys earned. The results of the economic depression have recently stimulated bar associations and law schools to consider this question. A few local studies have already been completed and others are being made. The data available as yet, however, are even more fragmentary and inconclusive than are those on the number of lawyers and the demand for their services.

A portion of Dean Garrison's Survey of the Wisconsin Bar was devoted to income.[1] The specific subjects investigated were the effect of the depression on earnings, a comparison of the incomes of lawyers with those of physicians, and the relation of earnings to the localities in which attorneys were situated and the number of years they had been in practice. Since income tax reports are available for public inspection in Wisconsin, information was obtained by analysis of the returns of lawyers actively practicing in the state from 1927 to 1932. Those whose earnings from their profession were nominal in comparison with income from business or other non-legal activity were excluded from the study; so also were retired lawyers, full-time law professors, and supreme court and federal judges. Other judges and district attorneys were included.

When the tax returns of 1,876 lawyers for 1932 were com-

[1] For further information, see Wisconsin Law Review, February, 1935, pp. 150–169.

pared with the returns made by the same lawyers in 1929, it was found that 66 per cent had a lower net professional income in the later year. Those who had had lucrative or fairly substantial practices in 1929 tended more often to suffer a reduction in income than did those whose net incomes had been small. Of 1,247 lawyers whose professional net incomes were less in 1932 than in 1929, nearly one-half had undergone reductions of from 35 to over 100 per cent. There were 626 lawyers, on the other hand, whose net incomes increased during this period, and 42 per cent of these 626 increased their earnings by from 35 to over 100 per cent. In general, however, few of those who reported gains had very large incomes at any time during the six years.

When earnings were investigated by year during the designated period, it was discovered that changes between 1927 and 1930 were not very striking. In 1931, however, incomes dropped substantially, and by 1932 the numbers in all the higher categories had shrunk. In the latter year almost half of the total number of attorneys reported incomes of less than $2,000, whereas only a third had reported so small a figure in 1927.

Since law and medicine are professions similar in size, requisite educational qualifications, and ethical restrictions upon soliciting business, information concerning the earnings of physicians was deemed desirable for comparative purposes. An examination was undertaken, therefore, of corresponding income data for 1930 compiled by the State Medical Society for physicians who were in active practice in that year. When surgeons, specialists, and general practitioners were taken as a group, it was concluded that the variation in their net earnings in 1930 was strikingly like that for attorneys.

In determining the influence of locality on earnings of lawyers, the average net professional income for the six years, 1927 to 1932, was used. Upon tabulating the results by size of community, Milwaukee, the largest city in the state, was found to be the only area in which any attorney had earned an average as high as $45,000 for the six years. What was more significant, however, was the fact that 8 per cent of the 728 attorneys in that city averaged less than $1,000 a year and 19.5 per cent averaged between $1,000 and $2,000. The combined percentage earning less than $2,000 per year was higher for Milwaukee than for any other size-of-community category. Cities of from 10,000 to 70,000 population had larger percentages of lawyers earning an average of from $5,000 to $9,000 yearly than did Milwaukee. Even communities of from 2,000 to 5,000 had a higher percentage of incomes between $3,000 and $9,000 than did Milwaukee. Incomes of this size, moreover, naturally provide greater comfort in the smaller places than they do in large urban areas.

Another fact revealed by the survey which is of interest is that the smaller communities offer lawyers relatively more opportunities for public service. In Milwaukee only 11 per cent of the attorneys held during the six-year period such public offices as district attorney, sheriff, judge, legislator, clerk of court, and so on, whereas the proportion was much larger for all groups of smaller places. In cities of from 5,000 to 10,000 population, 32 per cent held offices of this kind.

Finally, the survey suggested, on the basis of incomes from 1927 to 1930, that the lawyers making the highest earnings are those who have been in practice between twenty and forty years. After forty years at the bar, a few attorneys still have large incomes but the general level, it appears, begins to decline at about that time and continues progressively with age.

In the survey of the New York County Lawyers Association in 1934 a questionnaire, dealing in large part with the earnings of attorneys, was sent to 19,000 lawyers assumed to be residing or practicing in New York County.[1] Subsequent reports of changes of address, deaths, and so on led the Committee to believe that there were about 15,000 attorneys practicing there. Of this number some 5,000 replied to the questionnaire. The facts assembled from these replies constituted, in the estimation of the Committee, a representative picture of conditions in New York County.

About 28 per cent of those who answered the questionnaire had been admitted to practice during the five years immediately preceding the investigation, and nearly 60 per cent had been admitted within ten years. Although so large a proportion of young lawyers may appear surprising, the Committee concluded that it fairly portrayed recent trends. These high percentages should be borne in mind, however, when examining the figures for earnings, since attorneys, particularly if in private practice, generally have small incomes during the early years.

Of some 5,000 replies obtained, 3,210 afforded information about net incomes in 1933. The median earnings in that year for these 3,210 lawyers were $2,990. Fifteen per cent earned less than $1,000, and another 18 per cent between $1,000 and $2,000. At the other extreme 3.6 per cent received more than $25,000, and 10.6 per cent from $10,000 to $20,000. It is interesting to note that 82 of the attorneys responding were reported as having had net incomes in one of the worst years of the depression of from $25,000 to $50,000, 27 of from $50,-000 to $100,000 and 7 of more than $100,000. It must be

[1] Survey of the Legal Profession in New York County, pp. 6–38.

borne in mind that New York City provides the most lucrative area of legal practice in the entire country, and it is not improbable that the proportion of lawyers in the upper income brackets disclosed by the study was too low to be representative. However that may be, the earnings of relatively few men were so large that the arithmetic average income was $6,230, or more than twice the median. The aggregate income of the 34 men, who earned more than $50,000 each and comprised only one per cent of the whole group, exceeded the total earnings of the lower 50 per cent of the group.

Attempt was made to obtain information concerning average net income from 1928 to 1932. On the basis of the 2,452 replies to this question, it was concluded that nearly 5 per cent earned under $1,000 per year during the five-year period; 30 per cent earned from $1,000 to $3,000; 36 per cent from $3,000 to $7,500; and 29 per cent earned more than $7,500. Although these percentages are more favorable than those for 1933, they still show a large proportion of low earnings. Further utilization of material by the Committee disclosed that, in general, for those lawyers whose earnings averaged less than $3,000 during the period of five years, there was some improvement in 1933, while, for those who had earned more than $3,000 annually during the earlier period, there was a decrease in 1933. From another source the Committee learned that in 1935 about 1,500 attorneys, presumably 10 per cent of the Manhattan bar, had qualified for relief under a pauper's oath.

Statistics revealed, as was expected, that there was average improvement in earnings with increase in years of experience. The median income was lowest for those most recently admitted to the bar and highest for those admitted before 1900. The group of older lawyers included in the study was, however, probably not so large as actual facts would warrant, and no attempt was made to subdivide the small number admitted to the bar before 1900 in order to show the earnings of those who had been in practice forty or more years.

In reference to academic and professional training the survey disclosed the fact that, not only in 1933 but in the previous five years, the incomes of college graduates and of full-time law-school graduates were some 50 per cent higher than were the incomes of non-college and the part-time law-school graduates. The Committee believed it fair to conclude that a college education and training in a full-time school tended to improve financial returns in the practice of law. It recognized, however, that many men who had the advantage of the best education came from homes whose financial condition and social standing were such as to assure them more remunerative clients than lawyers less fortunately situated.

The fact that 55 per cent of the reporting Manhattan lawyers practiced for themselves, rather than as members or employes of law firms, was surprising to those who had thought of legal work as being highly concentrated in large law offices in New York City. Twenty-four per cent of the attorneys were members of law firms, and 21 per cent were employes in law offices of firms or individuals. As might be expected, the proportion of employes was largest among those groups most recently graduated from law schools. With years of experience these employes tend either to become partners in law firms or to open offices for themselves. Graduates of college and full-time law schools were apparently more often able to obtain employment in law firms.

The median net income in 1933 for those attorneys who said that they practiced alone was $2,310. For those who were the head of their own offices but employed other lawyers to assist them, it was $3,940. For the equal partner median earnings amounted to $5,220; for the junior partner $6,630; and for the senior partner $11,530. Attorneys who reported that they were junior or senior partners were probably members of large and well-established firms which were relatively prosperous.

All the figures presented have been for net income. From those instances in which lawyers submitted data both on gross and net income, the Committee learned something of the cost of conducting legal business. It concluded that in 1933 overhead expense was about 35 per cent of the gross and 50 per cent of the net income. Expenses tended to be relatively higher, naturally, among the lowest income groups, but even for attorneys earning from $25,000 to $50,000 a year, they were almost 30 per cent of gross income. During the preceding five years operating expenditures had been considerably less—about 26 per cent of the gross income for the entire group. Difficulties of collection and shrinkage of business in 1933 probably accounted in large measure for the increased costs of that year.

The California bar has concerned itself, in investigations in 1932 and again in 1937, with the economic situation among young attorneys.[1] Of the 1,466 lawyers who had been admitted by examination in 1929, 1930, and 1931 to practice in California, nearly 1,200 sent to the bar association in 1932 replies to requests for information. Their responses showed very low earnings for the group. In their first year after admission 51 per cent had been unable to earn enough from practice to sup-

---

[1] Brenner, James E., "A Survey of Employment Conditions Among Young Attorneys in California," in Proceedings of the Fifth Annual Meeting of the State Bar of California, 1932, pp. 32–36; Digest of a Survey of the Economic and Professional Status of California Lawyers During the First Five Years of Practice, mimeographed report issued by the State Bar of California, 1937.

port themselves and their dependents, and 71 per cent had not earned more than $1,000 net income. Of those who had had two years of practice 37 per cent had not made enough in the second year to support themselves and their dependents, and 42 per cent reported not more than $1,000 from their practice. Of those who were graduated in 1929, 33 per cent did not earn enough to support themselves and their dependents in the third year of practice, and 42 per cent had again earned not more than $1,000. Average net income began at $978 in the first year, increased to $1,602 in the second, and to $2,078 in the third. Even these averages would have been considerably less had it not been for the effect of a few unusually high incomes in each year.

In 1937 the California bar instituted another survey to determine what progress had been made by attorneys who had been in practice five years. Of the 535 living persons who were admitted to the bar in 1931, 336 replied to the questionnaire. Their median net income in 1932 was roughly $1,250; in 1936 it was around $2,250. Only 15 attorneys were earning $3,000 or more in the former year, and only one $7,000 or more; by 1936, 85 had earnings of at least $3,000, and 7 were in the $7,000 category.

The only data dealing with lawyers' incomes throughout the United States are those presented by the Bureau of Foreign and Domestic Commerce of the United States Department of Commerce in its study of National Income in the United States, 1929–1935.[1] To the figure set down by the federal census for the number of lawyers in 1930, the Bureau applied an index of the number of lawyers listed in the directories of a selected

[1] United States Government Printing Office, Washington, 1936, pp. 203, 214–215, 292.

group of some 60 cities. Thus it was able to estimate the total number of lawyers for each succeeding year through 1934. It also sent a questionnaire covering the years 1929 to 1934 to a supposed random sample of attorneys throughout the United States. The returns were subdivided into those of lawyers who were entrepreneurs and those of professional employes.

Since we do not know how large or representative was the sample obtained and since some adjustment of figures was necessary, the results of this study must be used with great caution. The Bureau set down figures, presumably for arithmetic averages, which showed a drop in the net income of lawyers who were entrepreneurs from $5,534 in 1929 to $3,868 in 1933, and then a rise to $4,218 in 1934. The per capita income of professional employes did not exhibit so great a fluctuation. It had been around $2,200 in 1929, rose slightly in 1930, declined during the next three years, and then gained again in 1934, reaching about $1,800.

The Bureau found that the number both of entrepreneurs and their employe lawyers increased in each year during the depression, except in 1934 when those engaged as employes decreased slightly. It should be borne in mind that the curtailment of ordinary business transactions subsequent to 1929 lessened the need for legal service, but this tendency was counteracted in part, at least, by the extraordinary expansion in foreclosures, receiverships, bankruptcies, and other activities requiring legal service.

From the foregoing facts and others which cannot be reviewed because of lack of space,[1] it is apparent that the law af-

[1] Converse, C. C., "Lawyers' Incomes and Others," in Proceedings of the North Dakota State Bar Association, 1923, pp. 118–119; Rutledge, Wiley B., "A Survey of the Welfare of the Missouri Bar," in American Law School Review, April, 1935, pp. 129–134.

fords a few attorneys ample opportunity to earn large incomes. Extended educational preparation and professional training in law schools having national reputations, social contacts, location in centers where the demand for legal service is brisk, and fortuitous circumstances play an important role in aiding individual lawyers to win affluence, prestige, and influence. For the majority of lawyers, however, earnings are not large at the present time, and although the situation may have been somewhat more favorable prior to 1929, attorneys on the average apparently have never had very large incomes.

The financial situation during the early years of practice presents a particularly serious problem for those who do not find themselves in that small favored class that is immediately received into the large law firms or the legal departments of vast corporations. Men who open offices of their own almost always have to undergo a period of distressing underemployment that sometimes verges upon unemployment and often continues for a long interval. For those who become clerks in small offices, salaries are generally very meager. In a letter published in the New York World Telegram for April 19, 1937, a young attorney declared that much has been written deploring starvation wages paid to those engaged in manufacture and industry, but little has been said about similar conditions in the legal profession because it is thought that professional ethics demand dignified silence. "The fact that a man seeks employment in a profession does not render him any less a man whose simple necessities cannot be satisfied by $5.00 a week." Lest anyone believe that $5.00 a week is a gross understatement of what some clerks earn, it should be recalled that, as early as 1929, Professor I. Maurice Wormser pointed to the large number of advertisements in the New York Law Journal of attorneys seeking jobs, many of whom were even willing to serve clerkships in reputable firms without compensation.[1]

So serious did the situation become for many attorneys during the depression that the Lawyers Security League was organized in New York City in 1935, for the purpose of securing work-relief projects for needy members of the profession. Branches of the League were also established in several other large cities. Since certain chapters of the National Lawyers Guild have absorbed some of the former constituency of the League, they too have been concerned with the problem of the needy lawyer. Such work as has been done, however, has been largely in the nature of improving critical conditions rather than of preventing the occurrence of other similar conditions. That there is much which the profession could achieve, through requiring that only able and competently trained persons be admitted to the bar, has been suggested in the preceding section. Subsequent pages will indicate that there are fields of legal work, not yet cultivated, that could probably absorb a considerable number of attorneys.

The problem of the meager earnings of a large sector of the legal profession is one that merits attention from the laity as well as from the bar, for the public has much at stake. No society can be healthy so long as a substantial portion of any group is partially or wholly unemployed. It has been clearly demonstrated in this country that "whenever lawyers are unable to make a living practicing in an ethical way, there is a strong temptation to resort to ambulance chasing, solicitation of business and a commercialization of practice."[2] It is likely, there-

---

[1] "Fewer Lawyers and Better Ones." In Report of New York State Bar Association, 1929, p. 355.
[2] Editorial in Bar Examiner, December, 1936, p. 25.

fore, that the present movement toward raising state requirements for admission to the bar will not only continue but become
accelerated.

OUTSTANDING WEAKNESSES IN THE
ADMINISTRATION OF JUSTICE

In the foregoing discussion attention has been centered primarily upon the legal profession and its problems. Emphasis
will now be shifted to the service rendered by that profession
in promoting justice. It has long been part of the philosophical heritage of this country that there should be equal justice
for all persons, and that justice should be a right and not a privilege. The translation of this philosophy into practice, however,
has presented many grave problems. When one considers the
changes that have occurred during the past century whereby the
United States has been transformed from a relatively simple
society into a highly complex urban and industrial nation, it is
not surprising that the forces promoting the administration of
justice have failed to keep pace with so rapid an evolution, and
that the administration has been characterized by some of the
very evils which have accompanied the development of other
basic institutions. As a result of its failures and shortcomings,
lawyers, judges, and courts have been subjected to a vast amount
of criticism. Such criticisms are not new. Roscoe Pound once
aptly remarked, "Dissatisfaction with the administration of
justice is as old as law."[1] Dissatisfaction is also continuous.
Although there are periods when it is particularly current, it is
never lacking. As this page is being written, the New York
Times remarks editorially that Attorney General Cummings is

[1] "The Causes of Popular Dissatisfaction with the Administration of Justice." In Journal of the American Judicature Society, February, 1937, p. 178.

"still following hard on the heels of that inveterate enemy of justice, delay."[1]

Note should be made of the fact that lawyers, when considered individually and not as members of the legal profession, occupy an anomalous position in reference to the administration of justice. In our competitive society an attorney is brought into a case by only one party. It is his duty—limited by a sense of professional restraint, to be sure, but without immediate concern for the attainment of the most just result—to advance the claims and interests of his client. Thus our system of administering justice demands partisan advocates on the one hand. On the other, it demands impartial judges, and juries, who, after having been enlightened by partisans for each side of the controversy, will supposedly be better able to reach a just decision. Under such a system lawyers can be held individually responsible for shortcomings in the promotion of justice only to the extent that they are lacking in integrity, ability, adequate training, or a willingness to co-operate with their colleagues in remedying conditions.

Upon the bar as a whole rests a far greater degree of responsibility, for its function as a body is exclusively that of administering and promoting justice. That the legal profession has failed to do everything possible in creating an efficient organization for achieving this purpose is the consensus of many leaders of the bar and bench. They have repeatedly pointed to five weaknesses in current methods of furnishing justice: (1) delay and uncertainty in the courts; (2) prohibitive expense of litigation; (3) unprofessional conduct and the slowness of the bar in ridding itself of unscrupulous members; (4) insufficient interest

[1] January 4, 1938.

on the part of the bar in the promotion of justice; (5) failure of the profession to accept its social responsibilities.

DELAY AND UNCERTAINTY IN THE COURTS

In 1906 William Draper Lewis declared before the American Bar Association:[1]

> On the side of the administration of the law, both civil and criminal, our failure to perform the service which the community may of right expect is almost complete. The two fatal words "uncertainty" and "delay" are interwoven in all our methods of doing legal business. . . .   To a modern business man, accustomed to modern and efficient methods of dispatching business, the delays and uncertainties of our administration of the law have become intolerable. . . .   The absurdities of the administration of our criminal law have allowed the hysteria which exists in a more or less positive form in every community to find outward expression in the crime of lynching; the delays of the civil law, tending to deprive the economically weak of justice, have been a potent factor in creating that wide-spread disrespect for law and distrust of courts which renders it increasingly difficult for us to meet the new and complicated problems of our social life.

In the same year Roscoe Pound, then dean of the College of Law of the University of Nebraska, made his memorable speech before the national organization on "The Causes of Popular Dissatisfaction with the Administration of Justice." So significant did his words seem even thirty years later that in February, 1937, the Journal of the American Judicature Society reprinted his paper with a description of its reception written by Dean Wigmore, who had been present at the time it was read. In his detailed analysis of the causes for dissatisfaction, Dean

---

[1] "Legal Education and the Failure of the Bar to Perform Its Public Duties." In Reports of the American Bar Association, 1906, pt. 2, pp. 35–36.

Pound pointed to the waste of judicial power and the resulting delays in court procedure.

A comparison of the volume of business disposed of by English and by American courts will illustrate the waste and delay caused by archaic judicial organization and obsolete procedure. In England there are twenty-three judges of the High Court who dispose on the average of fifty-six hundred *contested* cases, and have before them, in one form or another, some eighty thousand cases each year. In Nebraska there are twenty-eight district judges who have no original probate jurisdiction and no jurisdiction in bankruptcy or admiralty, and they had upon their dockets last year forty-three hundred and twenty cases, of which they disposed of about seventy percent. England and Wales, with a population in 1900 of 32,000,000, employ for their whole civil litigation ninety-five judges. . . . Nebraska, with a population in 1900 of 1,066,000, employs for the same purpose one hundred and twenty-nine. But these one hundred and twenty-nine are organized on an antiquated system and their time is frittered away on mere points of legal etiquette.[1]

In the years that have intervened since Messrs. Lewis and Pound delivered their scathing criticisms, there has been some, but still very inadequate, improvement in conditions. What is most encouraging is the growing awareness among the bench, bar, and the informed public that such conditions are deplorable. Many investigations, printed articles, and speeches have called attention to a problem seriously in need of remedy. In 1934, for example, the distinguished Commission on the Administration of Justice in New York State issued its final report of the study which had been authorized by the legislature some years earlier. It made the unequivocal statement that the major criticism of justice in New York State is that it is slow. It

---

[1] Pound, Roscoe, "The Causes of Popular Dissatisfaction with the Administration of Justice." In Journal of the American Judicature Society, February, 1937, pp. 185–186.

found unwarranted delay in nearly every court of the jurisdiction. "In some courts and in some counties the delay amounts to positive denial of justice."[1]

Of the 8,016 law cases disposed of by the New York Supreme Court by trial during 1930–1931, one per cent was five or six years old, 4 per cent were four or five years old, 13 per cent were three or four, and 17 per cent were two or three. In about 58 per cent of the instances trials occurred a year or more after the cases were placed on the calendar. Delay in the Supreme Court was discovered to be slight compared with that in the inferior courts of New York City. At the end of 1929 the Municipal Court of that city had nearly 300,000 cases pending; at the end of 1932 it had more than 550,000 cases, in spite of the fact that it disposed of 142,000 more cases in the latter than in the former year. In the City Court, as of January 1, 1933, average delay in tort actions ranged from forty-nine months in Kings County to twenty months in Queens County. Delay in commercial actions ranged from fifteen months in New York County to three months in Kings. On the other hand, there was very little delay in the inferior courts outside of New York City.[2]

When the Judicial Council of the State of New York, the permanent agency that is the outgrowth of the Commission on the Administration of Justice, rendered its third annual report in 1937, it was able to point to very considerable reduction in congestion of calendars.[3] It stated that delays had been so

[1] Report of the Commission on the Administration of Justice in New York State. Legislative Document 50, 1934, p. 11. For a description of the way in which delay may result in denial of justice, see I. Maurice Wormser's "The Law's Delay and Its Consequences," in America, March 3, 1934.

[2] Statistics pertaining to New York State have been quoted from the Report of the Commission referred to, pp. 12–13.

[3] Third Annual Report. Legislative Document 48, 1937, pp. 24–28.

localized and decreased in number that they were less serious than for generations. This improvement was largely the result of the fact that many of the recommendations presented by the Commission and the Council had been put into operation. In spite of encouraging trends, however, there were, on June 30, 1936, 10 counties of the 62 in the state where delay in the Supreme Court exceeded six months for tort cases and two for commercial cases. Although the number of cases on the calendar of the City Court of New York City had been reduced by 50 per cent between June, 1934, and June, 1936, delays ranging from twenty to thirty-seven months in tort jury cases still existed in three of the five counties comprising the city, and even tort non-jury cases lagged far behind in New York County. In the Municipal Court of New York City delay had been largely eliminated in all non-jury cases and in commercial jury ones. Tort jury cases in New York and Kings Counties continued to present a real problem.

Although the situation in New York has been and still is more serious than that obtaining elsewhere, Herbert Harley, secretary of the American Judicature Society, has pointed out that before a city attains a population of a million, complaints concerning delay in the courts are almost invariably frequent and well justified.[1] Evidence substantiates the validity of his statement. The Milwaukee Circuit Court, for example, before which virtually all civil suits for any considerable amounts are tried, was reported in 1934 to be two years behind in its calendar.[2]

Delay is the result of a number of factors. One of the chief

[1] "Administering of Justice in Cities." In Annals of the American Academy of Political and Social Science, March, 1928, p. 88.
[2] Garrison, Lloyd K., "Congestion in the Milwaukee Circuit Court." In Wisconsin Law Review, June, 1934, p. 325.

of these is the lack of flexibility in the organization of the courts. As needs have arisen, new courts have been created without much attempt to make them an integral part of a planned system for the administration of justice. Consequently, courts differ in facilities, jurisdiction, efficiency, and prestige. Artificial barriers have been built around them, whereby it is often impossible to use the facilities of those that are not continuously busy to assist those whose calendars are badly congested. Judges attached to a higher court frequently may not be assigned to a lower court, even though the two courts sit in the same building, and the judge of higher rank is unoccupied while his colleague cannot possibly keep abreast of the accumulated work.

Closely connected with the problem of inflexibility is that of lack of business organization and methods within the system of courts. Judge Joseph M. Proskauer has complained of the fact that attorneys do not even attempt to be practical in their trial work, but use methods of procedure, which were designed to assist the jury, to befog both judge and jury.

> Most of the time in our courts of law is not consumed with the adducing of evidence; it is largely occupied with controversy and discussion as to the manner in which the evidence shall be adduced. . . . The meaningless mumble of the objection as incompetent, irrelevant and immaterial sounds through our court rooms like the drone of destroying locusts.[1]

Judges themselves are often at fault for the unbusinesslike manner in which they conduct the work of the courts. They have frequently been criticized for their long vacations, their frequent recesses, and the few hours spent daily in the court-

---

[1] "A New Professional Psychology Essential for Law Reform." In American Bar Association Journal, March, 1928, p. 124.

room even when calendars are overcrowded.[1] Later note will be made of methods utilized in some cities for planning the court routine so that it will be operated in a systematic and efficient manner. In many of the large urban areas, however, there are still no agencies vested with administrative powers for using such methods. Scarcely anywhere as yet is there a centralized tribunal charged with the duty of supervising and controlling the administration of justice throughout an entire state.

Another difficulty that has commonly prevented dispatch arises from the situation existing within courts of limited jurisdiction, generally known as city or municipal courts. In the estimation of many, such institutions exercise the most difficult and important functions of the entire judiciary.[2] For the majority of persons their only knowledge of the administration of justice is gained in these lower tribunals. The successful trial of small causes demands expeditious procedure and judges of high ability. Unfortunately, courts of this type make little appeal to able lawyers who are eager to become judges. The work is less pleasant, less remunerative, and has less prestige attached to it than has work in a court of general jurisdiction. Judges in these courts, furthermore, are largely deprived of the assistance and stimulating criticism of the better element of the bar, and are subjected to the importunities of inexperienced lawyers and even shysters. The result is often serious delay and inefficiency.

Congestion in all courts is increased by the presence of cases on the calendars that will never be tried on their own merits. They are known as "dead wood." In the Supreme Court in New York County in 1932, 60 per cent of the cases upon being

---

[1] See report made on April 15, 1934, by Paul Blanchard to Mayor La-Guardia concerning magistrates' courts in New York City.

[2] Harley, Herbert, "Administering Justice in Cities." In Annals of the American Academy of Political and Social Science, March, 1928, p. 87.

reached were marked settled or discontinued, or were crossed off the calendar. The bringing of unfounded litigation into the courts greatly impedes their work. Judge Marshall F. Mc-Comb of the Superior Court of Los Angeles has recently described the experience that he encounters almost daily of cases brought for trial where a suit should never have been instituted.[1] When the attorney is asked why litigation was begun, he frequently replies that he knew he had no case but that his client insisted on having the suit filed. Judge McComb declares that attorneys should assume responsibility not only for protecting the right of clients but for protecting the public from baseless litigation.

It is also recognized that because of delay in the courts unnecessary litigation is stimulated and made profitable. Solicitor General Jackson has pointed to the large amount of litigation that is introduced by disadvantaged persons against the massed resources of an insurance company, a financial house, or the company that employed the person.[2] In such instances delay and technicalities are favored by the corporation, because it knows that the cost of waiting will probably be so prohibitive to the man of meager resources that the suit will be dropped or a small settlement accepted.

The presence of cases of a purely technical or even dishonest nature, therefore, both complicates the problem of the administration of justice and is a problem in itself. If a case is ill founded, some defendant is put to the cost of defending himself against it. If the case is well founded and is marked off the calendar, it is often because the plaintiff has been so long

[1] "Are the Law Schools Adequately Training for the Public Service?" In American Law School Review, December, 1935, p. 298.
[2] "The Bar and the New Deal." In American Law School Review, April, 1935, p. 154.

delayed in the prosecution. The Commission on the Administration of Justice that has already been quoted comments on the method of procedure followed in this country, which leaves the conduct of litigation almost entirely to the counsel for the two litigants.[1] It maintains that the judiciary should exercise greater control over pending cases by promptly ascertaining their merits and by attempting to prevent surprises at trial and the use of obstructive tactics.

Two other well-known causes of delay must be mentioned: the excessive use of jury trial, and the marked tendency to appeal to a higher court cases that should have been settled once and for all in the court of original jurisdiction. The method of jury trial, upon which many persons insist as their constitutional right, is, in the opinion of numerous authorities, slow, cumbersome, inefficient, and expensive. The lack of intelligence or broad educational background among the jurors, the possibility of their being bribed, prejudiced, and swayed emotionally; the delay and expense resulting from a mistrial caused by the dissenting vote of only one juror—these are some of the factors cited by Judge A. G. Burr of the Supreme Court of North Dakota that have led to frequent demands in recent years for the abolition of jury trials in most civil cases.[2] A few states have attempted to remedy the problem by permitting a verdict to be rendered by a majority of the jurors, by reducing its size, or by making provision whereby a jury of experts may be called to decide special, highly technical cases. Throughout the United

[1] Report of the Commission, p. 14.
[2] For further discussion of this subject, see Judge Burr's "Progress in Trial by Jury," in Annals of the American Academy of Political and Social Science, March, 1928, pp. 75–81. For a more sympathetic opinion of juries, see Joseph N. Ulman's A Judge Takes the Stand, Alfred A. Knopf, New York, 1933, pp. 21–52.

States, moreover, there is some movement toward replacing juries by trial judges.

The remark has been made that 50 per cent of the law's delay is caused by appellate proceedings. If there were real justification for so many appeals in the United States, the problem would be one of improving the lower courts. Unfortunately, it is a fact that in a vast number of appeals no substantial question is raised. We are appeal-mad in this country, in the opinion of Judge Proskauer. "There is no disposition on anybody's part to let well enough alone. An appeal on the off chance that some error may somewhere be found is a matter of course. . . . The waste of time, of money and of effort in futile appeals is staggering."[1]

Closely allied with the problem of delay is that of uncertainty to which reference has already been made in the quotation from William Draper Lewis.[2] So important a part does it play in impeding the rendering of justice that a further word must be said about it. There is great uncertainty regarding the law itself. Frequently judges have reached no consensus about the common law as it relates to a given case. Statutory law also tends to be differently interpreted and enforced in various localities and at various times. To a considerable degree, however, uncertainty is the by-product of the lapse of a long period of time between the beginning and the conclusion of a case. The outcome of litigation, moreover, is frequently unpredictable. Because of various factors that may enter into the situation, such as over-refinement of rules or dishonesty on the part of witnesses, results may be totally different from those that would normally

[1] "A New Professional Psychology Essential for Law Reform." In American Bar Association Journal, March, 1928, p. 125.
[2] See p. 198.

be expected. The hazards of a lawsuit, therefore, are such as to deter many persons from seeking to obtain their rights.

Prohibitive Expense of Litigation

The present director of the budget for New York City has stated in a particularly illuminating article on the expense of litigation that "there are few even among the ultra-conservative of the bar who will argue that the cost of litigation is not excessive."[1] The expense to a litigant includes many items. First, there are "fees," or the sums that a person must pay to a court or a public officer in connection with some step in the litigation or for the rendering of some specific service. Originally these fees were compensatory to the officer who rendered the service. Today they generally accrue to the state and bear no relation to the expense of the service rendered. Next there are "costs," or the sums generally paid by the losing person to the successful litigant. Costs are looked upon either as partial compensation for the expenses borne by the one who wins the case, or as a penalty imposed upon the unsuccessful person for having brought suit. As compensation, they seldom bear the slightest relation to the expenses incurred. Among other items are compensation to counsel for his legal services, and all the other out-of-pocket expenses involved in preparation for and conduct of the trial and in any appeal that may be taken. There must also be included, under the expense of litigation, the intangible losses that accrue from the interruption of a person's business, from having capital tied up in a suit, and from the destruction of goodwill.

A study of the courts of New York City, made a few years

---

[1] Dayton, Kenneth, "Costs, Fees, and Expenses in Litigation." In Annals of the American Academy of Political and Social Science, May, 1933, p. 34.

ago by the Institute of Law at Johns Hopkins University, presented a startling situation relating to fees. The Institute found that in the Supreme Court, which deals generally with cases over $3,000 in amount, litigants paid 13 per cent of the expense of maintaining the court. In the City Court, that handles cases usually between $1,000 and $3,000 in amount, they contributed only 7 per cent the expense. In the Municipal Court, designed to care for small cases involving less than $1,000, they paid 72 per cent of the expense of operation. It is unnecessary to point to the injustice indicated by these figures. The poor man, suing to recover $50 in wages, pays nearly three-fourths of the expense of the court maintained for his benefit; the wealthier person in the higher courts pays roughly one-tenth. The real discrepancy, however, is even greater, because one pays the same fees for a $50 claim that another pays for a $1,000 claim, and no distinction is made between a case disposed of in a few minutes and a case requiring several days.

Attorneys' fees are, in Mr. Dayton's estimation, modest and reasonable for the amount of work performed.[1] They are unduly high, however, because of the needless routine and duplication in the American system of litigation. And, even when they are modest, they are beyond the capacity of the poor to pay them. As a result, there are only two ways in which the indigent can procure legal service: through legal-aid organizations, to be described at length in a later section, and by contracting with a lawyer who agrees to render service for a contingent fee. This means that if the attorney succeeds in winning the case, he will be reimbursed by the client for his services and for all expenses incurred. Usually he demands, before agreeing to act as coun-

[1] *Ibid.*, p. 43.

sel, that he be given a minimum sum or a percentage of the amount he is able to collect.

The contingent fee presents one of the serious problems with which the legal profession is faced. It is peculiarly an outcome of the industrial era. As factories grew in number and size and emphasis was placed upon enlarged production rather than upon safety, thousands of accidents occurred for which workers could collect compensation if they were able to pay court expenses and lawyers' fees. Since they did not customarily have the necessary money in hand, lawyers began to offer service on a contingent basis. With the growth of workmen's compensation acts, the need of industrial employes for private counsel has decreased. The practice, however, has been extended to accident cases outside of industry and to other cases where there is possibility of any substantial collection.

Many honorable lawyers have taken cases on a contingent basis, as Reginald Heber Smith has pointed out, and have claimed for themselves only a reasonable proportion of the recovery.[1] The system, moreover, has been of real benefit to those who had no other way of obtaining the settlements to which they were entitled. On the other hand, it has been subject to grave abuse. Julius H. Cohen has written:

Lawyers who try to get business by charging nothing unless they succeed, even though they leave the size of their fees to be determined by the amount and character of their services, are constantly tempted to promote groundless and vexatious suits. Those who go further and bargain that, if successful, their fees shall be fixed sums or percentages are not only apt to become public pests, but are in constant danger of abusing or betraying their own clients. When making such a bargain the lawyer's superior knowledge and experi-

[1] Justice and the Poor. Carnegie Foundation for the Advancement of Teaching. New York, 1924, p. 85.

ence give him an advantage which tempts him to over-reach his client. By making it, he, in effect, purchases an interest in the litigation. Consequently, unhappy conflicts between his own and his client's interest, in respect to the settlement or conduct of the suit, are always likely to arise; his capacity to advise wisely is impaired; and he is beset by the same temptations which beset a party to be dishonest in preparation and trial.[1]

Mr. Smith has spoken even more emphatically of the evils of the contingent fee, asserting that the system has attracted undesirable persons to the bar; has induced the lawyer, "runner," and physician to conspire in the winning of fraudulent cases; has degraded expert testimony; and has served as a cloak for robbery through extortionate fees. "Unquestionably it has done more than anything else to bring the bar into deserved disrepute."[2]

In spite of all the criticisms made, the use of the contingent fee has persisted and has become officially recognized under qualifying conditions. One of the canons of the code of ethics of the American Bar Association reads, "Contingent fees, where sanctioned by law, should be under the supervision of the court, in order that clients may be protected from unjust charges." Similar canons have been adopted by many of the local bar associations.

UNPROFESSIONAL CONDUCT AND DISBARMENT OF LAWYERS

The foregoing discussion of the system of contingent fees brings us directly to a consideration of the related subjects of unprofessional conduct by members of the bar and disciplinary

---

[1] The Law—Business or Profession? G. A. Jennings Co., New York, 1924, p. 206.
[2] Justice and the Poor, p. 86.

proceedings. Under unprofessional conduct have been included, for convenience, those illegal acts which should rightly
be classified as misconduct, as well as other acts upon which the
bar looks with disfavor. Since the legal profession has never
been able to define exactly what constitutes unprofessional conduct but depends in many instances upon interpretations of acts
and motives as they appear,[1] the simplest method of approach-
ing the subject is to examine a list of some of the offenses for
which lawyers have been disbarred.

In New York, for example, attorneys have been disbarred for
conversion of clients' money to their own use; for misapplying
funds received from clients for specific purposes; for charging a
client for services not rendered and for other kinds of frauds
upon clients; for falsely stating in a suit that the plaintiff was
the true owner of stocks; for collusion in a divorce case; for
assisting a client to leave the state in order to put him beyond
the reach of the law; for procuring the release upon bail of a
person held as a fugitive from justice and then conspiring for
his escape; for using a threat of criminal proceedings as a means
of forcing a compromise in a suit; for trying to secure a verdict
in favor of the client upon testimony known to the attorney to
be false; for aiding and abetting a witness in perjury; and for
procuring from an injured person incapable of signing his name
or realizing what he was doing apparent authority to begin an
action.[2]

It will thus be noted that lawyers have been disbarred for a

---

[1] Professor John S. Bradway takes the position that any lawyer who does
something that materially lowers the prestige of the profession or substantially interferes with the administration of justice should be disbarred. For
further elaboration of this idea, see his article, "Moral Turpitude as the Criterion of Offenses That Justify Disbarment," in University of California Law
Review, November, 1935, pp. 9–27.

[2] Cohen, Julius H., The Law: Business or Profession? pp. 15–17.

wide range of causes. They have also been suspended for a variety of reasons. This is a particularly important fact to bear in mind. So much attention in the press and elsewhere is given to the problem of solicitation by lawyers of personal injury cases—popularly known as "ambulance chasing"—that it would be easy to conclude erroneously that practically all action in regard to unethical practices centered around this one question. As a matter of fact, Professor Taeusch observed some years ago that the majority of disciplinary proceedings result from a very few types of misconduct: conversion or misappropriation of funds, deceit, forgery, and fraud.[1] He pointed to the fact that lawyers are frequently aware that some colleague should be disbarred, but will not proceed against him because they do not want "to get mixed up in such a dirty mess."[2] It is this very attitude that has done much to discredit the legal profession in the eyes of those interested in the better administration of justice.

This attitude, moreover, is inconsistent with the official point of view of bar associations. The twenty-ninth canon of the code of ethics of the American Bar Association reads:

Lawyers should expose without fear or favor before the proper tribunals corrupt or dishonest conduct in the profession, and should accept without hesitation employment against a member of the Bar who has wronged his client. The counsel upon the trial of a cause in which perjury has been committed owe it to the profession and to the public to bring the matter to the knowledge of the prosecuting authorities. [This admonition should be compared with the statement by Samuel Untermyer, "Perjury is so rampant in the courts that the defendant can with impunity swear to any kind of concocted

---

[1] Taeusch, Carl F., Professional and Business Ethics. Henry Holt and Co., New York, 1926, pp. 38–39.
[2] *Ibid.*, p. 36.

defense."]¹ The lawyer should aid in guarding the Bar against the admission to the profession of candidates unfit or unqualified because deficient in either moral character or education. He should strive at all times to uphold the honor and to maintain the dignity of the profession and to improve not only the law but the administration of justice.

A few local bar associations have expended much time and money in the investigation and hearing of cases, in the disciplining of members of the bar, in recommending to the courts the disbarment or suspension of individual persons, and in answering questions concerning legal ethics. The Association of the Bar of the City of New York has at times appropriated as much as $20,000 annually to such work. During the ten years between 1925 and 1935 nearly 22,800 complaints were received by this body.² Some 900 of them were fully tried by the Committee on Grievances. Three hundred fourteen attorneys were found guilty, and 275 of these were prosecuted before the Appellate Division of the Supreme Court. It is instructive to note the disposition of these 275 cases by the Court: 108 attorneys were disbarred or had their licenses revoked after trial; 69 asked to have their names struck from the rolls after charges had been brought against them; 39 were suspended; 16 were censured; and in 43 instances proceedings were dismissed or discontinued, sometimes because of deaths. Thus only 26 per cent of the lawyers tried by the Committee and only one per cent of all those against whom complaints had been brought received sentences from the Court.

A state bar association which is particularly active is that of California. During the entire history of California until the

¹ "What Every Present-Day Lawyer Should Know." In Annals of the American Academy of Political and Social Science, May, 1933, p. 174.
² Association of the Bar of the City of New York Year Book, 1935, p. 166.

introduction of an integrated bar,[1] few disciplinary proceedings were undertaken. Subsequent to 1927, however, many complaints have been submitted to the state bar and many hearings have been held. Between October 18, 1935, and September 30, 1936, 109 cases were reviewed by its Board of Governors. Of these, 58 were dismissed; private reprimands were administered to 7 attorneys and public reprimands to 10; suspensions were recommended to the Supreme Court in 16 instances and disbarments in 13; and 5 cases were reviewed and ordered filed because of the previous disbarment of the respondent.[2]

The accomplishments of these two associations are not characteristic of the country as a whole. In many areas almost nothing has been attempted. Henry W. Jessup, who long served on committees of ethics of bar associations, ventured the estimate that in 90 per cent of the cases brought before committees nothing more was done than to administer "a liberal coat of whitewash" upon an attorney's agreeing "not to do it again."[3] Professor Sunderland, who has given attention to this problem, believes that this failure to act more incisively results from the lack of power vested in a grievance committee on the one hand, and to the realization, on the other, that disbarment is so drastic a proceeding that it should be used only as a last resort.[4] He points to the need for more flexible forms of discipline, which can be adjusted to various degrees of dereliction and can be

---

[1] See pp. 283–288 for a discussion of the integrated bar. In those states where such a bar has been established it generally brings more disbarment proceedings than do local bar associations.

[2] Wittschen, Theodore P., "President's Annual Address." In Proceedings of the Ninth Annual Meeting of the State Bar of California, 1936, p. 4.

[3] "The Ethics of the Legal Profession." In Annals of the American Academy of Political and Social Science, May, 1922, p. 21.

[4] Sunderland, Edson R., "Progress Toward a Better Administration of Justice." In Journal of the American Judicature Society, August, 1933, p. 54.

used as deterrents upon the first manifestations of unprofessional conduct.

LACK OF INTEREST IN THE PROMOTION OF JUSTICE

There has been a persistent feeling among members of the bar and many others that the legal profession has shown insufficient interest in making law more responsive to social needs. Earlier sections have indicated that the legal profession tends to be conservative, to be still somewhat bound to the tradition of law "as a body of absolutely fixed principles hovering over and above human affairs,"[1] and to be insufficiently aware of the evolution of social institutions and the contributions to law of economics, sociology, anthropology, political science, psychology, and psychiatry. Lawyers also are far too busy serving the interests of clients, and judges are too occupied with court routine, to give adequate attention to some of the less immediate aspects of the administration of justice. It has been said, probably with some justification, that the courts and the legal profession are really concerned with the law and not with justice. Unfortunately, the administration of law and the administration of justice are not synonymous.[2]

Many years ago Albert M. Kales pointed to the American method of selecting judges and the custom of permitting all lawyers to practice before the courts as one of the major causes of inefficiency and of failure in the promotion of justice. He recalled the fact that judges are chosen from the mass of lawyers in a given community rather than from a specially prepared group, like the English barristers who devote themselves exclu-

---

[1] Cohen, Morris R., Law and the Social Order. Harcourt, Brace and Co., New York, 1933, p. 199.
[2] Richmond, Maurice W., "Lawyers and the Public." In Law Quarterly Review, London, October, 1902, p. 403.

sively to arguing cases in the courts. It was ridiculous, in his opinion, to compare the results gained by such a selection with what might be obtained if judges were drawn from among advocates who spent their lives in the courtroom, becoming thoroughly acquainted with its rules instead of devoting themselves to serving special interests and clients.[1] Kales also referred to the inefficiency in court of lawyers as well as judges. He deplored our failure to have a class of barristers. Instead of such experts as would be found in England, he stated, our courts were overwhelmed by large numbers of client caretakers—lawyers who were not only ignorant of the rules of the court, but who attempted to impede the administration of justice in behalf of their clients. He concluded:

> There is grave reason to believe that the slow progress made in law reform and the reform in judicial organization and procedure in the large centers of population where it is most needed, is due to the fact that the solicitors or client caretakers represent, and almost wholly compose, the profession. . . . The more important and able the lawyer, the more he is in touch with the most important business interests of the community, and the more clear it is that he cannot propose or advocate any reform of an extensive character which will not be unwelcome to some particular client's interest. These are the men who stand as leaders of the bar. Their clients are not interested in reform.[2]

The situation seems to have changed little since the days when Kales was writing. Many lawyers continue to ally themselves with the interest of their clients, even when those interests run counter to public welfare. Professor Llewellyn has spoken in recent years of the attorney's emphasis upon duty to

[1] "A Comparative Study of the English and the Cook County Judicial Establishments." In Illinois Law Review, December, 1909, pp. 316–317.
[2] *Ibid.*, pp. 319–320.

his client as having resulted in his taking advantage of "each technicality the law may show, however senseless."[1] It has resulted in "distortion of evidence and argument to the utter bounds of the permissible." If emphasis were shifted to duty to the court, all judicial agencies would be used to the fullest extent to increase the more efficient functioning of the administration of justice, and to determine the probable truth of the question at issue.

In the light of such indictments the question arises, whether reform is more needed in substantive law[2] or in procedure. In 1916 Mr. Justice Brandeis inquired: "Has not the recent dissatisfaction with our law as administered been due, in large measure, to the fact that it had not kept pace with the rapid development of our political, economic and social ideals? In other words, is not the challenge of legal justice due to its failure to conform to contemporary conceptions of social justice?"[3] Of late years legal realists have sought to show that the law is not only out of touch with the facts of social life, but is frequently in plain contradiction to those facts.[4] Assistant Attorney General Thurman W. Arnold maintains that the realist can easily prove that law is not what it pretends to be and that its theories are sonorous, rather than sound; that its definitions run in circles; that applied by skilful attorneys in the forum of the courts, it can only be an argumentative technique; that it constantly seeks escape from reality through alternate reliance on ceremony and verbal confusion.[5]

[1] "The Bar Specializes—With What Results?" In Annals of the American Academy of Political and Social Science, May, 1933, p. 181.
[2] That is, law relating to rights, as distinguished from adjective law, which concerns administration or procedure.
[3] "The Living Law." In Illinois Law Review, February, 1916, p. 463.
[4] Robinson, Edward S., Law and the Lawyers. Macmillan Co., New York, 1935, p. 69.
[5] The Symbols of Government. Yale University Press, New Haven, 1935, p. 44.

Regardless of numerous criticisms of the apparent lag in legal concepts,[1] there is considerable agreement that the substantive law does not present so pressing a problem as does procedure. It has even been argued that there is no general basis for attacking substantive law. Some of the principles are anachronistic, some illogical, and some are "the defective offspring of mistaken loyalty to precedent," but they represent only a small minority of the whole.[2] Valid criticism must, therefore, be confined largely to the mechanics by which justice is administered and to the psychological attitude of the bench, bar, and litigant toward that administration.

Judge John J. Parker of the United States Circuit Court of Appeals has added his testimony by stating that, although the law is not perfect and has not solved all the problems that have arisen, it has made many necessary adjustments in a manner which should command the respect and gratitude of every serious student.[3] As illustration of what has been accomplished, Judge Parker mentions the changed conception of the relationship of employer to employe, the alteration in fundamental ideas about rights of private ownership, and the new emphasis upon the responsibility of public service utilities and other agencies for serving social welfare. He is unable, however, to find a similar degree of change in the field of procedure.

With this attitude William L. Ransom is in agreement.[4] He notes the existence of a broadened and quickened social con-

[1] Britt, Steuart Henderson, "Blood-Grouping Tests and the Law: the Problem of 'Cultural Law.'" In Minnesota Law Review, May, 1937, pp. 700–701.
[2] Dayton, Kenneth, "A Program for Legal Reform in the United States." In The Consensus, October, 1931, p. 8.
[3] "Social Progress and the Law." In American Bar Association Journal, November, 1930, pp. 701–708.
[4] "Improving the Administration of Justice." In Journal of the American Judicature Society, April, 1937, pp. 222–236.

science, which is being reflected in recent interpretations of the common law and in the enactment of new statutory law. His great concern is whether juridical machinery will keep pace with legal doctrine. In an era when the conduct of private and even public business has become more direct, exact, and expeditious, procedure is still much the same as in the period of stage coaches and tallow dips.

Judging the court by present-day efficiency standards and looking upon it as a mechanism for bringing about a result, the average court is the most indirect, inexact, inefficient, uneconomical and unintegrated instrumentality in the modern state, and the wonder is, not that justice is at times so inexactly and tardily administered, but that substantial justice between man and man is so often the outcome of proceedings in such a tribunal.[1]

Failure of Profession to Accept Social Responsibilities

Over a quarter of a century ago Woodrow Wilson reminded the American Bar Association that lawyers had ceased to handle the general miscellaneous interests of society and to concern themselves with the universal aspects of the social order. "Lawyers are specialists, like all other men around them. The general, broad, universal field of law grows dim and yet more dim to their apprehension as they spend year after year in minute examination and analysis of a particular part of it." The result seemed to him to be very serious in an age of law, "when society depends more than ever before upon the law-giver and the courts for its structural steel, the harmony and co-ordination of its parts, its convenience, its permanency, and it facility."[2]

[1] *Ibid.*, pp. 229–230.
[2] "The Lawyer and the Community." In Reports of the American Bar Association, 1910, p. 425.

Note has frequently been made in the foregoing discussion of the trend away from general practice, much of which used to be before the courts, and toward specialization in a particular type of work or for a particular type of client. This trend has been so pronounced that it is easy to overemphasize the amount of specialization that exists. Comprehensive figures would probably show that the general practitioner still plays the predominant role in the less densely populated areas and an important one even in large cities. The fact remains, however, that corporate business early realized the need for the most competent legal assistance, and it has gradually drawn some of the best minds into the field of business. So marked has this tendency become that a few of the finest law schools in the country train their students primarily to be members of big law firms and corporations.[1]

Karl N. Llewellyn[2] has traced in the Annals of the American Academy of Political and Social Science the inevitable results to the legal profession and to society of the change from advocacy to the giving of business advice. It is not surprising that many distinguished and successful lawyers show little interest in the criminal courts, in the adjustment of small claims, and in relatively unremunerative litigation, if they can occupy themselves with serving a few large clients. And so, as Professor Llewellyn says, a large number of the most ingenious and capable attorneys have deserted the fields where their predecessors once rendered a very necessary service to society in general, in order to devote themselves to the remaking of old legal tools, tech-

---

[1] Berle, A. A., Jr., "The Law and the Social Revolution." In Survey Graphic, December, 1933, p. 592.
[2] "The Bar Specializes—With What Results?" In Annals of the American Academy of Political and Social Science, May, 1933, pp. 177–192.

niques, and institutions to serve the needs of large-scale business and finance.[1]

Unfortunately, the interests they serve frequently contravene the welfare of other social classes. Corporation lawyers have made it possible for business men to accumulate more and more wealth at the expense of the general public.[2] They have devised methods, as William Howard Taft once pointed out, for fighting organized labor and lay groups concerned with labor legislation.[3] And, ironically enough, they have played an important role in the creation of title and trust companies, insurance companies, and other agencies which carry on useful functions in a generally efficient manner but which have succeeded in depriving the legal profession itself of a large portion of its former business. At the dedication a few years ago of the Law Quadrangle of the University of Michigan, Mr. Justice Stone spoke excoriatingly of the alliance between lawyers and the corporate interests:

At its best the changed system has brought to the command of the business world loyalty and superb proficiency and technical skill. At its worst it has made the learned profession of an earlier day the obsequious servant of business, and tainted it with the morals and manners of the market place in its most antisocial manifestations.[4]

Because so many of the most able members of the bar are concerned chiefly with business law, the whole administration

---

[1] *Ibid.*, pp. 178–179. See also I. Maurice Wormser's "Legal Ethics in Theory and in Practice," in Annals of the American Academy of Political and Social Science, May, 1933, pp. 196–197.

[2] Clark, Charles E., "Legal Education in Modern Society." In Tulane Law Review, December, 1935, p. 6.

[3] Ethics of the Law. Hubbard Lectures, Albany Law School, May 21, 1914, pp. 15–16.

[4] Stone, Harlan F., "The Public Influence of the Bar." In Harvard Law Review, November, 1934, p. 7.

of justice suffers serious loss. What is almost equally serious is that the psychology of the corporation lawyer has permeated thousands of less successful attorneys. For them standards of public service are largely devoid of meaning. As a result, the number of competent and honest lawyers willing to struggle for civil liberties and personal rights rather than property rights, and to care for the interests of the poor and of persons of inadequate means is distressingly small. Newman Levy, a New York attorney, once made the searching comment:

> There is no other profession quite so smug and self-satisfied, and at the same time quite so lacking in a sense of social obligation. An occasional rare soul, a Clarence Darrow, may dedicate his energies to the defense of unpopular causes and earn the supercilious disapproval of his more orthodox brethren. Here and there in the lower courts may be found some obscure lawyer battling for the poor, the needy, and the oppressed without regard for the pecuniary rewards that spell professional success. But these are the freaks of the profession; they are, to use that most devastating epithet, the radicals. Most lawyers prefer to seek the more comfortable and reputable rewards of pecuniary success.[1]

NEW TRENDS IN THE PROMOTION OF JUSTICE

Having reviewed some of the major criticisms of the administration of justice in the United States, we now turn to a survey of new trends of a constructive nature for promoting justice. First, there are changes in the law itself. They are of two kinds: the changes that are constantly being made more or less automatically as law strives to adjust itself to evolutionary forces, and those that are the result of the work of agencies cre-

---

[1] "Lawyers and Morals." In Harper's Magazine, February, 1927, pp. 293–294.

ated for the express purpose of improving the law. Although changes of the first kind are of primary importance, they fall outside the scope of the present discussion. Something must be said, however, about those agencies that seek to effect alterations. They are at present attempting to make law more uniform in the several jurisdictions, to restate and recommend changes in the substantive law, and to improve the rules of procedure and conditions in the courts. Some of them have already achieved much that is of value; others have accomplished relatively little. Even when the results have been disappointing, they assume significance as witnesses of the recognition that improvements in law are needed and should be fostered through concerted and planned effort.

Another trend of perhaps greater current importance is that relating to our tribunals. Some reform in the courts has been achieved, although tardily; and, under the impetus of judicial councils and an awakened public opinion, the efficiency of business methods seems more likely to be instituted within the vast judicial system in the not distant future than has heretofore seemed possible. Moreover, new devices for obtaining quick and expert settlement of cases, such as administrative commissions and arbitration tribunals, are replacing trials before the courts.

In recognition of the fact that justice is denied to a great segment of the population because of economic inability to purchase legal assistance, various agencies have appeared of late for extending legal services to the poor. The work of these agencies will subsequently be reviewed, as will plans that are now being made for greatly enlarging the volume of legal assistance, at small fees, to persons of moderate means.

Finally, there is a growing appreciation among members of

the bar, which must be noted, of its professional responsibility for improving the administration of justice. In this connection the recent movement, known as the integrated bar, assumes potential significance.

IMPROVEMENT IN THE LAW

Uniform State Laws

The National Conference of Commissioners on Uniform State Laws, created in 1890 as an adjunct of the American Bar Association, is a semi-official body engaged in the preparation and promotion of uniform legislation. It is composed of three or more commissioners from each state, who are appointed by their respective governors, usually under official statutory sanction. The commissioners are judges, lawyers, and law-school teachers of outstanding ability, who contribute their services without compensation to the drafting of statutes that are submitted to all the states in the hope that uniform laws may be obtained. Each year during the week preceding the annual convention of the American Bar Association the Conference holds its regular meeting for the purpose of passing upon acts that have been drafted by committees during the intervening months.

In the forty-six years since the Conference made its appearance, it has met with a considerable degree of success chiefly in the field of commercial law. Some of its model acts that had been most widely accepted by 1937 were its Uniform Negotiable Instruments Act, which had been adopted in every state and the District of Columbia; the Uniform Warehouse Receipts Act, adopted in 45 states; the Uniform Sales Act, in 34; the Uniform Bills of Lading Act, in 28; the Uniform Stock

Transfer Act, and the Declaratory Judgments Act, in 24 each; and the Aeronautics Act, in 21.[1]

In the domain of legislation concerned with social welfare, the Conference has unfortunately been able to achieve relatively little. Although it has carefully prepared uniform acts on such subjects as marriage, divorce, child labor, and vital statistics, little response has been found in the legislatures of the various states. Only two of its statutes in this field have been favorably received; the Desertion and Non-Support Act, which had had 17 enactments by 1937, and the Narcotic Drug Act with 31 enactments.

In spite of the fact that the work of the Conference has generally been looked upon favorably, certain criticisms have been heard. Some members of the bar believe that any bill, which is drafted in a way to command uniform enactment in a large number of states, must be the result of so many compromises that it fails to represent the type of legislation suitable for more advanced states. The criticism has also been made that so much time elapses during the preparing of a uniform law that individual states frequently draft bills dealing with the particular subject without waiting for the model to be presented to them. The Conference recognized the validity of this second criticism in 1937, by amending its constitution so that it might give final approval to an act at the same session at which the act is introduced.

Because of the extensive demand for new legislation dealing with economic and social problems, another constitutional amendment was recently adopted by the Conference, which gives it the power to draft model acts dealing with "subjects suitable for interstate compacts" and "subjects in which uniformity will

---

[1] Report of the American Bar Association for 1937, pp. 1163–1168.

make more effective the exercise of state powers and promote interstate co-operation."[1] This amendment was the result of several decisions of the United States Supreme Court which denied to Congress the power to legislate on certain questions, and which indicated that the particular fields of legislation belonged exclusively to the states. In order to render drafting service to the states in these areas that seemed likely to require immediate consideration, the Conference decided to broaden its own powers.

Restatement of the Law

In reviewing the work of the Association of American Law Schools, reference was made to its participation in the creation of the American Law Institute. The Institute was established in 1923, as a permanent, incorporated, organization, "to promote the clarification and simplification of the law and its better adaptation to social needs, to secure the better administration of justice, and to encourage and carry on scholarly and scientific legal work."[2] In conferences held prior to the formation of the Institute, emphasis was placed upon the need for some plan to deal with the growing uncertainty of law. Attention was called to the fact that judicial decisions and legislative statutes had become so voluminous that it was almost impossible for the practicing lawyer to consult all those dealing with any one topic. Decisions on the same subject, moreover, differed widely. As a result of this unfortunate state of affairs, it was agreed that a thorough restatement of the law was of primary importance.

[1] "Current Events." In American Bar Association Journal, February, 1937, p. 149.
[2] Pound, Roscoe, "American Law Institute." In Encyclopaedia of the Social Sciences, 1930, vol. 2, p. 30.

The Institute, formed to attempt this restatement, is composed of elected members from the bar, and official delegates consisting of the chief justice of the highest court of each state and deans of the leading law schools. At the time of its establishment the Carnegie Corporation contributed more than a million dollars to finance its work during the first ten years.

Two projects have been undertaken: restatement of the substantive law and formulation of a model code of criminal procedure. The model code was completed and approved in 1931. Although it was widely acknowledged as a highly competent technical document, it appeared at a time when interest in the administration of criminal law was so slight that it received little consideration. Dean Herbert F. Goodrich of the University of Pennsylvania Law School noted in 1936, however, that the marked reawakening of concern about criminal justice had resulted in bringing the code to attention.[1] He pointed to the frequency with which it was being discussed by committees of bar associations, state commissions, and other bodies, and to the fact that each year portions of it were being enacted into law by various states.

The main project, restatement of the substantive law, is well under way. Eleven volumes have already appeared, devoted to such subjects as contracts, torts, agency, trusts, and conflict of laws. Three are in preparation, and four others will probably be published before the task of restatement is brought to a close.

When a study is undertaken, it is placed under the supervision of a "reporter," who is aided by assistants. Members of the bar and bench, and particularly law teachers serve as advisers. Frequent conferences of the director of the Institute, the

---

[1] "What Would Law Teachers Like to See the Institute Do?" In American Law School Review, May, 1936, p. 494.

reporter, and the advisers are held. When the material begins to assume shape, it is submitted to the Institute's council for discussion. Finally it is presented to the entire membership for further criticism. Thus the views of judges and attorneys from all parts of the United States are obtained. Committees of state bar associations annotate the drafts for the various jurisdictions, stating and discussing the pertinent local decisions and statutes if there are any, or noting that there is none. These annotations also indicate the relation of the restatement of the general law to local peculiarities.

Since the model code of criminal procedure has been completed and the work of restatement is well advanced, the future program of the Institute is receiving much consideration. One project proposed is investigation of substantive criminal law. Co-operative relations have already been established with the group at the Harvard Law School sponsoring research in international law, and with the New York Commission on Law Revision. The Institute has made an arrangement with the National Conference of Commissioners on Uniform State Laws whereby certain acts will be drafted by the two bodies jointly. It is also considering extensive independent drafting of statutes in instances where legislative action seems essential to supplement the common law.

The accomplishments of the Institute have received nationwide attention and much general approval. Dean Merton L. Ferson of the College of Law of the University of Cincinnati has said of its work that it is "perhaps the largest undertaking of its kind in all history. Certainly nothing comparable to this task has been accomplished since the days of Justinian."[1] Al-

---

[1] "Standards of Legal Education." In North Carolina Law Review, December, 1926, p. 40.

though this statement appears somewhat extravagant, Dean Charles E. Clark and William O. Douglas reported in Recent Social Trends in the United States that many persons regard the Institute as the outstanding contemporary development in the law.[1] There are others who regret the preoccupation of the organization with law as it is rather than as it should be, and fear that its restatements may have a deadening effect upon growth and reform. Restatement is not codification, although Roscoe Pound admits that there has been hope that it would result in some of the benefits of codification.[2] Whether such benefits could be achieved without the loss of a degree of flexibility essential to all evolution is a debatable question.

Among the criticisms that have been made of the work of the Institute, a recent one by Professor Hessel E. Yntema of the University of Michigan may be summarized.[3] The initial plan, as he understood it, contemplated a statement that would embody not only the law as it exists, but whatever improvements might be recommended by exhaustive study. The actual work has been substantially limited to restatement. "This departure from the original conception . . . is a material nullification of the major objective of the Institute."[4] Professor Yntema noted, moreover, that no definite position had been taken concerning modern statutory trends as contrasted with currents in judicial

[1] "Law and Legal Institutions." In Recent Social Trends in the United States, p. 1465.
[2] "American Law Institute." In Encyclopaedia of the Social Sciences, 1930, vol. 2, p. 30.
[3] "What Would Law Teachers Like to See the Institute Do?" in American Law School Review, May, 1936, pp. 505–506. For other criticisms and replies to them, see Robinson, Edward S., Law and the Lawyers, p. 36; Goodrich, Herbert F., "Institute Bards and Yale Reviewers," in University of Pennsylvania Law Review, February, 1936, pp. 450–453; Arnold, Thurman W., "Institute Priests and Yale Observers—A Reply to Dean Goodrich," in the same Review, May, 1936, pp. 812–824.
[4] *Ibid.*, p. 505.

decision. This ambiguity has been reflected in the material that has appeared, which fails to show any clear policy as to either the inclusion or the exclusion of statutory law. No citation and no critical discussion of any specific legal sources, furthermore, is included in the volumes, although a complete discussion of all relevant materials was originally prescribed. The proposal for studies in the field of legal procedure and the administration of justice has been disregarded except for the work in criminal procedure, and no specific provisions have ever been made for the comparative study of foreign experience, or for the consideration of pertinent data accumulated in the other social sciences.

In conclusion, he remarked that the affirmative evidence concerning the influence of the restatement of the law in alleviating defects in the legal system is as yet negligible. The burden of the mass of the law has been increased by the additional volumes rather than lessened.

Whether the total result will be to clarify uncertainty, to eliminate diversity, to create greater precision in legal terminology, or to enlighten the ignorance of judges and lawyers, is, in view of the limited scope of the Restatement, the generality of its rules, the absence of a critical explanation of the authorities, disputable to say the least.[1]

In replying to these criticisms and some presented by other speakers at the same meeting, William Draper Lewis, who has been director of the Institute since its inception, pointed to one defect in Professor Yntema's argument. He maintained that the restatement was conceived as an attempt to give orderly form to the existing law; it was not visualized as a method for correcting the defects in the law.[2] From this point of view,

[1] *Ibid.*, p. 506.　　　　　　　　　　[2] *Ibid.*, p. 511.

therefore, the work of the Institute in connection with the common law must be considered as only the first step, although a very important one, in what should be a continuing study. Such a study should utilize the many sources not yet drawn upon, and should have as its purpose the recommending of needed improvements in the law.

Law Revision Commission

In 1921 the late Mr. Justice (then Judge) Cardozo published in the Harvard Law Review a now famous article in which he pointed to the need for state ministries of justice that would concern themselves with examining the substantive law and recommending changes in it. He argued:

The courts are not helped as they could and ought to be in the adaptation of law to justice. The reason they are not helped is because there is no one whose business it is to give warning that help is needed. Today courts and legislature work in separation and aloofness. The penalty is paid both in the wasted effort of production and in the lowered quality of the product. On the one side, the judges, left to fight against anachronism and injustice by the methods of judge-made law, are distracted by the conflicting promptings of justice and logic, of consistency and mercy, and the output of their labors bears the tokens of the strain. On the other side, the legislature, informed only casually and intermittently of the needs and problems of the courts, without expert or responsible or disinterested or systematic advice as to the workings of one rule or another, patches the fabric here and there, and mars often when it would mend. Legislature and courts move on in proud and silent isolation. Some agency must be found to mediate between them.

This task of mediation is that of a ministry of justice. The duty must be cast on some man or group of men to watch the law in action, observe the manner of its functioning, and report the changes needed when function is deranged. . . .

Discharge of such a task requires an expenditure of time and energy, a single-hearted consecration, not reasonably to be expected of men in active practice. It exacts, too, a scholarship and a habit of research not often to be found in those immersed in varied duties. . . . A single committee should be organized as a ministry of justice. . . . How the committee should be constituted, is, of course, not of the essence of the project. My own notion is that the ministers should be not less than five in number. There should be representatives, not less than two, perhaps even as many as three, of the faculties of law or political science in institutes of learning. Hardly elsewhere shall we find the scholarship on which the ministry must be able to draw if its work is to stand the test. There should be, if possible, a representative of the bench; and there should be a representative or representatives of the bar.

Such a board would not only observe for itself the workings of the law as administered day by day. It would enlighten itself constantly through all available sources of guidance and instruction; through consultation with scholars; through study of the law reviews, the journals of social science, the publications of the learned generally; and through investigation of remedies and methods in other jurisdictions, foreign and domestic. . . .

A ministry of justice will be in a position to gather . . . recommendations together, and report where change is needed. Reforms that now get themselves made by chance or after long and vexatious agitation, will have the assurance of considerate and speedy hearing. Scattered and uncoordinated forces will have a rallying point and focus. System and method will be substituted for favor and caprice. . . . In the end, of course, the recommendations of the ministry will be recommendations and nothing more. The public will be informed of them. The bar and others interested will debate them. The legislature may reject them. But at least the lines of communication will be open. The long silence will be broken.[1]

Judge Cardozo's conception of a ministry of justice received wide attention. It was supported in many addresses and articles by leading members of the bar, and particularly by Dean

[1] Cardozo, Benjamin N., "A Ministry of Justice." In Harvard Law Review, December, 1921, pp. 113–114, 124–125.

Pound. In spite of all the favorable consideration that it received, only one state has, as yet, created such a ministry. That state is New York and the agency is known as the Law Revision Commission.

In 1934 when the Judicial Council was created in New York to advise the legislature and the courts about desirable changes and improvements in judicial procedure, the Law Revision Commission was set up simultaneously to make suggestions concerning the substantive law. The Commission was charged with the duty of examining the common law and the statutes of the state, as well as current judicial decisions, for the purpose of discovering defects and anachronisms in the law and recommending needed reforms.[1] It was also expected to consider changes in the law recommended by the American Law Institute, the National Conference of Commissioners on Uniform State Laws, bar associations, or other learned bodies. Finally, it was to receive and examine suggestions as to defects and anachronisms submitted by the bench and bar, public officials, and the laity. The Commission was directed by statute to report its proceedings annually to the legislature, and to accompany its report with proposed bills for carrying out any of its recommendations.

The Commission is composed of the chairmen of the committees on judiciary of the Senate and the Assembly, who serve in an ex-officio capacity, and of five members appointed by the governor for five-year terms of office. At present they are two law teachers, two members of the bar, and a layman. Professor John MacDonald of the Cornell University Law School is executive secretary and director of research.

When the Commission made its first report in 1935, it stated

---

[1] Facts concerning the Commission have been taken from the annual reports published by that body.

that it had begun the study of the common law and the statutes of the state. At the request of a member of the judiciary, an examination had also been begun of the reports of the courts during the last quarter of a century in order to see to what extent these bodies had been controlled by rules of law badly adapted to current needs. Thirteen bills had been introduced into the legislature at its recommendation. Nine had become law.

Since then the large research projects have continued, and the Commission has authorized study directed toward a revision of the penal law of the state. This will involve consolidating in one chapter of the law all of the penal provisions, which are now widely scattered. Inconsistencies and duplications are to be eliminated, and the material will be reclassified on a scientific basis. Suggestions for several hundred projects have been received. Many of these have had to be rejected, as being inappropriate subjects for study or for other reasons. Some, however, have furnished valuable subjects for investigation. In addition to the reports, accompanied by bills, that have been submitted to each legislative session, the Commission has made several studies in highly specialized fields that warranted examination but which have not led to recommendations for legislation. Other studies, undertaken at the express request of the governor, have dealt with the law as it relates or might be made to relate to the "public enemy," psychiatric examinations in criminal trials, and so on.

The degree to which the Commission will succeed in effecting the purposes for which it was created only time will reveal. When other states will set up similar bodies is also unknown. As has been fittingly said, however, the existence of the New York agency may represent the beginning of a movement to subject our substantive law, civil and criminal, "to expert examination with the legislators acting as final arbitrators of the conflicts of interest which any large-scale scheme of reform is bound to develop."[1]

Judicial Councils

Progress in effecting much needed improvements in the regular courts has been made very slowly. One of the reasons may long have been the absence of any official body charged with this responsibility. During recent years a new agency—the judicial council—has been formed in about half of the states for the express purpose of examining their judicial structure and procedure and of suggesting desirable changes. Although this agency is not primarily engaged in improvement in the law to the same extent as are the other agencies already described, it has been included here because it occasionally has responsibility for studying the substantive law and nearly always is expected to examine the law of procedure.

A judicial council is an official agency by virtue of the fact that it is created by statute. Its members are generally appointed by the governor or chief justice, or are otherwise carefully selected. They are usually representative of both bench and bar, and sometimes of the legislature, the laity, and the law schools. For many years the American Judicature Society has emphasized the potential merits of these councils, and it is largely through the efforts of that organization that such bodies have come into being. The first one was created in 1923 in Ohio. Massachusetts, Maryland, and California established similar agencies in 1924. Since then growth has been continu-

[1] Warner, Sam B., and Cabot, Henry B., "Changes in the Administration of Criminal Justice during the Past Fifty Years." In Harvard Law Review, February, 1937, p. 609.

ous, although slow. In 1930 a National Conference of Judicial Councils was formed for discussion of problems relating to its constituency. Recently the Carnegie Corporation has offered financial assistance to the Conference, and, beginning with the autumn of 1938, Roscoe Pound will devote part of his time to its work.

The function which judicial councils have most readily, and perhaps most successfully, performed is that of collection of statistical data about the courts. When they entered this field the lack of such data was everywhere apparent. Some councils have evolved a statistical system comparable to that which has existed in European countries and which can be used as a basis for making recommendations concerning needed changes.

This leads us directly to the second function that councils have widely assumed: the task of submitting proposals for executive action by the governor or court, or for legislative action, about reorganization and reform of judicial administration. Two illustrations will portray the type of recommendations that may be made. The first, a recent suggestion by the well-established Council of Connecticut, is of interest because it seeks to eliminate, on a statewide basis, abuses similar to those to be described later as existing in Chicago before the creation of its municipal court. This Council advised the creation of a district court with branches in 33 localities to supplant 65 town, city, borough, and police courts, and "innumerable" justices of the peace, "which now operate as independent courts, having no common practice, no common standards, and which are accountable to no one in particular."[1]

The second illustration is drawn from the current report of

---

[1] "Review of Judicial Council Reports." In Journal of the American Judicature Society, June, 1937, p. 18.

the Judicial Council of the State of New York.[1] Among numerous recommendations appearing in that official document are three of broad significance, which are of particular concern here because they were designed to create a greater degree of centralization of judicial administration and a considerable amount of reorganization. These recommendations would require amendments to the state constitution. The Council unanimously suggested that the ultimate administrative supervision of all courts in New York State should be vested in the Court of Appeals or the Appellate Division of the Supreme Court. Although the Appellate Division now has certain supervisory powers over both the Supreme Court and some of the lower courts in New York City, it recommended that these powers be consolidated and broadened. It believed, furthermore, that the administrative body should be permitted to make temporary emergency assignments of certain judges to courts other than their own. After stating that it was not yet prepared to offer definite suggestions for reorganization of courts outside of New York City, it advised that the five county courts of that city be abolished and their jurisdiction be combined in the Supreme Court. It counseled, finally, that the present City Court and Municipal Court be wiped out and one new court be created in their place, and that the same procedure be applied to the Court of Special Sessions and the Magistrates' Courts.

In a few states the Council is vested with power to make rules for some or all of the courts. A fourth function, which has been granted only to the Judicial Council of California—although it is badly needed elsewhere—is administrative control of the courts. Through such control judges are transferred

---

[1] Fourth Annual Report of the Judicial Council of the State of New York. Legislative Document 48, 1938, pp. 39–40.

from one court to another as need arises, thus equalizing work and aiding congested institutions to keep abreast of their calendars. The latest report of the California Council tells how cases before the several courts of appeal have been spared long delays by aid from judges of the superior courts.[1]

The degree of success with which councils have met has differed widely from state to state. The councils of Massachusetts, California, and Connecticut were reported in 1933 to have achieved far more than those of other states.[2] The success of these three bodies was attributed to the fact that they consisted of reasonably small numbers, had adequate supervision and technical knowledge, and had sufficient funds. The Council created in 1934 in New York has made a notable record as an investigating, advisory, and recommending body. In several states little has been accomplished because of almost insuperable problems. Only in California have councils been permitted to exercise authority over the courts; they have been accorded scant attention by bar associations; and most of them have been seriously handicapped by lack of financial resources.[3]

The potential value of judicial councils will probably not be fully realized until more power is vested in them. Kenneth Dayton has insisted that they should have both regulatory power over the courts, and disciplinary power over judges, clerks, and other employes, so that inefficient persons could be removed from office.[4] Their authority, moreover, should be so extended

[1] "Review of Judicial Council Reports." In Journal of the American Judicature Society, June, 1937, p. 17.
[2] Clark, Charles E., and Douglas, William O., "Law and Legal Institutions." In Recent Social Trends in the United States, p. 1462.
[3] "Review of Judicial Council Reports." In Journal of the American Judicature Society, June, 1937, p. 16.
[4] "A Program for Legal Reform in the United States." In The Consensus, October, 1931, p. 39.

that they would be free to make all court rules regulating practice and procedure. They should be as responsible for the satisfactory administration of justice within a state as the governor and legislature are responsible for their respective tasks. Mr. Dayton confessed in 1931 to skepticism about how much councils would be able to achieve. He pointed to the hesitancy of legislatures to grant authority necessary for undertaking any extensive reforms; the "suspicion" of those bodies toward recommendations offered; and their failure to act favorably upon many of the proposals. Thus any council that "attempted . . . a thorough-going examination of the law not only would be unable to secure adoption of sweeping proposals, but it would be likely to find itself legislated out of existence."[1] It is significant to note, in this connection, that the New York Constitutional Convention, now in session, may provide that the Judicial Council be given constitutional power to effect, and not merely to recommend, changes in court practice and procedure, possibly subject to legislative veto.

DEVELOPMENTS IN THE COURTS AND IN NEW TRIBUNALS

Reform in the Courts

Although the American Judicature Society long ago advocated the desirability of having all the courts of a state knit together in a single structural organization, nothing has been achieved on so extensive a scale. Constitutional conventions have been held in New York, Illinois, and Missouri that have incorporated, in proposed amended constitutions, programs for complete or partial unification of courts. In all three instances the plans were rejected by the voters in statewide political con-

---

[1] *Ibid.*, p. 40.

tests, waged only in small part around the question of changes in the judicial system. Charles G. Haines, professor of political science at the University of California, has stated that opinions differ widely, among those acquainted with the problem, of the extent to which it would be practicable to unify all the courts of some states.[1] He recognized that existing arrangements were indefensible, but maintained that situations in large or sparsely settled areas such as Texas, California, and Montana differ radically from those in small or densely populated commonwealths like Connecticut and Rhode Island. He doubted, therefore, whether general principles of centralization could be applied without doing violence to local conditions and requirements.

If unification has not been achieved in any jurisdiction on a statewide basis, it has been tried in certain of the courts of an occasional city or county. This has been particularly true of a few of the municipal courts that have replaced the archaic, extremely inefficient, and sometimes dissolute justices of the peace and police courts.

Chicago was the first city to create a unified municipal court.[2] The situation that existed prior to its establishment would seem almost incredible to one unacquainted with judicial administration in American cities. The Chicago courts as a whole were in a disorganized condition, functions overlapped, and calendars were years in arrears. In an address presented before the Louisiana State Bar Association on May 8, 1915, Mr. Harley said: "This disgraceful situation would have been more poignant were it not for the pestering bites of a whole swarm of petty

---

[1] "The General Structure of Court Organization." In Annals of the American Academy of Political and Social Science, May, 1933, p. 5.

[2] For further details see Edward B. Boies' "The Executive Judge," and Herbert Harley's "The Argument for Judicial Rule-Making," in Annals of the American Academy of Political and Social Science, May, 1933, pp. 13–14 and 91–93 respectively.

judicial officers, fifty-four in number, who, as justices of the peace and police magistrates, acted as an effective counter-irritant against all other shortcomings of the courts." In addition there were 100 constables, many of whom, according to Mr. Harley, were common criminals. "They made false returns, they extorted money, and even shot down those who resisted them. In the world's greatest melting pot where all the tongues of Christendom are spoken, the opportunity for such licensed rogues to prey upon ignorant aliens was unexcelled."[1]

In 1906 the independent justice of the peace and police courts were eliminated, and their jurisdiction was conferred upon a new Municipal Court. In criminal matters this Court had authority over all misdemeanors, and could examine and hold for trial persons who had committed felonies. In civil matters its authority extended to all contract cases, regardless of the amount at stake, and to cases of tort where not more than $1,000 was involved. Provision was made, moreover, for transferring cases from any of the other local courts in order to secure prompt trial.

Significant as was the formation of a single, strong court to replace the large number of petty ones, the provisions designated for its administration were equally significant. To the chief justice was assigned the responsibility of being the administrative head of the organization, and of directing and controlling its operations as would a general manager. In addition to superintending the business of the Court, he was authorized to preside at a monthly meeting of the associate judges; to assign these judges to duty wherever necessary for prompt disposition of cases; to supervise preparation of the calendars of

[1] Willoughby, W. F., Principles of Judicial Administration. Brookings Institution, 1929, p. 283.

cases for trial; and to receive every month from his associates reports of the time they had spent in attendance in court. The purpose in authorizing the chief justice to preside at a monthly meeting of the municipal judges was to create a council that would consider all matters affecting the proper administration of justice in the court. Finally the right was conferred upon the Court to formulate its own rules of procedure. Because it did not have to follow rules determined by statute, it was able to create simple and direct methods that would conform to the needs of the several special branches into which the Court was organized and could be modified when necessary.

In operating the Court on a businesslike basis it soon became apparent that, if cases of a similar type were assigned to the same judge, he would shortly become an expert in the handling of them. This principle of specialization was applied to all work of the institution with resulting increased efficiency. Finally, it was carried even farther when special branches began to be created to deal with problems needing very different methods of treatment. These branches included domestic relations, morals, boys, traffic, small claims, and so on.

Although the Municipal Court had a notable history under the guidance of Harry Olson, who held the chief justiceship for nearly a quarter of a century, judicial unification in Chicago did not extend beyond the substitution of that tribunal for the unrelated inferior courts of the city. The Recorders Court, established in Detroit in 1920, carried the process of centralization one step farther.[1] In it was vested complete jurisdiction over all criminal cases, whether of the grade of misdemeanors or felonies. As a result, it was possible to establish an efficient system of specialization for the trial of cases. To one division

[1] *Ibid.,* p. 290.

of the Court, for example, were given all ordinance cases; to another, petty misdemeanors; to a third, major misdemeanors; and so on.

Even where unification of courts has not been attempted, some improvement in the administration of justice has been gained through the application of methods of business management, and of specialization; through simplification of procedure; and through general improvement in the tone of the tribunals and in the attitude of the participating counsel.[1] Illustration of what has been achieved in these ways—and could be achieved in hundreds of other places—has been recorded by Edward B. Boies, a New York attorney, in his description of the Cleveland Court of Common Pleas and the Circuit Court of Wayne County, Michigan,[2] and in Chief Justice Homer G. Powell's account of his own work in the Cleveland Court of Common Pleas.[3]

Administrative Commissions

One of the most striking innovations in this country in recent times is the rise of administrative commissions or boards composed of non-judicial officers. It is the function of these commissions to exercise control over certain aspects of the economic and industrial system where regulation is deemed necessary in the interest of public welfare. They often perform tasks that are both supervisory and judicial in character. Hence they occupy a position between the legislative and executive branches of government on the one hand and the courts on the other. In

[1] Harley, Herbert, "Administering Justice in Cities." In Annals of the American Academy of Political and Social Science, March, 1928, pp. 88–92.
[2] "The Executive Judge." In Annals of the American Academy of Political and Social Science, May, 1933, pp. 14–22.
[3] "The Cleveland Court of Common Pleas." In Annals of the American Academy of Political and Social Science, May, 1933, pp. 24–31.

order that they may be restrained from the assumption of unauthorized power or from the abuse of administrative discretion, provision has generally been made for appeal to the courts of cases coming before them. There is a growing tendency, however, for legislatures to grant them increasingly greater power in the making of final decisions. The trend of judicial review, moreover, has been toward enlarging the area on which the less expert and farther removed judicial body may not impinge.

Commissions are of two types: federal and state. The first important federal one was the Interstate Commerce Commission, created by act of Congress in 1887. Conspicuous among the long list of other federal bodies that have been established since the beginning of the twentieth century are the Federal Reserve Board, Federal Trade Commission, Employee's Compensation Commission, Federal Power Commission, Federal Communications Commission, Securities and Exchange Commission, National Industrial Relations Board, and so on.

Important as are these agencies, the administrative tribunals of the several states are far more numerous and pervasive in their influence.[1] State boards, which were originally limited to supervision of public works and tax assessments and to management of state institutions, now regulate vast areas of our social life. Among the almost innumerable state bodies are public utility commissions; motor vehicle commissions; boards supervising and enforcing labor laws; commissions controlling the marketing of securities; workmen's compensation boards; zoning boards; commissions, often vested with disciplinary powers, for licensing professions and even trades; education commissions for maintaining standards of public education; health

---

[1] Clark, Charles E., and Douglas, William O., "Law and Legal Institutions," in Recent Social Trends in the United States, pp. 1470–1471.

boards with licensing and inspection prerogatives; banking commissions for the regulation of banks, credit unions, and small loan companies; and various agencies for controlling sports and amusements, forests, water power, minerals, game, fish, and so on.

Why should judicial functions have been granted to commissions instead of the courts? The answer is that the judicial system has been too slow, cumbersome, and ineffectual to deal with situations where speed, flexibility, and specialized knowledge are essential. In an era when institutions are highly complex in nature, many of the problems that arise are too technical to be handled by the average judge. There has been a demand, therefore, for bodies of experts whose training has been other than that of the law.[1]

Commissions have been the result of this demand. They relieve the courts of a vast amount of work. At the same time they serve purposes that are foreign to the judiciary, and their procedure is frequently very different. Although the rights of the individual are protected because they are obliged to act within the law, they emphasize the public interest and minimize the old individualistic common law conceptions of legal relationships.[2] They determine cases upon the basis of considerations drawn from sources other than the traditional ones of law. Investigation and the collection of factual material play an important role in their work. Through the data secured they are able to render decisions based on more complete information than can be readily obtained from partisan testimony in court.

In their executive, as contrasted with their judicial, capacity

[1] Landis, James M., "The Implications of Modern Legislation to Law Teaching." In American Law School Review, April, 1935, p. 158.
[2] Blachly, Frederick F., and Oatman, Miriam E., "Administrative Courts." In Encyclopaedia of the Social Sciences, 1931, vol. 4, p. 532.

these commissions attempt to substitute a greater degree of regulation for the partial control that courts provide. Borrowers, for example, are protected from loan sharks through the licensing and supervision of lenders and not solely by the bringing of cases before the courts. Because of the examination and licensing of physicians, the sole protection of the patient is no longer an action for malpractice. Scores of new procedures and techniques different from those used by the courts have been evolved to effect nicer adjustments of social conditions.

In spite of the continuous growth of administrative tribunals and the great power that has been vested in them by legislative bodies, they have not acquired the high sanction and dignity accorded the courts. Their actions have been considered bureaucratic, the wisdom of their rulings has been criticised, and their fairness challenged.

It may be that their phenomenal rise to places of importance in modern life in a relatively short period of time, the informality of their proceedings, the speed of much of their activity, the absence of elaborate procedures, the direct and intimate contact with parties affected, the absence of aloofness and independence associated with courts, and their occasional political complexion all militate against a ready acceptance of them as vital and important governmental agencies.[1]

If these tribunals have failed to win warm popular support, they have received even less approval from the bar. Vigorous protests have been uttered whenever a new one has been created. Solicitor General Jackson has stated that the efforts of the law to extend its function and to reduce the area of economic or

---

[1] Clark, Charles E., and Douglas, William O., "Law and Legal Institutions." In Recent Social Trends in the United States, p. 1479. See also Thurman W. Arnold's, The Folklore of Capitalism, Yale University Press, New Haven, 1937, p. 372.

social anarchy and lawless irresponsibility have always met with opposition from the average lawyer. He has never adapted himself to the administrative method. "In spite of abstract reverence for law and order, he fears extension of the field of law. He thinks of his Constitution, not as a source of power to advance the general welfare but only as a document of limitation."[1] So great has been the disapproval of the bar that it has asserted that these agencies are "threatening the whole machinery of justice," and it has demanded that "the decision of controversies of a judicial character must be brought back into the judicial system."[2]

An alert bar, in Mr. Jackson's estimation, would have made the reforms necessary to prevent the decision of such controversies from being taken out of the judicial system. Yet nearly all efforts at reform have been defeated by lawyers and by legislators, generally with approval of the bar associations. Recognition of the need for a new attitude toward administrative agencies and of the responsibility of the legal profession in this matter was expressed in 1937 by a representative of the House of Delegates of the American Bar Association as follows:[3]

Complete return in administrative matters to stiff, cumbersome, dilatory and expensive procedure of courts and legislatures is unthinkable. . . . Those of us who would complain that the judicial function is slipping away from the judicial system and our profession, may well consider why and by whose motion (or default) this is taking place. Administrative boards have sprung up because they have held promise of expeditious, accurate, effective, and inexpensive

[1] Jackson, Robert H., "The Bar and the New Deal." In American Law School Review, April, 1935, p. 156.

[2] *Ibid.*, p. 155.

[3] Gambrell, E. Smythe, "The Improvement of Administrative Law: An Opportunity for the Legal Profession." In American Bar Association Journal, February, 1937, p. 93.

action. Their creation represented in part the public's revolt against a court system which exalted contentiousness. The necessity for the establishment of some of these agencies might have been obviated by our seasonably dredging the existing channels of justice. We of the legal profession must be ceaselessly aware of the fact that the continued existence of the legal profession, the courts and other social and political institutions will, and ought to, be influenced and determined by the extent of their abiding social usefulness.[1]

Arbitration

Arbitration is another device for the settlement of controversies out of court.[2] In respect to its purpose and method it is similar to conciliation, that will be described later. It has, however, one significant advantage: arbitrators are not restricted merely to seeking to induce the parties concerned to reach an agreement regarding the matters at issue. They have authority to render decisions that not only are binding upon the parties but are enforceable in court. Arbitration provides all the advantages that characterize conciliation tribunals and administrative commissions: promptness, convenience, elimination of heavy court costs, avoidance of technicalities, specialized personnel, emphasis upon justice rather than the strict letter of the law, relief of the courts, and so on.

The almost exclusive field of arbitration until recently has been that of commercial disputes, where matters of fact rather than of law are involved. Commodities valued at billions of

[1] Since the foregoing pages were written, the New York Times noted on June 19, 1938, that a committee on administrative law of the American Bar Association has recently issued a report in which, among other criticisms of administrative agencies, it points to the tendencies of such bodies to yield to political pressure at the expense of law.

[2] Although arbitration has been used extensively for a long period in some countries and has had a limited application in the United States since colonial days, it has been utilized here widely only so recently that it must be considered as a new trend in the administration of justice.

dollars are bought and sold every year under contracts which provide that differences be arbitrated according to specified rules.

An important feature in the use of arbitration by a trade association is the selection of certain of its members to whom disputes may be referred. These members are men thoroughly familiar with all the technical features and trade customs of the business to which the association relates. Consequently, they do not have to be instructed through testimony or otherwise, as would judges in the ordinary courts, regarding technicalities, but can proceed at once to a consideration of the particular facts at issue.

Arbitration may be resorted to in one of two ways: either by the agreement of parties at the time of entering into a contract that all disputes arising under it shall be adjusted by arbitration; or by the participants in a dispute agreeing, after the difference has arisen, to submit the matter to arbitration. The desirability of the first in preference to the second method is obvious. In fact, little development of arbitration can be expected unless business men contract in advance to utilize this method for the settlement of subsequent difficulties.[1]

Arbitration has not advanced in the United States so far as in England, but it has made substantial progress. Forty-six states have laws of some kind pertaining to it. In many of them arbitration is ineffective because parties can withdraw from the proceedings at any time before the award is made; because the awards are not deemed final but subject to revision by the courts; and because insufficient provision is made for arbitrators to secure rulings from the courts upon points of law. New York has the distinction of being the first jurisdiction to secure

---

[1] Willoughby, W. F., Principles of Judicial Administration, pp. 54, 71–72.

an effective statewide statute. Since its enactment in 1920, 13 other states have passed acts generally modeled after it.

Upon the tenth anniversary in 1936 of the founding of the American Arbitration Association this organization issued a report of the progress that had been made in arbitration since 1926.[1] A brief résumé of the report will furnish information about recent developments in this important field. In 1926 the protection of merchandise and traders was the chief concern of arbitration. During the last decade arbitration has been extended to include not only the relations of buyers and sellers, but those of some brokers and customers, architects and builders, contractors and owners, authors and publishers, landlords and tenants, debtors and creditors, engineers and clients, doctors and patients, lawyers and clients, and so on through a long list. Whole fields of controversy, for example, those pertaining to the theater, have been withdrawn from litigation by the voluntary acceptance of arbitration for the settling of disputes.

Until recently arbitration was looked upon as a small claims remedy. This is no longer true. Large sums of money are sometimes involved in the cases presented. If measured in financial terms alone, arbitration has expanded since 1926 to an unprecedented extent. Arbitrators, moreover, have finally come to command the confidence of the public. Most phenomenal of all, in the estimation of the Association, has been the recent change of attitude of attorneys in New York and to some degree in other cities. Although the American Bar Association has warmly endorsed and promoted the use of arbitration there was long much distrust of it and even active opposition from many members of the bar who feared that it would interfere with the

[1] Decennial Report of American Arbitration Association on the Progress of Commercial Arbitration. Published by the Association, New York, 1936, pp. 8–14.

practice of law. That this distrust is gradually disappearing is evidenced by the fact that hundreds of lawyers are appearing in organized tribunals to argue cases for their clients, while other hundreds are serving on panels of arbitrators.

Before bringing this discussion to an end something should be said of the American Arbitration Association, that was

formed . . . for the purpose of establishing and maintaining a national system of commercial arbitration, and to carry on the education and research necessary to the development of such a system, and to provide an arbitration tribunal available in any part of the country in which commercial disputes could be settled in record time and at little cost by submitting them to impartial arbitrators of the parties' own choosing.[1]

The American Arbitration Tribunal, maintained by the Association, offers a quasi-judicial system of arbitration operated in accordance with the prevailing laws of the several states, which is open to any parties willing to arbitrate under its rules. The functions of this Tribunal are limited to controversies that the parties have agreed, in writing, to submit to arbitration.

The arbitrators who handle disputes referred to the Tribunal are drawn from a permanent body, known as the National Panel of Arbitrators. This body is composed of some 6,000 members, representing a wide diversity of occupations and organizations, in 1,600 cities of the United States. About 2,000 of these persons are located in New York City, where the largest volume of arbitration is carried on. Representatives of a special panel of lawyers, maintained by the Association, are subject to call when questions of law are involved or when the parties concerned prefer that the arbitrator be a lawyer.

---

[1] Quoted from pamphlet entitled, American Arbitration Association, New York, n.d., p. 11.

Administration of the Tribunal is vested in a committee which appoints and maintains the National Panel. It receives requests for arbitration, and makes complete arrangements for subsequent hearings. The Tribunal is supported largely by the administrative fees that are charged the parties, or by appropriations made by trade or other commercial organizations which use it and exempt their members from payment of individual fees. Costs are fully standardized, and parties know in advance what the expenses will be. The arbitrators themselves receive no compensation.

Between 1926 and 1936 more than 5,600 controversies were referred to the Association for arbitration, and the settlement of almost an equal number of disputes was facilitated without arbitration. These figures do not include the many arbitrations conducted in special trade tribunals where the Association assisted in an administrative or advisory capacity. The spirit in which the awards were accepted is evidenced by the fact that in 88 per cent of the cases the decision was immediately complied with, and did not have to be filed in court for enforcement.

Besides the work that the Association carries on through its Tribunal, it engages extensively in research and promotional activities. Until its creation, there had been no national agency concerned with the collection and dissemination of knowledge about arbitration, and the literature was very fragmentary. The Arbitration Journal that appears quarterly and is the only publication of its kind in the United States, attempts to present all aspects of arbitration, not only as they are evolving in this country but in others. The Association also maintains a technical information service, and arranges public meetings, which offer "the only open forum in the world for the discussion of industrial or commercial or economic subjects in which arbitration is given a specific place."[1]

LEGAL SERVICE FOR THE POOR

Earlier pages have pointed to the indisputable fact that our fine old philosophical concept of justice as a right and not a privilege has little meaning for thousands of poor persons. As Reginald Heber Smith and John S. Bradway have declared in their recent book on Growth of Legal-Aid Work in the United States, "Poverty today does stand in the way of complete justice, and it will continue to do so until public opinion forces a radical overhauling of our archaic system of court costs and fees."[2] The poor are faced, however, with the problem of obtaining legal assistance more often than with that of obtaining their "day in court." It is generally agreed that there can be no comprehensive reform in the administration of justice unless provision is made for furnishing the services of competent attorneys who will advise impecunious clients as to their rights and how such rights may be protected.

Assigned Counsel

Because the lawyer is bound by his professional oath to render gratuitous service to poor persons, it has long been customary for the court to assign counsel to those who cannot furnish their own attorney. Sometimes lawyers are paid nominal fees by the state, and in cases of murder they are paid more gener-

---

[1] Decennial Report of the American Arbitration Association, p. 21.

[2] U. S. Department of Labor, Bureau of Labor Statistics, Bulletin 607, 1936, p. 17. The discussion of Legal Service for the Poor, unless otherwise indicated, follows closely both the facts and interpretations presented by these two authors in Growth of Legal-Aid Work in the United States, or by Mr. Smith in his earlier book, Justice and the Poor, published by the Carnegie Foundation, 1919.

ously. The practice of assigned counsel has generally been followed only in criminal cases, although civil cases constitute the great volume of instances in which wage-earners find themselves in difficulty. Even when used in criminal cases, it has frequently been unsatisfactory. Service is often rendered by attorneys who have just entered the profession and hence may not have the requisite experience. What is even more serious, it is often provided by "jail lawyers," "shysters," or "ambulance chasers"—men who have succeeded "by intimidation, threats, extortion, and even worse, in putting the assignment system on a commercial basis."[1] They are generally attorneys of small practice who, because of poor legal preparation or insufficient practice of an ethical nature, have been forced to utilize the unethical methods of "professional" assigned counsel. No comment is necessary about a system of justice which permits such a situation to exist. When experienced attorneys are assigned to cases, they are inclined to neglect the poor for clients whose work is more remunerative.

Unsatisfactory as has been the practice of assigned counsel in this country, Smith and Bradway agree that it should not be abandoned but that its effectiveness should be strengthened through better legislation.[2] They point to notable steps taken by the New York Legislature in 1935, when it was decided that a poor person might "bring a special proceeding" as well as a suit. The court was empowered to assign counsel to serve without compensation unless there were a recovery. In instances of recovery, the court was entitled to allow the attorney a reasonable sum for his work and disbursements. The new law rendered more flexible the definition of "poor person" by raising

[1] Smith, Reginald Heber, Justice and the Poor, p. 114.
[2] Growth of Legal-Aid Work in the United States, p. 30.

from $100 to $300 the amount of cash or property that he might have without being disqualified. Besides the right of bringing a case into trial court, the poor were given the right to appeal their case to a higher court without the payment of fees to any officers.

Public Defender

Adequate provision for assignment of counsel can unquestionably do much to improve the administration of justice in small communities and rural areas. In great cities, however, where the need for much legal service is imperative, better means of solving the problem can be devised. One of these is the creation of the office of defender. The term commonly used is that of "public defender," although some lawyers who act as defenders are employed by private agencies and should more rightly be called voluntary or private defenders. Thus far the office of defender has been concerned almost exclusively with criminal cases, and hence the contribution of this method for aiding the indigent must be thought of as largely limited to one restricted field of legal work.

Although the concept of a public defender was discussed in America as early as the end of the eighteenth century, it was not until 1913 that provision was made for such an office. In that year Los Angeles County provided for the first defender in criminal cases. Shortly afterward defenders were brought into the municipal courts in Portland, Oregon, and in Columbus, Ohio; one was introduced to the Superior Court of Omaha; and the office of police court defender was created in the city of Los Angeles. In 1917, in New York City, the Voluntary Defenders Committee, a private agency, began to provide the service of a defender. Two years later its work was merged with that of the New York Legal Aid Society. A limited number of cities and counties have subsequently introduced the plan.

The following description is given of the Office of Public Defender in Los Angeles County, partly because it has developed extensive size and importance since its inception, but also because it has come to care for civil as well as criminal cases.

At the present time the work is handled by Frederick H. Vercoe, who occupies the position of Public Defender, and by twelve assistants all of whom are lawyers selected from a civil service list.[1] Its functions in criminal cases are similar to those of comparable agencies. In civil matters the Office has the authority to prosecute wage and other demands for plaintiffs financially unable to employ counsel, providing the sum involved does not exceed $100 and the claims appear valid and enforceable in the courts. The Office also defends poor persons who are being persecuted or unjustly harassed.

The magnitude of the work of the Los Angeles agency may be seen from figures presented by Mr. Vercoe for the fiscal year 1933–1934, when 43,071 persons applied for legal assistance in civil and criminal matters. Of the 26,953 who asked for aid in civil problems, 18,286 were advised about their rights under the law; 2,540 presented claims for wages due, property detained, and so on, which were handled and adjusted; 3,098 were refused assistance because they were able to pay an attorney or because their cases fell outside the jurisdiction of the Office; and 3,029 were referred to lawyers on a panel maintained and approved by the Los Angeles Bar Association. More than $38,000 was recovered for the poor in civil cases during the year.

On the criminal side, the Office handled 2,669 cases in the Superior Court of Los Angeles County. They represented nearly 60 per cent of all cases coming before that Court during the year. Twelve hundred of the 2,669 cases were set for trial, but 784 were

[1] Facts presented about the Office of Public Defender in Los Angeles County have been taken from a typewritten report submitted by Mr. Vercoe in January, 1935, and from correspondence with Hatch Graham, senior civil deputy.

disposed of by various means without trial, principally by changing the pleas of defendants from not guilty to guilty. Only 416 were actually tried. Mr. Vercoe believes that in each instance the rights of the defendant, under the law, were fully protected and accorded him. Had there not been a public defender, the Office estimates that at least 600 more cases would have been tried in 1933–1934. According to Mr. Vercoe this would have necessitated five more superior courts assigned to criminal work and functioning full time. Since it costs about $50,000 a year for Los Angeles County to operate one such court while the entire cost of the Office for both criminal and civil cases in 1934–1935 was only $56,000, the conclusion has been reached that the Office saves the taxpayers annually at least four times the expense of maintaining it.

Arguments both for and against the system of public defender have been numerous. Some years ago when the executive committee of the Cleveland Bar Association examined the plan, it cited many of them.[1] In favor of defenders was the belief that their offices would be more economical than the paying of fees to individual attorneys; they would provide, in general, better defense than the usual assigned counsel; the defendant would be assured of good preparation both in the law and in the facts of the case; a distinct saving of time would result; there would be a tendency to sift the deserving cases from the undeserving; they would aid the indigent defendant in obtaining a minimum sentence by entering a plea of guilty when such a plea was justified; fewer unscrupulous and perjured defenses would be attempted in court; the general tone of the criminal courts would be raised.

Arguments against the system were as follows: the defender would become so hardened to the stories of defendants that he might become indifferent to the justice of each case or he might

[1] "Cleveland Bar Opposes Public Defender Plan." In American Bar Association Journal, March, 1931, p. 141.

become inclined to disbelieve their stories; he would not show the same degree of enthusiasm as would the attorney assigned to defend a particular case; as the result of indifference and lack of enthusiasm, he would be likely to recommend that pleas of "guilty" be entered; the office of defender would create another political position with the likelihood of accompanying patronage and corruption; many cases would be prosecuted and defended by the same group of men, because the prosecutor and defender would often act together. On the basis of these criticisms the committee opposed the use of public defenders, and recommended continuation of the system of assigned counsel with certain changes and improvements in that system.

In their recent study, Smith and Bradway have reviewed and evaluated some of these criticisms and many others that have been made.[1] They maintain that there is now a sufficient body of experience to dispel many of the fears of earlier years regarding the value of the office of defender, and they find reason to hope that the plan will be extended in the future to all of the larger cities of the country. They point to the splendid work which is being done under public auspices in Los Angeles County, to the remarkable results obtained under private auspices in New York City, and to the creditable records of several other cities, including Chicago, Minneapolis, and San Francisco. They estimate that in 1933 some 38,000 persons must have received assistance in criminal cases. Yet they maintain that the position of defender has scarcely done more than make its appearance in the United States. It is still limited to a very few cities.

In spite of its present restricted use, Mayer C. Goldman, a New York attorney who has devoted himself for twenty years

[1] Growth of Legal-Aid Work in the United States, pp. 73-80.

to forwarding the movement by writing and lecturing, is much encouraged over prospects for the future. He points to the Conference of Senior Circuit Judges, presided over by Mr. Chief Justice Hughes, which lately approved "in principle the appointment of a public defender where the amount of criminal business of a district court justifies the appointment. In other districts the district judge before whom a criminal case is pending should appoint counsel for indigent defendants."[1] In this resolution Mr. Goldman sees promise not only of the extension of the public defender to district courts but of an added impetus to the entire movement.

Specialized Courts

Institutions that have proved highly successful in aiding the poor are courts dealing with special types of cases, such as small claims and domestic relations. Small claims courts generally have jurisdiction in matters involving $50 or less that relate to claims for wages, debts, disputes about rent, board and lodging, detention of property under claim of lien, damage to personal property, and so on. These are the cases in which wage-earners are most likely to become involved.

The concept of the small claims court is relatively very new. The first one was established in 1913 in Cleveland under rules of the Municipal Court. In 1915 the Oregon Legislature provided by statute for a small claims department of the District Court of the county in which Portland is situated, and two years later extended the plan to all counties. Chicago, in 1916, and Philadelphia and Spokane in 1920, instituted similar courts or divisions of municipal courts. A great forward step was taken

---

[1] "Public Defender Plan Approved." In Journal of the American Judicature Society, December, 1937, pp. 131–132.

in 1921 when Massachusetts created a statewide system of courts for the hearing of all small claims and of tort cases where the amount did not exceed $35. Since then the movement, on a statewide basis, has spread slowly but steadily. By 1934 there were 16 states in which statutes provided for the establishment of such institutions. In general, this type of court has been found most necessary in those areas which are highly industrialized.

These courts are authorized by law to disregard established rules of pleading, procedure, and evidence. Emphasis is placed on impartial hearing and reasoned determination upon the basis of ascertained facts. Thus delays are eliminated and unnecessary costs are abolished. The court is so simple in plan that, aided by a judge and a clerk, persons can conduct their own cases, thereby avoiding the expenses of counsel and jury. In cities where these institutions exist, it is generally agreed that they are performing meritorious service for persons of small means who would otherwise be unable to obtain justice. The extent to which they are used is evidenced by the fact that between 1924 and 1932 the Minneapolis court averaged 11,000 cases annually. During the fiscal year ending June 30, 1937 the Small Claims Court in New York City disposed of more than 29,000 claims.[1]

Unfortunately the plan is not applicable to many sections of the country. The wide discretion and summary power implicit in the informal small claims procedure require that the court to which this procedure is intrusted be a well-organized, responsible municipal court, or, when the plan is instituted on a statewide basis, all the lower courts must maintain a high standard.

---

[1] Fourth Annual Report of the Judicial Council of the State of New York, Legislative Document 48, Albany, 1938, p. 132.

In many jurisdictions entire counties lack any system of courts that would make possible this form of administering justice.

Domestic relations courts first appeared as a means for the administration of the laws against family desertion and non-support, which were generally being strengthened after 1900. The first one was established in 1910 when the City Court of Buffalo created a domestic relations division.[1] In the same year New York City was authorized by legislation to establish such a court as part of the system of Magistrates' Courts. It was given no authority in juvenile cases and was long entirely distinct from the Children's Court. In recent years reorganization has resulted in making it independent of the Magistrates' Courts and in bringing the Children's Court under its jurisdiction. It is now composed of two co-ordinate parts: the family court division and the children's court division. The former is primarily interested in cases of desertion and non-support; the latter in delinquency and neglect.

The tendency of late has been to combine in one court the older domestic relations functions and jurisdiction over delinquent and neglected children. This movement has grown out of the recognition that problems of juvenile delinquency cannot be solved without dealing with abnormal family situations. The Cincinnati Court of Domestic Relations may be regarded as the progenitor of this broader type of tribunal. It was created in 1913, and was given responsibility for cases pertaining not only to juveniles, desertion, non-support, and contributory delinquency but also to divorce and the establishment of paternity. Most governmental units, however, are hesitant to vest such wide powers in one court. Constitutional obstacles sometimes

---

[1] Seagle, William, "Domestic Relations Courts." In Encyclopaedia of the Social Sciences, 1931, vol. 5, pp. 194–198.

exist. Far more fundamental are conflicts of opinion about unification of functions, and the propriety of extending the authority of these specialized courts, particularly in divorce cases.

Regardless of whether domestic relations courts have juvenile
jurisdiction or not, the service they render the poor is very great.
In cases of desertion—an occurrence which is so prevalent
among low-income groups as to be called the "poor man's divorce"—they have met with marked success in speedily appre-
hending the husband and in forcing him to contribute to the
support of wife and children.

In spite of the fact that the wide divergency of philosophy
about the scope of both kinds of courts is reflected in their lack
of uniformity of organization and jurisdiction throughout the
United States, they have brought justice to many by eliminating
delays and court costs and by making the services of lawyers
largely unnecessary. The courts themselves provide probation
officers or social workers to investigate and prepare cases, and
to do follow-up work after judgment has been pronounced.
Sometimes a case is heard so informally that no counsel is
needed; in other instances the court grants the services of an
assistant district attorney or an assistant city prosecutor.

Conciliation Tribunals

Conciliation tribunals are being used to a very limited extent
for the purpose of settling claims for wages, debts, rent, dam-
age to property, breach of contract, disputes between individuals,
and so on. Conciliation is also used as a means for settling collective disputes between capital and labor, but, as such, is outside the scope of this discussion.

A conciliation tribunal is not a court but an official agency presided over by a judge or a conciliator who may be appointed by a judge. Its function is to try to persuade persons with differences to come to an agreement. It cannot render a decision or enter its own judgment. It rarely has even compulsory jurisdiction over the defendant. Parties are free to place their controversy before the conciliator, and to abide by or reject at any time the solution he proposes. Its lack of power is so great a source of weakness that few such tribunals exist in the United States. Even in cities where provision has been made for their creation, they are little used. In North Dakota it has been obligatory since 1921 for most persons with cases pertaining to claims to attempt conciliation before having the right to sue in court. The results have not been altogether satisfactory.

The future of these tribunals cannot be foreseen. In spite of their limited use, much informal procedure utilizing the principle of conciliation is apparently engaged in by courts and legal agencies of which there is no record.[1] The fundamental idea underlying tribunals of this type has made a strong appeal to those concerned with promoting justice, and from time to time much interest is manifested in the subject. Smith and Bradway have written:

To the extent that conciliation procedure may be utilized in greater measure in our judicial system, to that extent will the poor man be helped, because of all procedures ever invented none is so quick and so cheap as conciliation when intelligently administered and when buttressed by a strong tradition that men ought, whenever possible, to compose their differences, not by litigation which is the way of war, but by conciliation which is the way of peace.[2]

[1] For an instructive account of the successful manner in which one member of the bench has informally used conciliation, see Judge Joseph N. Ulman's, A Judge Takes the Stand, pp. 100–103.
[2] Growth of Legal-Aid Work in the United States, p. 49.

Administrative Tribunals and Officials

Another method of affording justice to the poor has been through the creation of certain administrative tribunals, generally known as industrial accident boards or commissions, and through the appointment of officials who are given some jurisdiction over claims for wages. Before the first workmen's compensation act was passed in 1911, employes who sought to recover damages for injuries which were due to the negligence of employers found themselves at great disadvantage. Not only were they faced with delays in court procedure and fees which were often more than they could pay, but with the law itself and its outworn doctrine of liability. As the various states (except Arkansas and Mississippi) have enacted statutes providing workmen's compensation, most of them have set up quasi-judicial agencies for the administration of these acts. By means of these industrial accident boards, costs, fees, and the necessity for counsel have been nearly abolished and delays have been largely eliminated. Thus, in 72 per cent of the 580 uncontested claims in Ohio in 1930, payments began within thirty-eight days after the injury. Of 403 uncontested claims studied in New York for the same year, 78 per cent received first payments within thirty days after the beginning of the disability.

Where claims are contested, the situation faced by the employe is more complicated. In such instances, the boards have done much to assist the injured man to prepare his case through their staffs of inspectors and through the provision of impartial medical experts. Such assistance is not always adequate. In any real contest the injured employe needs to be represented by counsel as much as does a litigant in any other case if his rights are to be protected fully. It is probably unwise, furthermore,

for the boards to serve as counsel. Although these boards are spoken of as quasi-judicial, they are essentially judicial in function, since their decision on the law is so generally taken as final that few cases are appealed to the courts. When viewed as judicial agencies, therefore, the wisdom of their providing counsel becomes decidedly questionable, for it is difficult for a commissioner to judge a case in which he is the advocate.

The problem then arises of how attorneys may be provided to give legal advice and assistance to injured employes in workmen's compensation cases. Pennsylvania has provided for lawyers on the staff of the state compensation board. In Boston, Chicago, and New York legal aid societies furnish trained attorneys to workers seeking compensation for industrial accidents. The Boston society, which has had twenty years' experience in this specialized legal field, is reputed to provide counsel as competent as that representing the employers and insurance companies.

Just as civil litigation is too slow, cumbersome, and expensive for the settlement of cases of industrial accidents, so it is for cases dealing with wage claims. In state after state, therefore, attempts have been made to devise new remedies. The most fruitful legislative effort has been the creation of an administrative official, generally called a labor commissioner, whose duty is the enforcement of wage-payment laws. Many states had long had laws regarding the payment of wages, but these statutes were not very effective because there was no state agency vested with authority to enforce wage-claim collections. There are now nine states in which the labor commissioner exercises a *de facto* authority and actually collects unpaid wages, and seven others in which the law specifically empowers him to handle wage collections. In California, for example, which falls in the second group, the law permits the commissioner and his deputies to take assignments and prosecute actions for the collection of wages of persons unable to employ counsel. In 1932 over 16,000 wage claims were settled and $775,000 collected.

Wage-payment laws have been seriously attacked on various grounds. Their constitutionality has been upheld, however, in several states, and it is believed that in places where the laws have been declared invalid redrafted legislation would be found constitutional. Regardless of all the opposition of conservative groups, proper wage-payment laws, put into effect by labor commissioners, afford a summary and inexpensive method whereby wage-earners may enforce their claims. In fact, the existence of such laws and officials tends to make the statutes self-executing; in states where they exist wages are likely to be paid, and the law needs to be invoked but rarely.

Legal Aid Organizations

In spite of the assistance rendered by the various persons and organizations already described, there are a large number of difficulties in which the poor may find themselves that cannot be cared for by these designated agencies. They need attorneys for the drawing of contracts and other documents, and particularly for advising them about their legal rights and the course of action they should pursue. It has been noted that lawyers' aid is often essential in contested cases dealing with compensation for injuries. Litigation in the courts and the service of lawyers are necessary for all cases of debts and contracts beyond the jurisdiction of small claims courts and labor commissioners; all accidents not within the scope of the compensation acts; family difficulties which do not usually come within the jurisdiction of domestic relations courts, such as divorce, judicial separation, custody and guardianship of minors; partnership disputes; bankruptcy; claims growing out of insurance, real estate titles, mortgages; administration of the estates of deceased persons; disputes concerning the ownership, conversion or loss of personal property, and so on.

The agency that has been created to render service to the indigent whose needs fall within any of the above listed categories is the legal aid society. Organized legal aid work began in New York City in 1876, when an office was opened and a salaried attorney was appointed to give legal assistance to German immigrants who were subjected to frauds and impositions. In 1886 the Protective Agency for Women and Girls was opened in Chicago to protect young girls from seduction under the guise of proffered employment. Two years later the Bureau of Justice, fostered by the Society for Ethical Culture, made its appearance in the same city. Unlike the first two organizations which served only special groups, this office attempted to supply legal services to all needy persons, regardless of race, nationality, or sex. It may, therefore, be justly considered the first true legal aid society.

In 1890 Arthur v. Briesen was elected to the presidency of the New York society, and for twenty-five years he played the leading role in shaping the development of legal aid work, both in that city and throughout the country. Under his guidance the program in New York was broadened to care not merely for the immigrant but for any person who, because of poverty, was in danger of being denied justice. During almost five decades which have elapsed since he undertook his task, the New York society has continued to grow and to extend its services to larger and larger numbers of persons.

By the end of the nineteenth century only New York, Chicago, and Jersey City were providing legal aid. Scarcely more than 10,000 cases were handled in the last year of the eighteennineties. Subsequent to 1900, however, there was a rapid growth in the founding of societies, and in 1936, 60 such agencies were in existence. The number of cases handled by legal aid organizations has grown even more rapidly. In 1876 the one agency recorded 212 cases for the year, collections for clients of $1,000, and operating expenses of $1,060. In 1936 the 60 organizations cared for 260,400 cases, collected $627,000, and expended more than half a million. Figures for the entire period through 1933 disclose the significant totals of 3,900,000 cases and $13,600,000 collected for clients. Collections, which form a considerable part of the work of legal aid societies, average little more than $15 a case, and the cost of rendering assistance to a client averages about $1.45 per case.

Two facts in connection with these figures must not be overlooked. First, it may appear to many that the amount collected in cases growing out of contractual relations is so small as scarcely to warrant the effort expended. To the poor, however, these sums frequently appear anything but small. What is of even more consequence than the actual amount recovered, is the existence of an organization to which those in legal difficulties feel that they may turn with assurance that their rights will be protected.

Second, the reader must guard against being misled by the impressive number of cases. Large as it is, it probably represents a mere fraction of the legal aid work that needs to be done. In places where societies exist, there are not adequate funds or sufficient publicity to reach thousands of potential clients. And there are still large cities without a legal aid office, as well as whole states, particularly in the predominantly rural sections, where the movement has not yet penetrated.

Because the demand for legal aid service is relatively small in agricultural communities, there was long a question of what form of organization, if any, would be suitable for such areas. The Legal Aid Clinic operated by the Law School of Duke University appears to be demonstrating effectively that it is possible for one agency to serve as a nucleus for the activities of an entire state. The Clinic has assumed leadership in creating interest in legal aid in North Carolina, and supervises the work that is being done throughout the state. It secures the co-operation of local attorneys in various parts of the state, who volunteer to interview clients and conduct necessary litigation. It prepares briefs and assists these attorneys in such ways as are advisable. This undertaking may provide valuable experience for other states that are not highly industrialized.

We now turn to the form of organization of legal aid societies. There are a limited number that specialize in one type of work, such as the National Desertion Bureau in New York, the Legal Aid Bureau of the Educational Alliance also in New York, and the Legal Aid Department of the Jewish Social Service Bureau in Chicago. The first deals only with domestic relations cases, the other two limit their work almost entirely to Jewish applicants and particularly to immigrants.

In societies that provide general legal aid, organization ranges from simple to complex forms. In small communities one lawyer often volunteers his services and social agencies refer clients having legal problems to him. In larger cities there may be a group of lawyers appointed by the local bar association who assume responsibility for handling legal aid cases. In cities of over 100,000 population it is almost imperative that there be a definitely organized office. In a number of cities such an office is sponsored or supervised by the bar association; sometimes it is a clinic operated by a law school; in at least nine urban areas[1] it is a public bureau, generally organized as a department of the municipal government; often it is a department of a social agency; most frequently of all it is a private charitable corporation that may or may not receive financial support from the community chest.

In their report Smith and Bradway expressed the opinion that the privately incorporated societies have consistently done the best work. Control has been vested in boards of directors chosen because of their interest in legal aid. These societies have been free to develop as they saw fit, and their directors and staffs have exhibited foresight and enthusiasm. Like other private agencies, however, the problem of financing their work has been a serious one, and lack of adequate support has greatly curtailed the service they could otherwise have rendered. The public bureaus have been comparatively free from financial worries, but they have normally been subject to control by city councils that were not specifically qualified to provide intelligent leadership in framing the general policies of legal aid. The authorities quoted above believed that in spite of this handicap, the public bureaus have been more successful than any other type of organization in reaching the persons who need their help. This has been partly because of their better financial support, but chiefly because they *are* public agencies and

[1] Kansas City (Missouri), St. Louis, Los Angeles, Bridgeport, Dayton, Omaha, Hartford, New Haven, and Dallas.

hence have become better known in the community than would private offices.

It was agreed by the two writers that if legal aid organizations were ultimately to become a definite part of our system of administering justice rather than charitable agencies, the public office would be the most logical form of development. They recognized the misfortunes that have marked the establishment of municipal bureaus—the high turnover in personnel, the tendency for the work to become routine, the closing of some of the offices, and the fact that appointments have not always been made on the basis of adequate qualifications for the position. Yet the theory of the administration of justice as a public function seemed to them unassailable, and they were confident that as the techniques of government in general improved so would the legal aid bureaus. In the meantime they recommended that existing private societies continue to provide the experimental approach and the guidance that might prove of great ultimate value to the cause of public legal aid.

Since the publication of their bulletin on the Growth of Legal-Aid Work in the United States, however, two events within the bar have led Smith and Bradway, as well as some of their colleagues, to a new conception of the future of public legal aid. One was the action taken by the American Bar Association in 1936, whereby it has become a more representative body. The other is the acceleration of the movement toward integrated state bar associations which will be discussed later at some length.[1] It is sufficient to note here that an integrated bar, unlike a private state bar association, is a public or quasi-public body created by the legislature or the highest court of a jurisdiction. All attorneys practicing within a state having such a

[1] See pp. 283–288.

bar are required to maintain membership in it. Certain obligations, particularly the enforcement of the code of legal ethics and of rules pertaining to admission to practice, are vested in this body. These two developments indicate that the organized bar should soon be in a position to assume a larger degree of responsibility for legal aid than it has formerly done.

When the Standing Committee on Legal Aid Work made its report to the American Bar Association in 1937, it urged that one of the responsibilities that the integrated bar undertake should be that of exercising control over legal aid work. It also suggested that the ultimate supervision of legal aid in its national aspects should be vested in the American Bar Association. Too little time has elapsed since the presentation of the report to know what practical plans may be evolved from this new and still imperfectly defined philosophy. It is possible, however, that emphasis will come to be placed, not upon the type of private or public legal aid office that has been known until now, but upon agencies under the jurisdiction of integrated bar associations that will be responsible to the public for the quantity and quality of service rendered.

Before bringing the subject of legal aid to a close, a word must be devoted to the National Association of Legal Aid Organizations, which is the successor to the National Alliance of Legal Aid Societies, founded in 1912. In 1922 representatives from several of the local societies agreed that a strong national federation was needed which would offer genuine leadership to the legal aid movement. At a convention in 1923 the purposes of the new body were set forth as follows:

The objects and purposes of this association shall be to promote and develop legal-aid work, to encourage the formation of new legal-aid organizations wherever they may be needed, to provide a central body with defined duties and powers for the guidance of legal-aid work, and to co-operate with the judiciary, the bar, and all organizations interested in the administration of justice.

In the years immediately following its creation the National Association was concerned with certain specific problems confronting legal aid work. Paramount among these were the standardization of classifications of records and the unification of financial accounting. During the same period several committees made studies of the various remedial agencies for bringing legal assistance to the poor. A special committee on publicity has attempted, since the creation of the Association, to gather and disseminate information concerning the work of the members—now 43—and legal aid in general. Recently a series of "standards" and "ideals" has been formulated, in the light of which local organizations may measure progress achieved and plan constructively for the future.

The Association has frequently co-operated with other national bodies concerned with improvement of the administration of justice, particularly in reference to poor people. It is especially interested in promoting co-operation with social agencies, the law schools, the bar, and government officials. Much of its attention is being devoted at present to this task.

Legal Service for Persons of Moderate Means

The foregoing pages have pointed to the serious problem of how justice may be obtained by that large sector of the population that is unable to pay for the services of lawyers and the expenses of court proceedings. Inadequate, both in number and facilities, as are the agencies that have been devised for meeting this problem, they represent a very substantial achievement in recent years in the promotion of justice.

There is another problem of great magnitude, however, that has as yet received little attention from the bar.[1] It is the question of how legal counsel may be provided persons of small means who are not entitled to the services of agencies designed to aid the indigent. Although many individual lawyers since the very beginning of the bar have furnished much legal assistance at small or no fee, it is generally agreed that the nature and amount of the service and the method in which it is rendered offer no adequate solution.

In the New York Times Magazine for March 25, 1934, there appeared an article by Professor Karl N. Llewellyn, entitled, "Bringing Legal Aid to the Little Man." Two months later William S. Weiss, a New York attorney, furnished another article on "The Small-Town Lawyer for Plain City People."[2] Both authors pointed to the need of great numbers of small business men, salaried employes, artisans, and private citizens for legal counsel that would protect their rights and keep them from getting into difficulties. In the opinion of these two writers there is a vast amount of potential legal business, much of which is of a preventive nature, that should be done. There are wills to be drawn, leases to be signed, small claims to be collected, questions to be answered in connection with insurance policies, taxes, titles to property, mortgages, debts, and so on. The recent Connecticut survey, referred to in a previous section, furnishes evidence that substantiates this opinion.[3]

Unfortunately, a large part of the professional services that would be of great value to the middle class, and would also benefit the legal profession through its very volume, is not be-

[1] Garrison, Lloyd K., "The Legal Profession and the Public." In National Lawyers Guild Quarterly, March, 1938, pp. 127–128.
[2] New York Times, May 27, 1934.
[3] See p. 181.

ing given. Persons who have had no experience in consulting lawyers often do not even know that they need counsel. They conceive of the attorney as one to whom to turn for guidance only after trouble has been encountered. Of preventive legal service they have heard nothing. Still more important is the distressing lack of knowledge of how to obtain aid from honest and efficient lawyers at such fees as persons of small means can afford to pay. This problem assumes grave proportions in large cities where people are not personally acquainted one with another, and where the very lawyer that the less privileged class is likely to meet is not infrequently one whose professional preparation or integrity is questionable.

If means are to be devised for serving this large sector of society, it seems essential that organized groups of lawyers rather than individual practitioners assume responsibility for performing the task. There are several reasons for this conclusion. A lawyer is not permitted by the ethics of his profession to advertise directly. Consequently, there is no efficient method available whereby competent attorneys willing to serve the lower middle class may be known to prospective clients. At present some of the legal aid societies refer applicants not eligible for their services to practitioners whose names they keep on file. These names are often presented to the societies by local bar associations. Since the use of this device is almost entirely restricted to legal aid organizations and to a few of the social work agencies and bar associations, it offers little promise of meeting the widespread need of the lower middle class for information. It is doubtful, furthermore, whether individual attorneys can or should afford to care for a great many very minor cases at fees that are within the range of persons of moderate means. Careful definition, on the other hand, should probably be made of the income level above which persons would not be entitled to a service designed exclusively for those with small earnings. Otherwise, lawyers in private practice might well raise strenuous objections to the existence of law offices that appeared to compete with their business.

Reginald Heber Smith, Professor Llewellyn, and Professor Bradway, the chief authors of the small amount of literature as yet available on the subject, are in general agreed that adequate legal assistance for this group can be made self-supporting, but only by careful organization, including group practice and detailed cost accounting, and by conducting a large volume of business of a relatively well-standardized nature. They suggest, furthermore, that law offices for this type of client be sponsored by bar associations. Under such auspices, offices could engage in a type of publicity that would at once make people conscious of their legal difficulties, and inform them of agencies where competent assistance would be given under the regulation of bar associations and at a cost stated in advance of work begun.[1]

Mr. Smith has recently attempted to foresee how a law office under the control of a professional organization could be established in a large city.[2] He believes that it should be a non-profit corporation in which the entire staff would be engaged on a salary basis. Both specialists and general practitioners would be necessary, for so intricate has the law become that it would be uneconomical to dispense with the services of men trained in particular branches. There would be need for one specialist in litigation to handle cases coming before the courts, another

---

[1] Llewellyn, Karl N., "The Bar Specializes—With What Results?" In Annals of the American Academy of Political and Social Science, May, 1933, pp. 191–192.

[2] "The Bar Association Law Office for Persons of Moderate Means." In Economics of the Legal Profession, pp. 118–133.

skilled in taxation, others in real estate and domestic relations, and finally one in corporations if there were enough clients with questions pertaining to incorporated businesses to warrant engaging in that type of practice. The great volume of the work could be done by general practitioners, however, and in this connection Mr. Smith would recommend that, when possible, able young men recently graduated from approved law schools be utilized. For much of the general practice their professional preparation would be adequate, and the experience of dealing with clients would be exceedingly valuable for them. Their position would be comparable to that of internes in hospitals, who work under the supervision of experienced physicians. Because they would be considered as engaged in practical training, they would be paid salaries that would be smaller than those that the office would be obliged to pay for older men.

Professor Bradway, in a companion article on this subject,[1] has attempted to visualize the form of organization that would be suitable for areas which are not densely populated and where such cities as there are have fewer than 100,000 persons. In his opinion, legal counsel for low income groups in these areas should be established on a statewide basis. He would favor the creation of a central office, preferably in the state capital, with local offices in various communities. It would be the function of the administrator and staff of the central office to acquaint the bench, the bar, and the public with the purpose of such an agency; encourage the formation of local associations, and assist them temporarily in a supervisory and perhaps financial way; provide a clearing house for and about local offices; assist in cases that were inter-county or inter-state; train personnel for

[1] *Ibid.*, pp. 133–148.

the local branches; furnish the aid of specialists in preparing briefs and pleadings; and formulate and promulgate standards.

County or groups of county bar associations would elect committees that would be responsible for operating the local offices. The nature of these offices would be determined by the demand for service and the financial situation. During an initial period it might be necessary to depend upon the services of a volunteer committee of lawyers. Later it should be possible to engage an attorney to serve as local administrator and probably as secretary of the local committee. Thereafter, further lawyers could be added to the office staff, as the demand for them arose. If all highly technical cases were referred to specialists in the central office, general practitioners only would be needed to fill these positions.

The question which appears most difficult for Professor Bradway to answer is how such a statewide organization is to be financed. Unlike legal work in urban areas, he fears that a program of this kind cannot be made self-supporting, at least in its early years. He mentions as one possible solution a system of prepayment for service that would utilize the principle of insurance. It would be comparable to methods for prepayment of hospital costs now in operation in many localities. Hospital insurance is bringing much needed revenue to the institutions concerned, and it is providing care at extremely reasonable rates to subscribers because of the distribution of risks over large numbers of persons. Two factors, however, are essential if any insurance plan is to be successful: recognition of the need for service and broad public education. So frequent and imperative is the need for medical care and so far advanced is education in health matters in this country, that it is relatively easy for people to see the advantage of budgeting for sickness and of spreading the risks by means of insurance. No such a situation exists, as yet, in reference to legal assistance. The need for legal service is not viewed with an urgency comparable to the need for medical care, and popular education has not even advanced far enough, as has already been noted, for great masses of the people to recognize the existence of potential difficulties. Consequently, it is doubtful whether introduction of the use of insurance holds much promise for the immediate future.

A few months after Mr. Smith and Professor Bradway had attempted to formulate designs for furnishing the "less poor" with legal assistance, the Chicago Chapter of the National Lawyers Guild adopted a Proposal for a Legal Service Bureau for the Metropolitan Area of Chicago.[1] The Chapter stressed the fact that the kind of bureau recommended as most desirable would engage in, explore, and develop fields of legal service required by the public but not furnished by the legal profession. As one of its duties, this agency would attempt to educate the low-income groups and the public at large about their needs for legal services. It was the opinion of the Chapter that the bureau should be entrusted to the collective bar of Chicago. (There are at least eight recognized bar associations in that city.) The bar should lend skill and experience in creating an adequate form of organization, and should secure for the bureau legal status as part of the general system for the administration of justice. A board of trustees, composed of representatives of local bar associations and law schools and of judges from the state supreme and local lower courts, would be expected to plan, direct, and control the practice in which the agency would engage. The board, furthermore, would select the administrative

[1] The complete text of this Proposal appears in the National Lawyers Guild Quarterly, March, 1938, pp. 149–155.

personnel and fix the compensation of all persons engaged by the bureau.

In the foregoing suggested plans the position has been taken that the law office or bureau should be public and under the auspices of one or more bar associations. Other proposals are being made. The Committee on Professional Economics of the New York County Lawyers Association has recommended the establishment of legal bureaus in residential neighborhoods for the purpose of rendering service at moderate fees.[1] It suggests that sponsorship or supervision be furnished either by a professional association or by a law school. A sub-committee of the Association of the Bar of the City of New York unofficially favors offices being public but under the control of the Appellate Division of the Supreme Court, since it believes that they would thus gain in prestige and have the confidence both of the public and the legal profession.

At least two other possibilities exist: enlarging the functions of legal aid societies to care for persons above the level of indigency, and furnishing service on an organized basis by private practitioners. Some years ago William J. Norton, secretary of the Detroit Community Fund, envisaged the possibility of extending legal aid to those whose cases would not be profitable to the average attorney but who, nevertheless, could pay modest fees.[2] Although Mr. Norton conceived of this plan primarily as a means for obtaining partial financial support for the legal aid movement, the desirability of the creation of special departments within these societies for the express purpose of assisting persons of restricted means warrants careful consideration. A

[1] Survey of the Legal Profession in New York County, p. 62.
[2] "The Problem of Financing Legal-Social Work." In Annals of the American Academy of Political and Social Science, September, 1929, p. 149.

few societies have discussed the question, but no actual experiments have been undertaken. Because of the invaluable experience that they have already had and the organizational facilities which are at their disposal, it is not improbable that legal aid agencies could furnish a useful alternative to the plan for independent offices sponsored by bar associations or the courts.

Plans to provide legal service under private management, but subject to certain standards formulated by a central agency, are now being made by two Philadelphia lawyers, George Scott Stewart, Jr., and Robert D. Abrahams.[1] Since these attorneys believe that much small legal work goes undone because many prospective clients will not visit law offices situated in the heart of a big city, they propose the creation of decentralized law offices in various community centers in and around Philadelphia where no practicing lawyers are at present situated. They suggest that competent young attorneys of sound professional training offer general practitioner service in all civil matters.

In order that the public may have confidence in these local offices, the proponents of the plan advocate that standards be created and their maintenance be supervised by some agency, preferably by a committee of the Philadelphia Chapter of the National Lawyers Guild. Attorneys accepting these standards would be entitled to display a legend to that effect upon their office doors and stationery. It is recommended that publicity be given the fact that local service is available, not by directly naming the specific offices, but by bringing to the community through

---

[1] Abrahams, Robert D., "Law Offices to Serve Householders in the Lower Income Group." In Dickinson Law Review, April, 1938, pp. 133–140. This plan is still in process of considerable revision, particularly in reference to the degree of participation of a bar association. It is presented here in tentative form, because it contains several features not emphasized in the preceding discussion.

local newspapers, radio broadcasts, and community organizations, information about the methods under which such offices operate and the standards with which they comply. One factor, strongly advocated in this proposal, is to do away with all mystery concerning fees. Rates would be established on the basis of the time spent in interviewing clients and in the preparation of documents. A printed set of standard fees would be available for inspection by all persons coming to such offices.

One further plan for the furnishing of assistance by private practitioners has come to our attention. Donald T. Winder, an attorney, has submitted to the Chicago Bar Association a proposal for a Legal Service Bureau in Chicago. He recommends that a board of trustees of 15 members be created from representatives of the state, county, and city courts, and of the local law schools and bar associations. This board would be vested with responsibility for selecting the staff of the bureau, fixing its compensation, and supervising its work.

Any lawyer residing in Cook County who had practiced law for at least five years would be entitled to register his name with the bureau for a fee of $1.00 a year. Registration cards would be filed according to the division of law indicated in the application. As requests for legal assistance were received, each client would be provided with the names and office addresses of three attorneys, taken from the appropriate division in the file. These names would not be submitted to another client until all of the registrants in the particular division had been recommended.

Clients would be free to visit any of the proposed lawyers. These members of the bar would be expected to render service at a low fixed schedule of fees to anyone paying in advance. No litigation or preparation of legal documents involving extensive legal study and research would be undertaken by attorneys rendering this type of work.

It will be seen from the foregoing pages that the concept of organized legal service for persons of moderate means is so new that the few existing designs have not progressed beyond the initial stage. Inherent weaknesses may be found in most, if not all, of them, and whether they will receive the support of the bar, be ignored, or be formally opposed by it still remains to be seen. When they will be perfected and put into operation, cannot be foretold. The fact remains, however, that the sorry economic plight of a vast section of the population and the equally sorry condition of great numbers of well-trained lawyers, who would welcome the opportunity to work on a salary basis or with some assurance of remuneration, are commanding the attention both of society and the bar. Just as the creation of organizations for caring for some of the legal needs of the poor has been largely the work of the last forty years, so the establishing of agencies for those whose needs are scarcely less great may become the great task of the present generation.

THE INTEGRATED BAR

Before bringing to a close our survey of new trends in the promotion of justice, we turn to a movement within the legal profession that has already been mentioned,[1] which is believed by many to hold great promise of enhancing the role of the bar in connection with the administration of justice. The legal profession occupies the position of first importance in this field. Its social responsibility, as has been pointed out, *is* the administration of justice. Unfortunately it has been so loosely knit together that, as Herbert Harley has repeatedly said, a bar has

[1] See pp. 271–272 and note one on p. 214.

scarcely existed, except in name. Consequently, the movement to institute what is most frequently called the integrated bar—but is also known as the self-governing, the inclusive, the incorporated, or the statutory state bar—is viewed by its proponents as a significant step in creating an effective organization that will be able to work cohesively for this end.

Educational work in behalf of such state bars was begun by the American Judicature Society some twenty years ago. In the very first bulletin issued by that organization in January, 1914, the statement was made that one of the reasons for the widespread dissatisfaction with the administration of justice lay in the fact that there was no integrated bar and hence little professional solidarity and constructive leadership. The bulletin pointed out that such organizations of lawyers as existed were social and voluntary, and in many instances included only a small part of the total number of lawyers of any one state. The Society suggested that a legally incorporated organization was needed in every jurisdiction, that would include all members of the bar by the simple process of fixing the fees to be paid and by requiring, as a condition of continuance in practice, that each lawyer should retain membership in the body. It was proposed, furthermore, that the governing board of this incorporated state bar should have power conferred upon it to enforce the rules of the highest court of the state as to admissions to the bar. It should also have power to enforce any authoritative code of legal ethics and to disbar members.

Since the appearance of that statement the American Judicature Society has steadfastly insisted that an integrated state bar is a necessity if the individual lawyer is to be made aware of his responsibility to the profession and if he is to be provided with power to discharge his duty. It long emphasized admission to practice and discipline of members of the bar, as the two cardinal tasks that the state bar should assume. They are tasks, in its estimation, which cannot be properly done by an overworked and underorganized bench or by local bar associations. Of late years, however, it has ceased to emphasize them, because it maintains that experience has shown that once an inclusive bar is effected these problems are dealt with as part of the general program of the organized body. The Society now stresses, therefore, "the means afforded by a responsible bar to educate itself as to its reason for existence—the administration of justice —and to accomplish this in a more acceptable manner."[1]

The Conference of Bar Association Delegates of the American Bar Association early accepted and promoted the idea of an integrated bar. In 1919 the proposed reform was discussed at a meeting in Boston presided over by Elihu Root, and the following year it was endorsed. Thereafter, the Conference not only supported it, but in 1926 arranged a special meeting in Washington, D. C., under the chairmanship of the Honorable Charles E. Hughes, for extensive discussion of future action. Mr. Harley, secretary of the Conference at that time, was able to report that in a number of states a formerly grudging acceptance of the idea had become an enthusiastic espousal.[2] In four instances bills dealing with incorporation of the bar had been passed by state legislatures, although in California the bill had been subsequently vetoed by the governor. In 1927 it was again passed and signed by the new state executive. Thereafter, the movement grew slowly but steadily.

Missouri attempted to pass a bar act in 1933 but it was de-

---

[1] Quoted from a letter of April 4, 1938 from Mr. Harley to the writer.
[2] "Special Meeting on Bar Organization Held in Washington." In American Bar Association Journal, May, 1926, pp. 323 ff.

feated by a slender margin. The Supreme Court, however, adopted rules whereby a considerable amount of integration was acquired. Although the "Missouri plan," as it is known, cannot be truly considered as bar integration, it has strongly influenced the profession in a number of states where the setting up of an inclusive bar would have presented particular difficulties. There are now all-inclusive bars in 18 states; state bar associations have given their approval to integration in about an equal number; and various plans toward partial integration, at least, are being developed in several others. In only a few states is there no interest apparent, and all of these, except New York, are very small jurisdictions. Because of political compromises resulting from opposition by judges, however, there is great variety in the functions of the existing integrated bars. This is particularly noticeable in the extent of control over admissions to the bar which has been accorded to these bodies in place of the court.

The movement has met with its greatest success in states west of the Mississippi River. In fact, the only states east of that boundary which have, as yet, achieved an integrated bar are Alabama, Mississippi, North Carolina, Virginia, Kentucky, and Michigan. Interestingly enough, Alabama was the first state to pass the requisite legislation, and in its most radical form. In 1937, however, the bars of Massachusetts, New Jersey, and Pennsylvania had bills presented to the respective state legislatures. Although none of these was passed, their introduction was a matter of primary importance to the future of the movement.

Those states with the largest and most heterogeneous bars, and with old voluntary bar associations to which great prestige was attached, had long shown little enthusiasm in any efforts toward integration. The prevailing attitude of the legal profession in places like Massachusetts, Illinois, and New York had probably been well expressed by the late William D. Guthrie, a New York City attorney, who declared, at the meeting in 1926, in Washington, that it would be extremely dangerous to vest the control of the future of the New York State bar in the hands of a body of lawyers "now wholly outside the bar associations, who have never shown the slightest desire for co-operation or any spirit of fraternity."[1] He was aware of the criticism that many lawyers in his city were indifferent to bar organizations because the existing groups appeared to them to be insufficiently representative or lacking in vitality, but he believed this criticism to be without justification.

Aside from those who have been opposed to the integrated bar for the reason expressed by Mr. Guthrie, there are others who have gravely questioned the wisdom of such an organization.[2] They have visualized it as a form of guild, and like other guilds, they have feared that its disadvantages might outweigh its advantages. To them the resulting cohesion of the bar, which has generally been considered one of its great virtues, has seemed a potential source of autocratic power that might be wielded to advance narrowly selfish or unwisely conservative professional ends rather than to serve the public good. Some of them have even spoken of it as a threat to the cause of democracy. While such fears would appear to most members of the bar and the laity to be extravagant, they are perhaps needed as signals for caution to a profession that has sometimes failed

---

[1] "Special Meeting on Bar Organization Held in Washington." In American Bar Association Journal, May, 1926, p. 330. See also Mr. Guthrie's "The Proposed Compulsory Incorporation of the Bar," in New York Law Review, May, 1926, pp. 179–192 and June, 1926, pp. 223–236.

[2] See Elliott E. Cheatham's Cases and Materials on the Legal Profession, The Foundation Press, Inc., Chicago, 1938, p. 119.

to see that the furtherance of its own interests could wisely be achieved only through the promotion of the social well-being.

CONCLUSION

The facts that have been set down in this study point to problems that are complicated in nature, and fraught with significance both for the future of the legal profession and for society as a whole. There is, first of all, the basic problem of legal education. In spite of very real progress during the past two decades, it can categorically be said that, until the last proprietary school is closed, the problem of the evening school resolutely faced and solved, the weak schools, full-time and part-time, strengthened, and all institutions put in a position to offer professional training which is in conformity with contemporary legal knowledge, there can be no fundamental solution of questions pertaining to legal service and the administration of justice. Professional education is the keystone on which the entire superstructure rests, because the product of the law schools determines the character of legal and judicial practice.

The function of licensure needs to be thoroughly restudied, and a more basic and general philosophy concerning it established. Regardless of the recent achievements of the National Conference of Bar Examiners, the extreme inadequacy of the scope, content, and method of bar examinations in most states militates against the establishment of a system that would permit only competently trained persons to be admitted to practice.

When we turn our attention from students of the law and the method whereby they are inducted into its practice, we find within the bar numerous signs of new life and an awakened professional and social consciousness. The recent reorganization of the American Bar Association, the emergence of the

National Lawyers Guild, the extension of integrated state bar associations to more and more states, the expansion of the program of the American Judicature Society—these are only some of the indications that lawyers are at last coming to recognize the value of and the strength inherent in organized forms of endeavor.

There is also discussion of the need for cohesion and unity within the profession, and for a broad policy of "public relations." Whether the bar has clearly visualized what these words imply and how they may be translated into a program of purposeful action is doubtful. As yet opinion has not crystallized, and such action as there is, is of a halting, uncertain, and unintegrated nature. If we may draw any general conclusions from these initial efforts, it seems safe to assume that we may look forward to broader and more adequate attempts, on the part of the legal profession, to explore questions such as the number of lawyers in relation to the demand for their services, and the effect upon income of geographic location, education, type of work performed, and standards of living. For the first time in the history of the bar in the United States, there appears the probability that the profession will undertake to gather the information about itself that is essential for any planned readjustment of number and distribution of lawyers in the terms of their own welfare and that of the social interest.

The present noticeable interest of the legal profession in "public relations" appears to be the outgrowth of several factors. Economic stringencies which have come from a prolonged depression, and the severity of the criticisms of bar and bench are probably responsible for creating this concern, quite as much as is any deep and abiding desire on the part of the profession to provide adequate legal assistance for all social classes. Whatever the causes may be, it is not unlikely that this inclination to find ways for the strengthening of relations with the public will lend impetus to the developing movement for extension of legal counsel to low-income groups, to efforts to increase the efficiency and raise the moral tone of the bar and the courts, and to the general promotion of justice.

How far the bar as an organized body will go in any or all of these several directions cannot be foreseen. All groups, as they grow in size and age, tend to become conservative. The indictment most frequently made of the American Bar Association, in the past, has been that of ultra-conservatism. Professions, in general, find it difficult both to initiate new services and to reform old ones. Even if they could preserve the flexibility and the forward-looking attitude necessary for this task, they would be restricted in what they could do, for each profession is but a single thread woven into the complex pattern of civilization. It is the duty, therefore, of the general public not only to alter or enlarge upon the social design, as needs arise, but to bring pressure upon all component groups to do likewise.

In fields like medicine and education, for example, it has been the laity who, time and again, have become aware of the need for making existing forms of service more widely available and for instituting new forms. In many instances they have not only assumed responsibility for instructing the public concerning these needs, but they have even created the requisite organization and obtained professional persons to provide the services. Sometimes a period of years has elapsed before they have been able to relinquish their task to an appropriate professional group or to an official body that was ready to assume the necessary leadership.

Such occurrences have been less frequent in connection with

the administration of justice. Law has become so intricate, while always standing somewhat apart from daily life, that few persons not trained in it have had the knowledge, interest, or courage to attempt any contribution to the solution of its ills. The present lag in the promotion of justice may be attributed, in considerable part, to the failure of the public to assume a legitimate share of the burden. Wherever intelligent and concerted public opinion has operated, change has become imminent. No better evidence could be furnished of the power of such opinion than the procedural reforms achieved in England in the nineteenth century in the very face of objection by the legal profession.

So strongly convinced was Franklin D. Roosevelt, when governor of New York State, of the desirability of allying laymen with judicial reform that he vetoed a legislative bill, designed to create a Commission on the Administration of Justice for the sole reason that no provision had been made for them to constitute part of the group. In his veto message he asserted that a commission of lawyers and legislators would probably be interested only in strictly legal and technical phases of judicial administration, rather than in broad general questions of policy and fundamentals. "No substantial benefit could possibly result from such a survey." He noted further that this was "not to be an investigation of the legal profession or of legal practices or of technical procedure, but rather of the underlying theories of civil and criminal judicial administration." Its aim was to remedy conditions more important to the public than to the lawyer. He concluded, therefore, "While the bar should have a part in this study it should not have an exclusive part."[1]

[1] Cheatham, Elliott E., Cases and Materials on the Legal Profession, pp. 452–453.

In the actual administration of the law, the layman can offer little assistance. A training which he has not had is essential. In the initial designing of new legal tools and the reconditioning of old ones, however, his general experience and broader perspective are likely to be of sufficient value to warrant his cooperation. The pressure, moreover, which he can bring upon legislative and judicial bodies to institute change, is almost indispensable. Gradually there is evolving the realization that the services of both the legal profession and the public are needed, and that only through their working together can there be broad and continued progress in the promotion of justice.

INDEXES

INDEX OF SUBJECTS

Administration of justice: agencies for improving, 222–287; bar's responsibility for, 197, 224, 283; criticisms of, 196–210, 214, 215–219; law schools' responsibility for, 288; lay responsibility for, 290–292; reform in, defeated by lawyers, 247. *See also* American Bar Association, Section of Judicial Administration; American Judicature Society; Judicial councils

Administrative commissions, 19, 59, 66, 72, 89, 223, 243–248, 264–266

Admission to bar. *See* Bar admission requirements

Alabama, 141, 173, 286

American Arbitration Association, 250, 251–253

American Bar Association, 49, 51, 52, 53, 64, 65, 105, 106, 115, 128–146, 147, 150, 153, 154, 155, 161, 164, 179, 182, 210, 212, 224, 248, 271, 272, 285, 288, 290; Conference of Bar Association Delegates, 130, 138, 144, 285; evaluation of, 141–146; form of organization, 128–134; membership requirements, 132; National Bar Program, 130–132; number of members, 129; program of, 143–146; publications, 143; sections and committees, 134; Section of Judicial Administration, 145–146; Section of Legal Education and Admissions to the Bar, 32, 37, 39, 45–50, 103, 110, 134–141, 154, 164

American Judicature Society, 133, 162–164, 235, 239, 284, 285, 289

American Law Institute, 133, 159, 226–231

American Medical Association, 33, 38, 49, 63, 106, 128, 129, 132, 184

American Society of Civil Engineers, 129

Appeals, misuse of, 206

Apprenticeship training, 22, 23, 25, 140. *See also* Supervised practice

Approved law schools: definition of, 45–46; length of courses in, 51–52; number, 48–49; number of full-time, 50; number of students in, 52; relation to university, 50; requirements for admission, 51; Stanford University School of Law, as example of, 55–57

Arbitration, 248–253

Arizona, 140

Arkansas, 116, 140, 264; University of, School of Law, 116

Assigned council, 253–255

Association of American Law Schools, 53, 65, 69, 79, 105, 106, 107, 116, 119, 133, 136, 143, 153–159, 162; investigation of member schools, 156; membership requirements, 154–157; publications, 155, 158

Association of American Medical Colleges, 33

Balboa Law College, survey of, 57–59

Bar admission requirements, 23, 29, 97, 114–127, 161, 162, 181–184; development of state regulation of, 24, 37, 139–141. *See also* National Conference of Bar Examiners

Bar associations, national, 127–153; state and local, number of, 131. *See also* Integrated state bar

Bar examiners, 115, 116. *See also* Examinations for admission to bar; National Conference of Bar Examiners

Boston University, School of Law, 83

California, 51, 117, 170, 213, 235,

INDEX OF AUTHORS